A-Z of Cult Films

and Film-Makers by Steven Paul Davies

B T Batsford • London

Printed by Kyodo in Singapore

ISBN 0 7134 8704 6

Volume © B T Batsford 2001
Reprinted 2003

First published in 2001 by
B T Batsford, The Chrysalis Building
Bramley Road, London W10 4SP

A member of **Chrysalis** Books plc

Distributed in the United States and Canada by Sterling Publishing Co., 387 Park Avenue South, New York, NY10016, USA

INTRODUCTION

What makes a cult movie? Italian philosopher Umberto Eco described a cult film as not one movie, but all movies. Some of the films discussed within these pages are enigmatic, some anti-establishment, most aren't mainstream, although there are films that made it into the mainstream on initial release and yet became cult favourites later on. Many of the films included do indeed fulfil Umberto Eco's definition.

All of the movies in this book are deemed to have achieved cult status. There is something about them that leads a loyal band of cultists to enthuse over scenes and memorable dialogue. Quirky, innovative or unusual, stylish or outrageous, these films span the 50s to the present day. The focus is on the cutting edge, films with a different attitude, films with something more than car crashes and big bangs. Most are still on the shelves of video stores and many have had a release on DVD; re-released in different formats because of demand, because of their place in cult film history.

Documented here are the great triumphs of cult movie history. Each film listed is reviewed, incorporating a plot synopsis, trivia and memorable dialogue. Cast and credits are given along with any notable soundtrack details. In addition, from Woody Allen to David Zucker, this A–Z is interspersed with profiles of renowned cult directors.

I've resisted splitting this book into genres because most of these movies are just too hard to categorise. If you're looking for information on *Titanic* or the latest Robin Williams flick, you have the wrong book. If you're looking for films that will challenge you, emotionally or intellectually, I trust this companion will fascinate, even educate. Enjoy reading and happy viewing.

Choose your future. Choose life. Choose movies...

THE ADVENTURES OF PrISCILLA, QUEEN OF THE DESERT

1994 / 99 mins / Australia / *DVD* / ▭ Video
Stars: Terence Stamp, Hugo Weaving,
Guy Pearce, Bill Hunter
Director: Stephan Elliott
Producers: Al Clark, Michael Hamlyn
Script: Stephan Elliott

Stephan Elliott's Australian road movie is about two drag-queens (Anthony/Mitzi and Adam/Felicia) and a transsexual (Bernadette) who are hired to perform a drag show at a resort in Alice Springs in the remote Australian desert. The flamboyant trio are Hugo Weaving and Guy Pearce (as the two queens) and Terence Stamp (as the world-weary transsexual). They take a tour bus (called *Priscilla*) west from Sydney, across the enormous outback, on a journey full of bitchy banter and outrageous incidents. En route, it is discovered that the woman they've contracted with is Anthony's wife. Their bus breaks down and is repaired by gruff mechanic Bob (Bill Hunter), a big fan from the past, who travels on with them. It's not long before our three favourite queens are performing their own inimitable version of 'I Will Survive'.

For all the tack and bitchiness, there are some really understated moments and emotional scenes. In one key development, Stamp is plunged into despair by the death of someone close to him and this is where the 60s British icon shines. He is totally credible and completely dignified.

The three main characters – one gay guy, one bisexual and a transsexual – represent three highly segregated communities. And they all detest each other. Only the danger and the hardship of the journey unite them. Viewers need to watch closely to pick up on the subtleties. In fact, viewing several times would help. In the end, Adam gets to fulfil his dream of climbing to the top of King's Canyon in a Gaultier frock, tiara and heels, Mitzi faces up to being a father and Bernadette gets her man.

Priscilla is a ready-made cult movie, complete with all of the vital ingredients, including countless memorable lines of dialogue (including many stabs at Abba: 'What are you telling me? This is an Abba turd?'). The camp 70s soundtrack is to die for: Abba, Village People, Ce Ce Peniston, Gloria Gaynor, M People, originals and exclusive dance remixes. The gaudy, outrageous costumes won a well-deserved Oscar and the photography is superb.

The success of *The Adventures of Priscilla, Queen of the Desert* led to America producing a similar offbeat road movie about drag queens, *To Wong Foo, Thanks for Everything, Julie Newmar* (1995). The Hollywood effort failed to tap into the same nerve that *Priscilla* did with its innovative subject matter and sensitive character portrayals. *Priscilla's* camp trio were far more impressive in a film in which the glitz and glamour seemed more stylish, less Hollywood and more appealing and believable to a gay audience.

`Memorable dialogue:`

Bernadette: I'll join this conversation on the proviso that we stop bitching about people, talking about wigs, dresses, bust sizes, penises, drugs, night clubs and bloody Abba!
Tick: Doesn't give us much to talk about then, does it?

Bernadette: Just what this country needs: a cock in a frock on a rock.

Bernadette: Why don't you light your tampon and blow your box apart because it's likely the only bang you'll ever get, sweetheart!

Bernadette: I've said it before and I'll say it again: 'No more fucking ABBA!'

Felicia: So anyway, back to me.

Felicia: Oh, for goodness sake! Get down off that crucifix, someone needs the wood.

AIRPLANE!

1980 / 88 mins / USA / DVD / ▭ Video
Stars: Robert Hays, Julie Hagerty, Lloyd Bridges, Leslie Nielsen, Peter Graves, Robert Stack, Kareem Abdul Jabbar, Lorna Patterson, Stephen Stucker
Directors: Jim Abrahams, David Zucker, Jerry Zucker
Producers: Jon Davison, Howard W Koch Jr
Script: Jim Abrahams, David Zucker, Jerry Zucker

Voted 'One of the top ten funniest movies ever made' by the American Film Institute, *Airplane!* is the satire film that all others are measured against. In the 1970s the disaster movie was king, with people getting blown up, killed and injured in every kind of natural disaster possible. It was only a matter of time before all this seriousness gave way to silliness.

The persons and events in this film are fictitious, thankfully! An extremely funny spoof of *Airport*-type disaster movies, a never-ending string of offbeat gags and dialogue ensured this film cult status.

The plot of *Airplane!* revolves around Ted Striker (Robert Hays), an ex-fighter pilot with an unfortunate fear of flying. His life has been rapidly falling apart and the final straw comes when his flight attendant girlfriend, Elaine Dickinson (Julie Hagerty), dumps him. In an attempt to save their relationship Ted follows Elaine on to her next flight. Things begin to go disastrously wrong when the crew are struck by some form of virus. The fate of everyone on the plane lies in the hands of Striker as he's forced to take over the controls of the airliner.

As well as Hagerty and Hays, the all-star cast includes Leslie Nielsen, Robert Stack, Lloyd Bridges and Peter Graves, who all add to this masterpiece of zany, off-the-wall comedy – the finest of its genre for sight gags. Watch out for the bouncing heart and Otto the inflatable autopilot. Surely the most memorable line is...well, there are so many. Oh, and don't call me Shirley.

Memorable dialogue:

Ted Striker: Surely you can't be serious.
Dr Rumack: I am serious, and don't call me Shirley.

Elaine Dickinson: You got a letter from headquarters this morning.
Ted Striker: What is it?
Elaine Dickinson: It's a big building where generals meet, but that's not important.

ALIEN

1979 / 117 mins / USA /DVD / ▭ Video
Stars: Sigourney Weaver, Tom Skerritt,
Yaphet Kotto, John Hurt, Veronica Cartwright, Harry
Dean Stanton, Ian Holm
Director: Ridley Scott
Producers: Gordon Carroll, David Giler, Walter Hill
Script: Dan O'Bannon, Ronald Shusett

Alien could be seen as too popular and mainstream to be labelled cult but there are elements to this movie that add cult appeal. It is completely diverse: a horror movie, an action thriller and philosophical thriller. It is not one movie but all movies, thus fitting perfectly under philosopher Umberto Eco's definition of a cult movie.

Alien has proved to be one of the most influential science-fiction movies of the past 30 years; it's also one of the most entertaining and genuinely terrifying, containing some of cinema's eeriest visual imagery. It's smart, graphic, gloomy and dark. *Alien* also boasts the presence of an intelligent female hero – a rarity in sci-fi – the excellent Sigourney Weaver as Ripley.

Director Ridley Scott provides pure unadulterated fear. As the movie's poster tag line reads, 'In space, no one can hear you scream'.

The film takes place aboard the *Nostromo*, a spaceship mining the galaxy for signs of life. Members of the crew include the captain, Dallas (Tom Skerritt), second in command Ripley (Sigourney Weaver), whiny Lambert (Veronica Cartwright), idiot supreme Brett (Harry Dean Stanton), a British member of the expedition, Kane (John Hurt), android Ash (Ian Holm) and Parker (Yaphet Kotto).

They receive an extraterrestrial transmission from what seems a desolate planet. When the crew touch down they find an uninhabited vessel. Dallas, Lambert and Kane go out to explore the ship. In it they find nothing but a bunch of egg-shaped objects. Kane gets too close to one, however, and it leeches on to his face. Against Ripley's wishes, he is brought back to the *Nostromo*, where the crew attempt to remove the being. However, it won't budge and the crew has no choice but to leave it there. The next time they come and check on him, the being is gone and Kane seems to be okay. They all sit down to cinema's most memorable evening meal and the gut-wrenching bloody arrival of an uninvited guest. In a final showdown with the alien, Ripley must destroy the slime-spewing creature that kills to live – and lives to kill...

Ridley Scott's attention to detail is phenomenal. He shows the alien only in little flashes and even then for a few seconds at the most. This works well, as the unknown is more terrifying than that which can be seen. Jerry Goldsmith's sparse musical score is perfect and the art direction is outstanding, creating a highly claustrophobic feel. Scott's movie has a bucket-load of fantastic, Oscar-winning effects and was followed by James Cameron's *Aliens*.

Memorable dialogue:

Kane: Quit griping!
Lambert: I like griping!

Kane: Oh, I feel dead.
Parker: Anybody ever tell you you look dead?

ALLEN, WOODY
(Allen Stewart Konigsberg)

Actor, director, writer
Born 1 December 1935, New York

At the age of 15, Woody Allen started selling material to gossip columns and comics. He began performing deadpan stand-up comedy in 1961 and got his first film job as screenwriter and actor in *What's New, Pussy Cat?* Next, in 1966's *What's Up, Tiger Lily?* Allen and several character actors (including his then-wife Louise Lasser) dubbed ridiculous dialogue on to an already silly-looking Japanese spy thriller. His first film as director was *Take the Money and Run* (1969) and from that point Allen would mostly direct his own material, most of it becoming commercially successful.

After his directorial debut came a series of dazzling comedies: *Bananas* (1971), *Everything You Always Wanted to Know About Sex But Were Afraid to Ask* (1972), *Sleeper* (1973), *Love and Death* (1975) and *Annie Hall* (1977). The latter won Allen a Best Director Oscar (he shared the Academy's Best Screenplay Oscar with co-writer Marshall Brickman and was also nominated for Best Actor). From that point on, his films became more serious, including the Bergman-influenced *Interiors* (1978), which received several Oscar nominations including Best Director and Screenplay, but little commercial success. *Manhattan* (1979) had Allen as an intellectual womaniser, while *Stardust Memories* (1980) had him as a beleaguered movie director – just two films in which the angst-ridden director gets to show a side of himself and also gets the chance to confront himself. 'I don't want to make funny movies any more. They can't force me to,' says his character Sandy in *Stardust Memories*. 'I don't feel funny. I look around the world and all I see is human suffering,' he continues.

'Human suffering doesn't sell tickets in Kansas City,' replies his manager.

Allen quickly settled into a regular film-a-year production schedule that included the self-referential comedy *The Purple Rose of Cairo* (1985), more Oscars with *Hannah and Her Sisters* (1986) and serious drama such as *Another Woman* (1988).

By the 90s he had found his niche. A strong cult following and encouraging producers allowed him to make whatever he wanted. His output ranged between the mediocre cinema verité of *Shadows and Fog* (1992), to the award-winning *Bullets Over Broadway* (1994) and *Mighty Aphrodite* (1995), and even musicals with *Everyone Says I Love You* (1996).

Despite mixed reviews for his recent films such as *Celebrity* (1998) and *Sweet and Lowdown* (1999), Allen has continued undaunted and *Small Time Crooks* (2000) received his best reviews in years.

There's no doubt Woody Allen has a devoted audience who know everything about all of his movies. Rather than the odd Allen film becoming a stand-alone cult classic, most devotees have come to realise that each stage of his film-making – the funny and the serious phases – all form part of the same artistic language and wonderfully rich body of work. Furthermore, the films of Woody Allen inspire a game for his fans, looking for further clues to this native New Yorker's life. To them, his films have always represented an ongoing autobiography, through which he has bared his self-deprecating over-analytical soul to the world. See Filmography, p.238.

ALPHAVILLE

1965 / 100 mins / France / Italy / ▭ Video
Stars: Eddie Constantine, Anna Karina, Akim Tamiroff,
Howard Vernon
Director: Jean-Luc Godard
Producer: André Michelin
Script: Jean-Luc Godard

This Jean-Luc Godard film is a science-fiction film-noir comedy, the story of Lemmy Caution (Eddie Constantine), an Outland agent, who checks into an Alphaville hotel as Ivan Johnson, a reporter from *Figaro-Pravda* – just one of many unusual alliances. He is sent to a futuristic city run by an electronic brain in search of the mysterious Professor von Braun. Shot in black and white, New Wave disciples will love this Godard film, which owes a lot to Raoul Coutard's amazing photography that creates the idea of a modern Fascist city.

Alphaville is a dark and very frightening thriller, a comic pastiche of detective films, a love story, a sci-fi movie with a power-mad (and asthmatic) computer that is far scarier than Hal. In other words, it's a real cult genre-buster.

Alphaville is an interesting French take on the 60s obsession with the perils of information and technology. Like Patrick McGoohan's cult television series *The Prisoner*, another futuristic vision which aired in 1967, the plot involves a lone individual battling against a rigged system. Both texts detailed a nightmare existence, based around science and computers gone wrong. Information? With the internet, are any of us safe?

Both works also ended as they began. In *Alphaville*, set in the circular city with actors walking and talking in circles, the film ended 24 hours after it began.

Be seeing you.

Memorable dialogue:

Alpha 60: Sometimes reality is too complex for oral communication. But legend embodies it in a form which enables it to spread all over the world.

Alpha 60: Time is like a circle which is endlessly described. The declining arc is the past. The inclining arc is the future.

Alpha 60: Everything has been said, provided words do not change their meanings, and meanings their words.

Alpha 60: Once we know the number one, we believe that we know the number two, because one plus one equals two. We forget that first we must know the meaning of plus.

ALTERED STATES

1980 / 100 mins / USA / (Not currently available)
Stars: William Hurt, Blair Brown,
Charles Haid, Bob Balaban
Director: Ken Russell
Producer: Howard Gottfried
Script: Paddy Chayefsky

A researcher (William Hurt in his debut film role) investigating different states of consciousness begins to use himself as a guinea pig. Hurt marries the gorgeous Blair Brown after a sex-charged romance and they have two children. But because he's too self-absorbed to be interested in his relationship and kids, his marriage crumbles and Hurt embarks on a trip to Mexico to engage in a consciousness-expanding ritual. This involves using the 'sacred mushroom'. Ingestion is supposed to revive the common experience of early humans and so after a mind-blowing experience, he returns with a sample to perform yet further experiments. The results are literally mind-bending and his use of an isolation chamber leads to disturbing physical changes in his body that point toward an evolutionary regression. Nevertheless, despite these freaky head trips, Blair's devotion is just strong enough to bring him back from the most altered state imaginable.

It's a credit the film was made at all, after production hit all sorts of problems along the way. Original director Arthur Penn walked from the project late in 1978; special effects wizard John Dykstra left soon after. Then the film transferred from Columbia to Warner Brothers as the proposed budget grew to $15 million. Problems remained once Ken Russell had completed the movie. Paddy Chayefsky was so enraged at the liberties taken by the director with his novel that the author had his name removed from the credits and replaced with his frequent alias Sidney Aaron.

Nevertheless, Russell's cerebral work – which couples his own baroque visual style with state-of-the-art special effects (by Dick Smith who worked on *The Exorcist* and *Taxi Driver*) – provides an unforgettable assault on the senses and a completely gruelling, climactic and off-the-wall story resolution.

Memorable dialogue:

Eddie Jessup: The purpose of our suffering is only more suffering.

Arthur Rosenberg: The way I feel, I don't expect to go to sleep for a year. I'm on fucking fire!

ANDERSON, LINDSAY

Director, writer
Born 17 April 1923, Bangalore, India

Son of a Scottish major-general stationed in Raj-era India, Anderson was educated at Oxford before co-founding (along with future directors Karel Reisz and Tony Richardson) *Sequence*, a highly influential film magazine. He emerged as a critic and journalist in the late 40s and early 50s, and became a major force in the reshaping of British cinema. In his essays for *Sequence*, *Sight and Sound*, and *The Times*, Anderson advocated a greater topicality and social awareness in British films. His writings along these lines contributed greatly to the 'Free Cinema' movement of the 50s, which favoured universalist subject matter and exhibited general disdain for Hollywood-type commercial product (although one of his heroes was director John Ford, about whom he wrote a book in 1981).

Anderson began as a film-maker in the field of documentaries during the late 40s and earned an Academy Award in 1954 for his short *Thursday's Children*; he subsequently worked as a director on television. He became a theatrical director in the late 50s and moved into feature film work in 1963 with *This Sporting Life*. This told the story of a disturbed rugby champion with low-key dramatics. Anderson is best known to American film buffs for his trenchant trilogy starring Malcolm McDowell as Mick Travis, a British 'Everyman' who survives the public school system. This and his subsequent movies, including *If...* (1968), *O Lucky Man!* (1973) and *Britannia Hospital* (1982) (all of which starred Malcolm McDowell) are characterised by a grim view of English society, government and institutions, and a generally nihilist view of the world, coupled with disconcerting elements of realism.

Also active as a stage director in London, he took occasional acting roles, most notably in *Chariots of Fire* (1981). In 1992 he adapted his book on John Ford into a television documentary which he hosted on-camera. See Filmography, p.238.

ASSAULT ON PRECINCT 13

1976 / 91 mins / USA / *DVD* / ⊡ Video
Stars: Austin Stoker, Darwin Joston,
Laurie Zimmer, Martin West, Tony
Burton, Charles Cyphers
Director: John Carpenter
Producer: JS Kaplan
Script: John Carpenter

A 1970s cult classic, complete with funky score, John Carpenter's *Assault on Precinct 13* was instantly hailed as 'the cult movie of the year' by noted critic Derek Malcolm on its release in the UK. It's a real treat for those who remember when cinema was daring, exciting and cool.

An almost abandoned LA police station finds itself under a state of siege by a youth gang, the members of which make a pact of blood to strike back at police who are guarding a prison on the night before its closure.

This riveting thriller is Carpenter's second film and a modern-day paraphrase of Howard Hawks' *Rio Bravo* (1959). There are visual and dialogue borrowings from various other films as well, including *Night of the Living Dead* (1968) and *Once Upon a Time in the West* (1969) – a move that always pleases cultists everywhere. Recognising lines of dialogue from older films proves just as pleasurable as witnessing the birth of new great lines. Although it must be said that Carpenter's own 'Why would anybody shoot at a police station?' was pretty damn good and instantly memorable. The writer–director also wrote the eerie music score and did the editing, under the pseudonym John T Chance – John Wayne fans will know where that came from. Careful viewers will also realise that the siege actually takes place at precinct 9, division 13, not precinct 13 (that title was given by the distributor of the film).

Memorable dialogue:

Wells: Look at that, two cops wishing me luck. I'm doomed.

Captain Collins: There are no heroes anymore, Bishop. Just men who follow orders.

Napoleon Wilson: Can't argue with a confident man.

Napoleon Wilson: In my situation, days are like women – each one's so damn precious, but they all end up leaving you.

BACK TO THE FUTURE

1985 / 112 mins / USA / ▭ Video
Stars: Michael J Fox, Christopher Lloyd, Lea Thompson,
Crispin Glover, Thomas F Wilson,
Claudia Wells, Marc McClure
Director: Robert Zemeckis
Producers: Neil Canton, Bob Gale,
Steven Spielberg (exec)
Script: Robert Zemeckis, Bob Gale

Skateboards, gadgets, sporty cars, a hip soundtrack – all a huge part of that 1980s phenomenon *Back to the Future*. Ironic then that most of the film takes place in 1955.

An eccentric scientist called Doc Emmet Brown (Christopher Lloyd) invents a time machine that hurls average high schooler Marty McFly (Michael J Fox) 30 years into the past and he's stranded there unless the 1955 Doc Brown can help him. To make matters worse for poor young Marty, he arrives just in time to interrupt and alter the meeting of his parents, who were 17 years old at the time. By meddling in this way, he threatens his own existence as his own mother (Lea Thompson), here a high-school teenager, is falling for him instead of his father. It's up to Marty to make sure nothing is disrupted and they do get married and have him. That's difficult when Mom develops a full-on crush on her own son!

The funniest moments in the movie are when the characters perform multiple roles as their older and younger selves, and as with all good cult films, it takes multiple viewing to get all of the back references. For instance, you see a van (in 1985) advertising for Mayor Wilson; when Marty travels back to 1955, he bumps into the past version of Wilson and gives him the idea to run for mayor.

Doc Brown is a great character in the film – he's all manic dialogue and exaggerated facial expressions. Huey Lewis, who sings the film's hit song 'The Power of Love', has a cameo as a high-school teacher. This wild and totally wacky feel-good comedy film was produced by Steven Spielberg and his company and was followed by two sequels, numerous imitations and an animated TV series.

Millions of cinema-goers joined Marty in the journey of a lifetime back in 1985 and made *Back to the Future* one of the biggest blockbusters of that whole decade. As a cult today, the film attracts those who were addicted in the mid-80s as well as a new audience who've discovered it through television, video. With its strands of inherent sci-fi, it is even beginning to emulate the cult of *Star Trek* and *Babylon 5*, evident in the immense hard work, organisation and following of the official fan website www.bttf.com which not only has all you need to know about the original film and its sequels but info on the original cast members' recent activities – from Huey Lewis gig details to the current Parkinson's Disease charity work undertaken by Fox. The site is also full of fan fiction based on the original *Back to the Future* characters and details of fans who've designed their own hoverboards!

The BTTF site also organises conventions and memorabilia fairs dedicated to the film. At Universal Studios in 2000, fans organised, via the internet, 'FutureCon2000', an event where people arrived in DeLoreans and dressed as Marty McFly and Emmet Brown. Although Fox and Lloyd were nowhere to be seen, other actors involved – such as the man who played Biff – did attend. The event is now held every year.

Memorable dialogue:

Marty McFly: Wait a minute, Doc. Ah. Are you telling me you built a time machine out of a DeLorean?
Dr Emmet Brown: The way I see it, if you're gonna build a time machine into a car, why not do it with some style?

Marty McFly: If you put your mind to it, you can accomplish anything.

Dr Emmet Brown: If my calculations are correct, when this baby hits 88 miles per hour you're gonna see some serious shit.

Dr Emmet Brown: Roads? Where we're going we don't need roads. (last line)

BADLANDS

1973 / 95 mins / USA / Video
Stars: Martin Sheen, Sissy Spacek, Warren Oates,
Ramon Bieri, Alan Vint, Gary Littlejohn
Director: Terrence Malick
Producer: Terrence Malick
Script: Terrence Malick

In 1959 a lot of people were killing time. Kit and Holly were killing people...

Until his role as Kit in *Badlands*, Martin Sheen was a popular TV movie actor but playing the young garbage collector in Terrence Malick's film really put him on the Hollywood map and in most critics' favourite-actor lists. And it *is* unusual for a big box-office success to have achieved such critical acclaim. In 1973, Terrence Malick made, without doubt, the all-time great American movie.

Based on the true story of the Charles Starkweather and Caril-Ann Fugate murders in 1958, Malick tells the tale of Kit Carruthers, a garbage collector in South Dakota, who gets it in mind to go on a killing spree with schoolgirl Holly Sargis (Sissy Spacek), after shooting to death her disgruntled sign-painter father (Warren Oates) – he happened to disagree with their relationship. On their way towards the Badlands of Montana they leave a trail of dispassionate and seemingly random murders.

Spacek sits and talks with terrified victims, even those bleeding slowly to death in front of her, as if they were school pals. She explains how Sheen can be a little odd sometimes; as if his violent acts could be down to the raging hormones of moody American youth. Sheen, meanwhile, looking very like James Dean, lives for potential fame and notoriety. He sees his behaviour as quite commendable, something to be imitated and often pauses to tape messages which he thinks will serve as fine moral examples: 'Listen to your parents,' he says, 'they got a line on most things.'

Narration is used to great effect. Spacek's dreamily detached voice adds to the film's haunting quality. Rather than attempting a detailed explanation of the couple's motives, the narrative cleverly refuses to judge. Malick's use of music is perfect and features a soundtrack that includes works by James Taylor, Erik Satie and Nat King Cole. Brian Probyn, Tak Fujimoto and Stevan Larner are credited for the beautiful photography.

Malick's stark, moody thriller has a cult following and is admired by movie-goers, critics and film-makers alike. There is no doubt that without *Badlands* there would be no *True Romance* (1993) or *Natural Born Killers* (1994) and Malick's film is still hipper than both. *Badlands* also anticipated Martin Scorsese's *Taxi Driver* (1976) – another movie about urban alienation and madness – and Sheen's son Emilio Estevez's directorial debut *Wisdom* (1986), which was a remake of *Badlands*.

So what happened to Terrence Malick? He not only directed *Badlands* but also wrote and produced it. Five years later he made *Days of Heaven* (1978), another superbly photographed work of art, this time about a group of farm workers in Texas and their relations with the owner of the land. Then he became a complete recluse and didn't direct another film until *The Thin Red Line* (1998) which, although one of the most intriguing war films around, simply failed to live up to the impossibly high standards of *Badlands*.

Memorable dialogue:

Kit Carruthers: I'll give you a dollar if you eat this collie.

Holly Sargis: At this moment, I didn't feel shame or fear, but just kind of blah, like when you're sitting there and all the water's run out of the bathtub.

BAD TASTE

1987 / 90 mins / New Zealand / ▭ Video
Stars: Terry Potter, Pete O'Herne,
Craig Smith, Mike Minett, Peter
Jackson, Doug Wren, Dean Lawrie
Director: Peter Jackson
Producer: Peter Jackson
Script: Ken Hammon

Bad Taste is a dark comedy gore-fest of a movie by New Zealand director Peter Jackson in which a sleepy coastal town is invaded by alien entrepreneurs searching for human flesh to use as meat in their intergalactic fast-food chain. Four dim-witted men from the New Zealand National Air and Space Defence League form the government hit squad who arrive in the small fishing town to investigate the reports of landing UFOs. It is these mere mortals who must take on a battalion-sized army of aliens who have massacred the town's population as part of their plans. Can the fearless foursome stop the man-hungry invaders before the entire human race is served up in a bun?

Jackson also acted in, co-wrote, edited, produced and did the make-up for *Bad Taste* which, not surprisingly, became a worldwide cult hit. Cast with amateur actors and shot with hand-held cameras, Jackson's movie became one of the most commercially successful movies ever made in New Zealand. It *is* cheap and it *is* nasty but then a lot of cult movies are. It also fails to take itself at all seriously, which is the secret of its success.

Bad Taste is full of gory gunfights and grotesque humour and if you like it, you'll love the other films by Peter Jackson: *Meet the Feebles* (1989) and *Braindead* (1992). But Jackson's more recent effects-laden blockbuster Tolkein trilogy may leave you yawning. Get back to the camcorder, Peter.

One element that has ensured cult movie status is the film's cast of wacky characters. In his acting role, Jackson plays nerdy Derek, member of the Astro-Investigation and Defence Service, last seen on his way to the alien's home planet. Barry, fellow member of the Astro-Investigation and Defence Service, spends most of his time covered in blood. Frank is the leader of AIDS and also sings the title song. Ozzy is equally as nerdy and violent as the other members, whereas Giles is the one who's almost eaten. The retarded alien Robert is also played by Peter Jackson.

Plus, as well as crazy characters and plot twists, there is still room for chicken guts.

Memorable dialogue:

Derek: Stick all the bits of brain in a plastic bag, Barry.

Derek: Suck my spinning steel, shithead!

Derek: I'm a Derek and Dereks don't run!

BANANAS

1971 / 82 mins / USA / DVD / Video
Stars: Woody Allen, Louise Lasser, Carlos Montalban,
Natividad Abascal, Jacabo Morales
Director: Woody Allen
Producer: Jack Grossberg
Script: Woody Allen, Mickey Rose

Consumer products tester Fielding Mellish (Woody Allen) becomes infatuated with Nancy (Louise Lasser as a political activist). He stalks her at demonstrations and tries to persuade her that he is truly worthy of her love. However, Nancy wants someone a bit less weedy and a bit more dynamic. Fielding runs away to San Marcos where dictator Carlos Montalban has seized control. Drunk with power, at one point, this arrogant leader proclaims Swedish the national language! Allen joins the rebels, is feted by Montalban and eventually becomes President of the country. On a return visit to the States, he meets Nancy again and, of course now that he has some amazing leadership qualities, she falls for him.

Most of the humour is hilarious, with some memorable sight gags and one-liners, but some of the jokes are very bad. It's Allen's bizarre ideas (his mild-mannered New Yorker character becoming involved in revolution and the cause for freedom is pretty hard to believe) that add cult appeal and make this worth at least one viewing. The quirky score is by Bond maestro Marvin Hamlisch. Watch out for Sylvester Stallone in a cameo as a hoodlum.

Allen's second feature as a director, *Bananas* was conceived as a tribute to the Marx Brothers' *Duck Soup (1933)*. Interestingly, this is probably the only American film that has revealed that J Edgar Hoover was really a black woman. When asked why he called it *Bananas*, Allen said: 'Because there are no bananas in it.'

Memorable dialogue:

Fielding Mellish: I object, your honour! This trial is a travesty. It's a travesty of a mockery of a sham of a mockery of a travesty of two mockeries of a sham.

Fielding Mellish: I once stole a pornographic book that was printed in Braille. I used to rub the dirty parts.

Woody Allen in Bananas: *'a travesty of a mockery of a shame of a mockery of a travesty of two mockeries of a sham.'*

BARBARELLA

1968 / 98 mins / France / Italy / DVD / ⊟ Video
Stars: Jane Fonda, John Phillip Law, Anita Pallenberg,
Milo O'Shea, Marcel Marceau
Director: Roger Vadim
Producer: Dino De Laurentiis
Script: Vittorio Bonicelli, Claude Brule, Brian Degas, Jean-Claude
Forest (also novel), Tudor Gates, Terry Southern, Roger Vadim,
Clement Biddle Wood

Barbarella is a great fun, camp, wild psychedelic ride through the cosmos with that gorgeous flame-haired Barbarella (Fonda) at the helm! Based on the popular French comic strip about sexy 41st-century space adventures, this movie includes Fonda's infamous strip-tease during the opening credits – a sequence which alone would have ensured this movie its cult status.

Peacefully floating around in zero-gravity Barbarella is suddenly interrupted by a call from the President of Earth. Planet leaders have worked hard to achieve intergalactic peace but a young scientist, Duran-Duran, armed with his latest invention, a 'positronic ray', is threatening the ancient universal peace. Barbarella, with a dazzling array of phallic weapons, is the one chosen to find him and save the world. She crash-lands her spaceship on the planet Lythion, where she encounters killer dolls, a hairy man called Mark Hand, a sightless angel called Pygar (Law), the cruel world of the Black Queen and the absent-minded, absolutely libidinous inventor Dildano. During her mission, Barbarella never finds herself in a situation where it isn't possible to lose at least part of her already minimal dressing.

Also known as *Barbarella: Queen of the Galaxy*, Roger Vadim's film has affected many people (the famed rock group Duran Duran derived its name from O'Shea's character), and many artistic styles of the particular era (late 60s, early 70s) are evident in its production. This is an example of great fantasy for that time period and boasts unique characters and lush artwork. It's a kind of female version of *Flash Gordon* but screenwriter Terry Southern, a satirist who co-wrote *Dr Strangelove (1964)*, takes it beyond comic-book fantasy with thinly veiled jabs at 60s counterculture.

Hollywood's latest babe of the moment Angelina Jolie is preparing to star as Barbarella in a forthcoming remake, which will not please Drew Barrymore who wanted to do the same in 1999.

Memorable dialogue:

Barbarella: A good many dramatic situations begin with screaming.

Pygar: An angel does not make love, an angel is love.

President: Your mission
Barbarella: Find Duran-Duran.

The Great Tyrant: Hello, pretty-pretty!

Barbarella: Make love? But no one's done that for hundreds of centuries.

BARTEL, PAUL

Actor, director
Born 6 August 1938, New Jersey

Paul Bartel was born in Brooklyn in 1938. Interested in animation from a very early age, at the age of 13, he spent a summer working at New York's UPA studio. He majored in theatre arts at UCLA and received a Fulbright scholarship to study film direction in Rome, producing a short that was presented at the 1962 Venice Film Festival. Roger Corman's brother, Gene, later hired Bartel to direct the low-budget horror movie *Private Parts* (1972). Roger Corman hired him as a second unit director on *Big Bad Mama* (1974), which led to his directing *Death Race 2000* (1975) about a cross-country race in which drivers were encouraged to mow down pedestrians.

Bartel could not persuade Corman to finance his pet project, the hilarious black comedy, *Eating Raoul*. The $500,000 was completely self-financed, made after his parents sold their New Jersey home! Shot in 22 days, mostly weekends, over the course of a year, *Eating Raoul* (1982) is a true indie movie which stars Bartel and Mary Woronov as gourmet cannibals who lure sex swingers to their apartment, smack them with a skillet, rob them and use the proceeds to buy a restaurant. Broad and violent satire, this film has been a favourite on video for the past two decades.

Lust in the Dust (1985) has enjoyed similar cult success. A Western spoof starring Tab Hunter, Lainie Kazan and Divine, the poster tag line stated 'He rode the West! The girls rode the rest. Together they ravaged the land!' An irresistible cult movie of the first order, *Lust in the Dust* had hard-living cowboys and hot-blooded wenches all lusting for wealth and each other in the wild western town of Chile Verde. But when the mysterious gunfighter Abel Wood and defiled singer Rosie Velez (Tab Hunter and Divine, reunited from John Waters' *Polyester*) come together with saloon-owner Marguerita Ventura (Lainie Kazan), fiery passion and unbridled greed turns the town upside down. Completely camp and outrageous!

As well as his time spent behind the camera, Bartel achieved some success in minor or cameo acting work. Over the years, his roles included parts in *Basquiat (1996)*, *Escape from LA* (1996) and *The Usual Suspects (1995)*.

The relatively lavish *Scenes From the Class Struggle in Beverly Hills* (1989), while far from achieving commercial success, was deemed something of a directorial comeback for Bartel. The film ended with Cole Porter's song 'Let's Be Outrageous (Let's Misbehave)', perfectly apt for a director who's always done just that.

His next film as actor–director was 1993's *Shelf Life*, about three adults who have been trapped in a bomb shelter for years and who behave as characters from television. Since television was their only guiding influence, their routine is an opportunity for Bartel to mock TV-reliant culture. Not released theatrically, it's a real curiosity and a tough one to track down.

'I'm very interested in doing eccentric, individual low-budget films,' said Bartel early on in his career. He never swerved from that low road. Sadly, this quirky director died of liver cancer in May 2000 but was last seen on screen in Michael Almerey's film version of Shakespeare's *Hamlet* (2000), starring alongside such big names as Ethan Hawke, Kyle MacLachlan, Sam Shepherd and Bill Murray. See Filmography, p.238.

Next page: Lainie Kazan, Tab Hunter and Divine in Paul Bartel's Lust In The Dust *(1985)*

BARTON FINK

1991 / 116 mins / USA / ▭ Video
Stars: John Turturro, John Goodman, Judy Davis,
Michael Lerner, John Mahoney, Jon Polito, Steve
Buscemi, Tony Shalhoub
Director: Joel Coen
Producers: Ethan Coen, Graham Place
Script: Ethan Coen, Joel Coen

In 1941, intellectual New York novelist Barton Fink is summoned to Hollywood to write his first script – a Wallace Beery wrestling picture. Staying in the Hotel Earle, Barton develops severe writer's block. His only friend is travelling insurance salesman Charlie Meadows (John Goodman) who is staying next door. He tries to help but Barton continues to struggle as a bizarre sequence of events distracts him even further. It's soon revealed the 'Average Joe' salesman has a horrific secret. Throw in a few unexpected killings, a mysterious box, an eerie hotel fire and the revelation of another character's sinister identity and you have one of the 90s' weirdest films.

The Coens' strange tale can be read a number of ways but it's clear the film deals with the directors' own Jewishness with some brilliantly cruel one-liners. By turns unsettling and hilarious, the film becomes a hellish vision of Hollywood that shows the terror behind the tinsel.

Its appeal to cultists lies in its strangeness. Like all great cult films, it is in part confusing, not necessarily plot-wise, but mood-wise. Sometimes we can't tell what's real and what's a dream. *Barton Fink* is full of constant surprises and unexplained occurrences. It's a satire in which the fascinating sense of the surreal is key – usual characters in most unusual circumstances.

Memorable dialogue:

Barton: Sex? He's a man! We wrestled!

Barton Fink: Have you read the Bible, Pete?
Pete: Holy Bible?
Barton Fink: Yeah.
Pete: Yeah, I think so. Anyway, I've heard about it.

Above: John Turturro, star of Barton Fink *(1991)*

BEAUTIFUL THING

1996 / 90 mins / UK / DVD / ▣ Video
Stars: Meera Syal, Linda Henry, Martin Walsh, Glen Berry, Scott Neal, Steven M Martin, Andrew Fraser, Tameka Empson
Director: Hettie MacDonald
Producers: Tony Garnett, Bill Shapter
Script: Jonathan Harvey

Scripted by Jonathan Harvey, *Beautiful Thing* is based on his original play. Set during a hot summer on a southeast London housing estate, this is one of the most tender love stories ever told on film. It's a story of sexual awakening, an urban fairy-tale, a heartfelt rites-of-passage story depicting what it's like to be 16 and in the throes of bashful first love.

Jamie, an unpopular kid who skips school to avoid games lessons, lives next door to Ste, a more popular athletic boy but who is constantly beaten up by his father and older brother. Jamie's mum, Sandra, offers refuge to Ste, who has to 'top-and-tail' with Jamie.

The story tells of their growing attraction for one another, from initial lingering glances to their irrefutable love, and covers the issues of coming to terms with one's sexuality and the reaction of others. The film also details Sandra's unconditional love, loyalty and defence of Jamie and the fear of repercussion should Ste's family find out. Girl-next-door Leah is another great character. She has been expelled from school and spends her time listening to Mama Cass records and tripping on a variety of drugs.

Understandably, the film has struck a chord with the gay community, and within this group there is undoubtedly a cult of *Beautiful Thing*. Those who spent their teenage years deep in denial about their sexuality have especially taken the film to their hearts. Looking at the numerous fan web sites, *Beautiful Thing* chat-rooms and email discussion pages, it seems the movie has affected people most powerfully if they've had a hard time accepting their own sexuality. One fan explained how the strongest reaction he heard came from a man he knew in his late 40s who came out recently to his wife and grown sons, straight after seeing the film. One other fan described how he'd been to London before but now planned to go to Thamesmead in the summer. 'Can you imagine,' he wrote, 'there'll be all these poofs walking around with maps looking for *Beautiful Thing* locations!'

Most film critics missed the groundbreaking nature of the film – and criticised the (deliberate) happy ending – saying it is unrealistic (unlike, apparently, *The Birdcage*, made in 1996). The film has, however, been taken up by many high-school teachers (mainly in the US) who play it to their classes to explain to both gays and straights that 'it's okay now', a nice change over the past decade that suggests teachers now admit that some gay people are students of theirs, and they don't just appear when full-grown!

Memorable dialogue:

Sandra: It's for his bird.
Tony: Do you have to use words like that? It really disempowers you.

Sandra: It's not natural, is it?
Jamie: What ain't?
Sandra: A girl her age being into Mama Cass.
Leah: She's got a really beautiful voice.
Sandra: And what's wrong with Madonna?
Leah: She's a slut.
Sandra: Hypocrite.

Sandra: What happened? School burned down, did it?
Jamie: Yeah.
Sandra: What was it this time? IRA bomb?
Jamie: Fundamentalist Muslim pyromaniacs.
Sandra: Oh, funny, that. Looked all right when I walked past it.

BEING JOHN MALKOVICH

1999 / 112 mins / USA / DVD / ▭ Video
Stars: John Cusack, Cameron Diaz, Catherine Keener,
Orson Bean, John Malkovich
Director: Spike Jonze
Producers: Steve Golin, Vincent Landay, Sandy Stern,
Michael Stipe
Script: Charlie Kaufman

Being John Malkovich is one of the most original and innovative films of recent times and is already the subject of endless internet discussion forums and chat-rooms – full of die-hard fans chatting about deeper meanings and what it would really be like to be JM.

Spike Jonze's directorial debut, *Being John Malkovich* is a darkly compassionate exploration of love and identity. Craig Schwartz (John Cusack) is coming to the end of his tether. A gifted street puppeteer, he nonetheless finds himself out of work – New York City has little use or tolerance for his special talents. His 10-year marriage to Lotte (Cameron Diaz), a workaholic pet store employee who literally brings her work home with her, has become habitual at its best. They have no money, no passion and no escape.

With no other prospects, Craig takes a job as a filing clerk at LesterCorp, a small company located on floor 7½ of Manhattan's Merlin-Flemmer office building. At his orientation, he meets the beautiful but uninterested Maxine (Catherine Keener) and for Craig, it's obsession at first sight.

Dejected and rejected, Craig retreats to his office to file. In a moment of exasperation, he slams a drawer shut, causing a folder to fall behind the cabinet. Upon moving the cabinet, a small boarded-up door is revealed. Prising open the door, Craig uncovers a passageway. Cautiously, he climbs in and is suddenly sucked through a dark wet tunnel. There is a flash of bright white light, and then, all at once, Craig realises he has discovered a portal that is an all-access pass to the unique experience that is John Malkovich. He is being John Malkovich...

Both absurd and simple at the same time, the movie really takes off when Craig realises he can *control* Malkovich and when he starts charging members of the public $200 to step inside. A success like this proves that obscure scripts don't have to be confined to the desks of art-house directors.

Memorable dialogue:

Lotte Schwartz: Don't stand in the way of my actualization as a man.

Craig Schwartz: Nobody's looking for a puppeteer in today's wintry economic climate.

Craig Schwartz: Do you know what a metaphysical can of worms this portal is?

Craig Schwartz: You see the world through John Malkovich's eyes. Then after about 15 minutes, you're spit out into a ditch on the side of the New Jersey Turnpike!

Maxine: Meet you in Malkovich in one hour.

Craig Schwartz: With all due respect, John, It's MY portal.
John Horatio Malkovich: It's MY HEAD, Schwartz. It's MY head!

Craig Schwartz: Can I buy you a drink, Maxine?
Maxine: Are you married?
Craig Schwartz: Yes, but enough about me.

Dr Lester: I've been very lonely in my isolated tower of indecipherable speech.

A BETTER TOMORROW

1986 / 95 mins / Hong Kong / DVD / ▭ Video
Stars: Ti Lung, Leslie Cheung, Chow Yun-Fat,
Emily Chu, Waise Lee, Fui-On Shing,
Kenneth Tsang, Hark Tsui
Director: John Woo
Producers: Hark Tsui, John Woo
Script: Hing-Ka Chan, Suk-Wah Leungy

Ying Huang Boon Sik or *A Better Tomorrow* is the film that started it all, full of its director's now-classic trademarks of jaw-dropping style, heart-stopping action and gunfire mayhem. Chow Yun-Fat stars in this epic story of suave gangsters and renegade cops who discover that in a world bound by honour, revenge comes at the speed of a bullet.

Written and directed by John Woo (*Face Off [1997]* and *Mission: Impossible 2 [2000]*), this was his breakthrough film and made an international superstar of Chow Yun-Fat (1992's *Hard Boiled* and 1998's *The Replacement Killers*).

The story is the tale of two brothers: gangster Ho (Ti Lung) who wants to go straight and his brother Kit (Cheung), a dedicated police inspector who blames him for their father's death.

John Woo's main theme is the importance of brotherhood. He sets brother against brother, gangster against gangster. Woo has stated that tight bonding between men is something that was lost among youngsters at the time of his movie. Brotherhood in the film is all about honour and love. The relationship between Ho and Kit is so strong that, eventually, there is nothing that can destroy it.

Groundbreaking when first released because of the stylistic depiction of the action scenes, its success inspired a new genre in Hong Kong cinema known as Heroic Bloodshed. These films were usually gangster pics characterised by gory shoot-outs, heavy action and gritty, violent drama. Hong Kong cinema in the late 80s was in the midst of a gangster film craze similar to Hollywood in the 30s and 40s, France in the 50s and 60s, Japan in the 60s and 70s, and Italy in the 70s and 80s. *A Better Tomorrow* is to Heroic Bloodshed what *A Fistful of Dollars* (1966) was to the Spaghetti Western.

Woo later made a sequel in which the mayhem moves from New York City to Hong Kong, where renegade gangsters and hot-shot cops take on the syndicate in another showdown of honour, loyalty and bullet-riddled revenge.

Memorable dialogue:

Mark: If you don't stop pointing that gun, you'll have to use it.

Mark: I never realised Hong Kong was so beautiful at night. It will vanish one day, that's for sure.

Ho Tse Sung: Do you believe there's a God?
Mark: Yes, I'm one, you're one. A god is someone who controls his destiny.

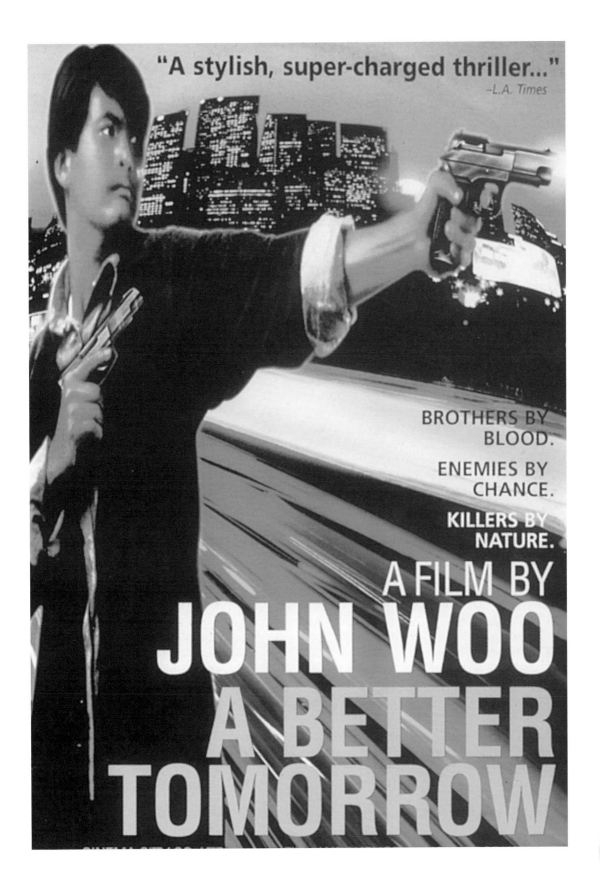

"A stylish, super-charged thriller..."
—L.A. Times

BROTHERS BY
BLOOD.

ENEMIES BY
CHANCE.

KILLERS BY
NATURE.

A FILM BY
JOHN WOO
A BETTER
TOMORROW

BILL AND TED'S EXCELLENT ADVENTURE

1989 / 89 mins / USA / DVD / ▭ Video
Stars: Keanu Reeves, Alex Winter, George Carlin,
Tony Camilieri, Dan Shor, Ted Steedman, Rod Loomis,
Al Leong
Director: Stephen Herek
Producers: Scott Kroopf, Michael S Murphy, Joe Soisson
Script: Chris Matheson, Ed Soloman

Two teenage airheads – Ted 'Theodore' Logan and Bill S Preston – will fail to graduate if they don't do well in their history presentation, and that could mean they'll end up in military school. Totally bogus and uncool! Only a miracle can save them. However, straight out of *Doctor Who*, a dude called Rufus (George Carlin) comes from the future in a telephone box to help them.

Reeves and Winter are great fun as Bill and Ted. Their real dream is to be internationally famous rock stars and they constantly plug their guitars into their amps and imagine themselves as the Wyld Stallyns – their band's name. Travelling through time in their phone booth, they meet (and round up) such historical figures as Napoleon, Socrates – whom they call 'So Crates' – Joan of Arc, Beethoven, Freud and Abraham Lincoln, all of whom can help the pair with their history presentation. Radical!

Herek's movie was followed by an animated TV series, a live-action TV series and a movie sequel, *Bill and Ted's Bogus Journey* (1991). If you enjoyed *Wayne's World* (1992), then you'll love this.

Memorable dialogue:

Bill and Ted: Excellent!

Ted: Be excellent to each other.
Bill: Party on, dudes.

Ted: Bill?
Bill: What?
Ted: I'm in love, dude.
Bill: Come on, this is a history report, not a babe report.

Ted: But, Bill, those are historical babes!
Bill: Okay, you're the ladies' man. How we gonna meet 'em?

Bill: You killed Ted, you medieval dickweed!

Ted to Socrates: All we are is dust in the wind, dude.

History Teacher: Who was Joan of Arc?
Ted: Noah's wife?

Bill: Excuse me. Do you know where there are any personages of historical significance around here?

Ted: Strange things are afoot at the Circle-K.

Bill and Ted meet themselves
Ted: OK wait. If you guys are really us, what number are we thinking of?
Both: 69 dudes!
Both: Whoa!
Quadruple air guitar solo

Rufus: Gentlemen. We're history!

Once...They Made History.
Now...They Are History.

BiLL & Ted's
BOGUS
Journey
IT'S A TRIP.

Clockwise from top: William Sadler, Keanu Reeves and Alex Winter in the movie poster for Bill and Ted's Bogus Journey *(1991), the follow up to* Excellent Adventure.

THE BIRDS

1963 / 120 mins / USA / *DVD* / ▭ Video
Stars: Rod Taylor, Tippi Hedren, Jessica Tandy,
Suzanne Pleshette, Veronica Cartright
Director: Alfred Hitchcock
Producer: Alfred Hitchcock
Script: Evan Hunter

Based on Daphne Du Maurier's novella, Hitchcock's 54th film shocked audiences at the time of release (very gory by Hitchcock standards), but succeeded in becoming an instant box-office hit. *The Birds* went on to influence a variety of work, including George Romero's *Night of the Living Dead* (1968), itself a great cult classic. Romero kept the element of unexpected menace but replaced the birds aspect of the story with zombies.

The virtually unknown Tippi Hedren was cast in the lead role as jet-setter Melanie Daniels, Rod Taylor as tough lawyer Mitch Brenner, Jessica Tandy as Mitch's fearful mother Lydia, and Suzanne Pleshette as one of Mitch's old flames, Annie Hayworth. Veronica Cartwright, Ethel Griffies, Charles McGraw, and Ruth McDevitt also put in fine performances.

Set in San Francisco, Melanie Daniels is shopping in a pet store when she meets Mitch Brenner who's looking to buy a pair of love birds for his young sister's birthday. He recognises Melanie and, knowing her as a prankster, he pretends to mistake her for an assistant and eventually storms out of the store. She decides to get her own back by finding him, buying the birds and driving her sports car up the coastline to Bodega Bay, where Mitch spends his weekends with his sister and mother. Shortly after she arrives, Melanie is attacked by a seagull. Mitch is there to attend to the startled young woman, but he is surprised to meet her again. However, this is just the start of a series of attacks by an increasing number of birds.

News of birds attacking people begins to spread around town. However, no one believes the reports until a school full of children, including Mitch's sister Cathy, are attacked and the authorities don't know what to do. Bodega Bay is finally evacuated. Only a few stay, including Melanie, Mitch, Lydia, and Cathy who are all trapped in buildings by the vicious army of birds.

The gory highlights include hordes of attacking, pecking birds and the bloody corpse that has its eye balls removed by the feathered friends. The school play yard scene is breathtaking. First there are only a few ravens sitting on the gym's climbing bars. Within minutes hundreds of the beady-eyed terror-makers arrive. They are waiting for the recess bell, when all the kids come out.

Like Hitchcock's complicated shower scene in *Psycho* (1960), the attic scene in *The Birds* took about a week to shoot. Since Hitch needed so many cuts for the film editor to build the torrid pace of the scene, Hedren had birds hurled at her for five days straight. That was in addition to the birds that she already had tied to her arms and legs.

'Filming the attic scene was terrifying,' Hedren recalled. 'I ended up under doctor's care for a week. People who saw the film will recall that there are very few scenes that I am not in. I was working every day. In six months, I had only one afternoon off,' she said. 'When Hitch heard the doctor say I couldn't go back to work for a week, he said, "We have nothing else to shoot – she has to come back." The doctor said, "Are you trying to kill her?"'

In fact, Hedren was so exhausted that she began losing track of day-to-day events:

'I don't remember driving to the studio, I don't remember anything,' she said. 'When I lay down on the sofa, the make-up man or hairdresser couldn't wake me. I hardly remember anything about that week.'

Despite the toll that the scene took on her, Hedren still had a tremendous amount of respect for Hitchcock's vision. 'He was a very complicated person – very deliberate in his thoughts and in his planning,' she said.

'He was very businesslike, and that spoiled you when it came to working with other directors...he used to tell funny jokes which made it fun at times. But he was a very psychological director, which sometimes made it very difficult. He knew what buttons to press to get the right performance out of you.'

In the end, Hitchcock reportedly derailed Hedren's career because she rejected his amorous advances.

ALFRED HITCHCOCK'S "The Birds"

TECHNICOLOR

...and remember the next scream you hear may be your own!

There is no happy ending in the movie either, only an increasing sense of doom. Hitchcock suggested that his film was about 'the Day of Judgement'. Blood and gore was rare on celluloid in 1963 and the director clearly came up with a completely original movie for that period in time. Hitchcock leaves his audience guessing as to why these birds have turned on humans but does give a few hints along the way.

Albert Whitlock's special effects are excellent, state of the art for the time. His crew used a combination of real and fake birds. Most of the time, it is hard to tell them apart. Hitchcock's humour is as dark as ever. And don't forget the director's trademark cameo, this time he's walking his dog. The nightmare ending is first-rate and Hitchcock devotees continue to look for deeper psychological or metaphysical meanings to this great thriller.

Memorable dialogue:

Melanie Daniels: I'm neither poor nor innocent.

Mitch: What do you want?
Melanie Daniels: I thought you knew. I want to go throughout life jumping into fountains naked.

Cathy Brenner: He's got a client who shot his wife in the head six times. Six times, can you imagine it? I mean, even twice would be overdoing it, don't you think?

BLADE RUNNER

1982 / 112 mins / USA / DVD / ▭ Video
Stars: Harrison Ford, Rutger Hauer, Sean Young, Edward James Olmos, M Emmet Walsh, Daryl Hannah, William Sanderson, Brion James, Joe Turkel
Director: Ridley Scott
Producer: Michael Deeley
Script: Hampton Fancher, David Peoples. Based on the novel
Do Androids Dream of Electric Sheep? **by Philip K Dick**

Los Angeles, 2019. Drowned in a grimly realistic urban landscape of stark metal, artificial light and pouring rain, Rick Deckard (Ford), a blade runner, is forced out of retirement and drafted back into the LA police department to destroy four escaped replicants (near-perfect androids): Roy Batty (Rutger Hauer), Leon, Zhora and Pris.

While hunting the foursome, Ford meets and falls in love with Rachael (Young), another replicant. At first, Rachael herself does not realise that she is a replicant. However, in her dealings with Deckard, she comes to understand her true origins and her ultimate destiny. Although Rachael is essentially an artificial construct, Deckard sees her as more than a collection of genetically engineered tissue and programming. She too has the very human desires for identity, growth and survival.

Scott's futuristic thriller quickly became a cult classic, with a fervent following and many devotees coming to prefer the Hauer character, the philosophical villain of the piece, to the lifeless Ford. Hauer's swan song is one of the most touching in modern film history: 'I've seen things,' he says, recalling the cosmic wonders he has witnessed in his lifetime. Then, clutching a dove in his hand, he remarks wistfully, 'All those moments will be lost in time, like tears in rain. Time to die.'

The director's restored cut (117 mins) has added to the film's reputation, making the noir tale darker and more complex. The ending of the original version was upbeat, with Deckard escaping with Rachael to Canada to live happily ever after. In the director's cut, the ending is more ambiguous, with Deckard and Rachael boarding the apartment elevator, the doors closing and their fate unknown. However, an even more intriguing aspect of the director's cut was new evidence suggesting that Deckard is himself a replicant. The key scene is a unicorn dream sequence. Gaff (Edward James Olmos), the enigmatic police officer who has been following Deckard around throughout the investigation, seems to know about Deckard's unicorn dream when he leaves an origami unicorn outside Deckard's apartment at the end of the film. The only way he could have known about Deckard's private thoughts would be if Deckard was a replicant and the unicorn dream was one of the standard memory implants that he possessed.

A bleak vision of the future, Scott's film questions what it is to be human and why life is so precious. Philip K Dick, the author of the book on which the film is based, died before the movie's release but did get to see footage before it hit cinemas. 'This is not like anything we have ever seen,' he remarked.

Memorable dialogue:

Tyrell: 'More human than human' is our motto.

Roy Batty: I want more life, fucker.

Deckard: All they'd wanted were the same answers the rest of us wanted, where have I come from? Where am I going? How long have I got?

Roy Batty: Quite an experience to live in fear, isn't it? That's what it is to be a slave.

Leon: Wake up! Time to die!

Rachael: I'm not in the business. I am the business.

Gaff: It's too bad she won't live! But then again, who does?

THE BLAIR WITCH PROJECT

1999 / 77 mins / USA /DVD/ ▭ Video
Stars: Heather Donahue, Joshua Leonard,
Michael Williams
Directors: Daniel Myrick, Eduardo Sanchez
Producers: Robin Cowie, Gregg Hale,
Michael Monello
Script: Daniel Myrick, Eduardo Sanchez

An opening screen explains that the film consists of footage found from three lost student film-makers who disappeared in the Maryland woods while searching for the legendary Blair Witch. Nothing in the film allows anything to shatter that illusion.

A young woman hires a film crew to accompany her into the Maryland woods to make a student film about a local urban legend, The Blair Witch. Together, during a two-day hike they chronicle local, age-old yarns and superstitions about witchcraft. But they never come back. When the threesome get lost, the terror begins. A year later, the students' film and video is found in the woods. The footage is compiled and made into a movie: *The Blair Witch Project.*

Mostly ad-libbed and despite a desperately low budget, those involved have created a real atmosphere of fear and anxiety. Eduardo Sanchez and Dan Myrick leave horror to the audience's imagination and have managed to create a truly scary film. Shot with hand-held cameras, *The Blair Witch Project* has the look of a student film and its accompanying out-takes, but more importantly, it feels real. The film relies on suggestion and implication, with the view that the imagination's thoughts of what might have happened generally horrify on a deeper level than knowing what did.

The Blair Witch Project is based on the legend of the Blair Witch that began in 1785 in the Township of Blair, located in north-central Maryland. The three protagonists investigate two centuries worth of mythology, including an 1809 book called *The Blair Witch Cult*, a newsreel from the 40s on a serial killer responsible for the deaths of seven children and maps of landmarks where mysterious mass killings in Maryland's Black Hills Forest occurred.

Heather Donahue, Joshua Leonard and Michael Williams, the three college students involved, follow the tales of the witch and the maps of Black Hills on their perilous documentary project until they become completely disorientated and totally alone in the woods. They've all heard horror stories about what may or may not have happened there and, as night falls, their imaginations run riot.

Completely isolated, they realise they are being hunted for their lives by something they cannot see and their experience takes a turn from just plain horrifying to a living and breathing bone-chilling nightmare.

Fuelled by an internet preview campaign, *The Blair Witch Project* generated a packet at the box office. Made on a pitiful $25,000 budget, virtually no crew and no special effects, the pseudo-documentary topped the US box-office charts throughout the summer of 1998 and scared everyone witless. Proof, were any needed, that a little bit of talent and goodwill and a huge helping of hype can make a winner.

Many followers of this film have tried to prove it is based on an actual event and that something sinister really is at work. Quite cleverly, Joe Berlinger (with Myrick and Sanchez's involvement) used exactly this notion to create the sequel – *Book of Shadows: Blair Witch 2* (2001), which returns to Maryland's ominous Black Hills region to reconstruct a ghastly series of crimes committed in November 1999. In the wake of the original movie and the prodigious media coverage devoted to its intermingling of half truths and long-forgotten myths, fans and curiosity seekers descend on the movie's real-life setting of Burkittsville, Maryland, to discover some truths for themselves. A rag tag of believers, sceptics and thrill-seekers prepare to spend their first night in the woods. Arguing among themselves regarding the first film's basis in fact or fiction, the group falls asleep. When they awake, they find a scene of destruction and none can remember the events of the previous evening...

Back in the real world, Momentum's excellent DVD release of this title provided haunting clues – not easily seen by the naked eye – to the 'Secret of Esrever'.

Memorable dialogue:

Joshua Leonard: You gonna write us a happy ending, Heather?

Heather Donahue: I'm scared to close my eyes. I'm scared to open them.

Heather Donahue: It's very hard to get lost in America these days, and even harder to stay lost.

Heather Donahue: Mmmm. Marshmallows. Soft.

Michael Williams: What's with that slime on your backpack?
Joshua Leonard: That's not slime, it's just water. No wait, it is slime, what the fuck?

Joshua Leonard: I heard two noises coming from two separate areas of space over there. One of them could have been a deer, but the other one sounded like a cackling.
Heather Donahue: No way!
Joshua Leonard: Yeah, it was like a serious cackling.
Heather Donahue: See, my problem is that I sleep like a fucking rock.
Michael Williams: If I heard a cackling, I would have shit in my pants!

Joshua Leonard: It's not the same on film is it? I mean, you know it's real, but it's like looking through the lens gives you some sort of protection from what's on the other side.

THE BLOB

1958 / 86 mins / USA / (Not currently available)
Stars: Steve McQueen, Aneta Corsaut, Earle
Rowe, Olin Howlin, Alden 'Steven' Chase,
John Bensom, George Karas
Director: Irvin S Yeaworth Jr
Producer: Jack H Harris
Script: Kay Linekar, Irving H Millgate,
Theodore Simonson

'Indescribable... indestructible... insatiable... Nothing can stop it! The indestructible creature! Bloated with the blood of its victims!' As you can guess from this 1958 movie's poster tag line, *The Blob* is a fine example of a cheesy, camp classic of cheap 50s sci-fi. Steve (billed as 'Steven' in his first starring role) McQueen is a misunderstood kid who leads teenagers into battle to save their small town from being swallowed up by a mysterious creature from another planet, resembling a giant blob of jelly. The residents of a nearby small town refuse to listen to some teenagers who have witnessed the blob's destructive power. In the meantime, the pink blancmange from Hell just keeps on getting bigger. It reaches the size of a house and becomes a danger to the free world in a film full of cheap thrills.

Not really very good at all and it certainly won't scare you (did the producers really think this film would scare people, even in the 50s, or was it all intentionally cheesy?) but you'll definitely smile, especially if you love kitsch. Burt Bacharach composed the title song. In 1979, Larry Hagman (yes, that one) directed a sequel, *Beware! The Blob* and Irvin S Yeaworth Jr's film was remade 30 years later by Chuck Russell.

Memorable dialogue:

Kate, the nurse: Doctor, nothing will stop it!

Lieutenant Dave: Just because some kid smashes into your wife on the turnpike doesn't make it a crime to be 17.

On the radio to Washington
Lieutenant Dave: I think you should send us the biggest transport plane you have, and take this thing to the Arctic or somewhere and drop it where it will never thaw.

Lieutenant Dave: At least we've got it stopped.
Steve Andrews: Yeah, as long as the Arctic stays cold.

THE BLUES BROTHERS

1980 / 133 mins / USA / _DVD_ / ▭ Video
Stars: John Belushi, Dan Aykroyd, Kathleen Freeman,
Cab Calloway, James Brown, Chaka Khan, Carrie
Fisher, Henry Gibson, John Lee Hooker, Aretha
Franklin, Ray Charles, Steve Cropper
Director: John Landis
Producer: Robert K Weiss
Script: John Landis

Originally based on a _Saturday Night Live_ sketch, the Blues Brothers are Jake (John Belushi) and Elwood (Dan Aykroyd). After the pair are released from prison, they go to visit the old home where they were raised by nuns. They discover the church has stopped funding the orphanage and plans to sell it to the education authority. The only way to keep the place open is if the $5000 tax on the property is paid within 11 days. Jake and Elwood decide to help by putting their blues band back together to raise some cash.

'We're on a mission from God,' Elwood repeatedly claims. So, they track down the other band members – at a soul food café, at a restaurant, and at a Holiday Inn lounge – reform and nearly destroy Chicago in the process. Completely off the wall with an amazing soundtrack, like loads of other great cult movies _The Blues Brothers_ also has a string of cool cameo performances. None other than the Godfather of Soul, James Brown, appears, playing a Baptist minister; Aretha Franklin is a waitress; Ray Charles a music shop owner; the late John Candy a cop and blockbuster director Steven Spielberg is the county assessor who stamps the cheque that saves the church orphanage. Other guest appearances include Frank Oz, Steve Lawrence, John Lee Hooker, British supermodel Twiggy and Paul Reubens (Pee-wee Herman).

There are lots of inside jokes about Chicago and the state of Illinois which may be lost on an international audience but the general mix of comedy, car chases and car crashes will always prove to be a real crowd-pleaser.

In 1998, a sequel starring Dan Aykroyd and John Landis – _Blues Brothers 2000_ – picked up 18 years later from the original. Elwood Blues is released from prison again and once more tries to re-form his old band with new lead singer Mighty Mac. This time round, BB King, Eric Clapton, Dr John and others join in the fun.

Memorable dialogue:

Donald 'Duck' Dunn: We had a band powerful enough to turn goat piss into gasoline.

Jake Blues: How much for the little girl? Your women – how much for the women?

Mrs Tarantino: Are you the police?
Elwood Blues: No, ma'am. We're musicians.

Jake Blues: I ran out of gas! I got a flat tire! I didn't have change for cab fare! I lost my tux at the cleaners! I locked my keys in the car! An old friend came in from out of town! Someone stole my car! There was an earthquake! A terrible flood! Locusts! IT WASN'T MY FAULT, I SWEAR TO GOD!

Elwood: You fat penguin!

Jake Blues: Ya see, me and the Lord have an understanding.

Cab Calloway: Boys, you got to learn not to talk to nuns that way.

BLUE VELVET

1986 / 120 mins / USA / *DVD* / ▭ Video
Stars: Kyle MacLachlan, Isabella Rossellini,
Dennis Hopper, Laura Dern,
Hope Lange, Dean Stockwell
Director: David Lynch
Producer: Fred Caruso
Script: David Lynch

On seeing *Blue Velvet* for the first time, Roy Orbison (whose 'In Dreams' provides perhaps the most unnerving scene) said, 'There was just no reference point in the culture to compare it.'

A triumph of weirdness and flamboyance, David Lynch's tale from 1986 details a young man's involvement in a small-town mystery. Jeffrey Beaumont (Kyle MacLachlan) returns to Lumberton, his hometown, to see his father recovering from a stroke in hospital, makes his way home and discovers a severed human ear in a field. Not satisfied with Detective Williams' (George Dickerson) handling of the case, Jeffrey and the police detective's daughter Sandy (Laura Dern) carry out their own investigation.

Sandy provides Jeffrey with eavesdropped information about the ear and its possible link to local nightclub singer Dorothy Vallens (Isabella Rossellini). Jeffrey breaks into Vallens' apartment but slips up big time and is caught. Dorothy bundles him into a closet on the arrival of a second guest, tragically unhinged Frank Booth (Dennis Hopper, devilish as ever, mesmerising in a perversely charismatic role). It was Frank, we learn, who cut off the ear of Dorothy's husband and it is he who is using Dorothy as a sex slave. He demands the lighting be set in a certain way and has Dorothy dressed in blue velvet as just one of his many sexual fetishes. Hopper's over-the-edge performance was his best for years and heralded something of a comeback for this acting legend.

But Jeffrey starts to become more like Frank as the story progresses. He suddenly changes from an average lover to a guy who beats Dorothy during sex sessions. Through flashback sequences we come to learn of his own 'perverted' nature within himself. However, unlike Frank, he doesn't remain in a state of self-pity and instead seems to learn from the experience. In the end Jeffrey is redeemed.

Hopper steals every scene that he is in. One key memorable scene takes place at a party at The Slow Club.

The charming Ben (Dean Stockwell) mimes to Roy Orbison's 'In Dreams' as Frank intently listens, giving a hint of homoeroticism. This scene is extended later as one of the party girls dances to 'In Dreams' on top of the car roof as Jeffrey is mockingly kissed and then pummelled by Frank and his gang. By this point *Blue Velvet* is at its most surreal.

On its release, the noted critic Pauline Kael remarked: 'The charged erotic atmosphere makes the film something of a trance-out, but Lynch's humour keeps breaking through, too.' There's no doubt Lynch's film paved the way for the lighter *American Beauty* (1999). All in all, *Blue Velvet* is an intriguing look at the evil behind the facade of a picture-perfect American town.

Memorable dialogue:

Jeffrey Beaumont: See that clock on the wall? In five minutes you are not going to believe what I just told you.

Sandy Williams: I can't figure out if you're a detective or a pervert.

Detective Williams: That's a human ear all right.

Frank: Suave! Goddamn you're one suave fucker!

Frank: Baby wants to fuck! Baby wants to fuck Blue Velvet!

Raymond: Do you want me to pour it Frank?
Frank: No I want you to fuck it. Shit, yes pour the fuckin' beer.

BRAZIL

1985 / 142 mins / USA / UK / 🖭 Video
Stars: Jonathan Pryce, Robert De Niro, Katherine Helmond, Ian Holm, Bob Hoskins, Michael Palin, Ian Richardson, Peter Vaughn, Kim Griest, Jim Broadbent
Director: Terry Gilliam
Producer: Arnon Milchan
Script: Terry Gilliam, Tom Stoppard, Charles McKeown

A Pythonesque take on *1984* and starring the wonderful Jonathan Pryce, Terry Gilliam's film has great production design paid for by American money. However, despite the American cash (and American director), the film has a distinctively British feel.

Set in a bleak, futuristic world, hapless technofile Sam Lowry (Pryce) is the ambitious civil servant who dreams of a life where he can fly away from technology and overpowering bureaucracy and spend eternity with the woman of his dreams (Griest). He sees himself as a winged superhero, soaring through the clouds to Xavier Cugat's 'Brazil' but is crushed by the State and a system he had never dreamt of questioning.

While trying to rectify the wrongful arrest of one Harry Buttle, Lowry meets the woman he is always chasing in his dreams, Jill Layton (actress). Landing a big promotion and now with access to the right computer files, he sets out to track her down – plunging himself further into the world of petty bureaucracy in order to escape it.

Meanwhile, Jill is running around trying to report a big governmental mistake. Her neighbour has been taken away by the police because he's been identified as a master criminal, stemming from a one-letter misspelling on the arrest form. But no one will believe her. At the same time, the real criminal continues, illegally, to fix plumbing and electrical problems for people. The man in question is Harry Tuttle (Robert De Niro). Tuttle was the man the Ministry were looking for in the beginning of the film and who quit the government because of too much paperwork

Tuttle lands a job fixing the air conditioning for Sam and his interception of a phone call lands him in trouble with the Department of Works, and two other weird repairmen, one being Spoor (Bob Hoskins). Sam is then suspected of organising a rash of terrorist bombings, and both his and Jill's lives are put in danger.

By the end, Sam is living inside his mind, flying in the clouds with his dream girl and humming the cool latino song 'Brazil'. The final torture sequence has him strapped into a metal chair in the middle of a huge dome.

Full of anarchic black comedy, the screenplay was written by Gilliam, Tom Stoppard and Charles McKeown. Classic subtle moments in *Brazil* include a man is buying 'clean air' from a vending machine in the street and the sequence where a small child tells Santa she wants a credit card for Christmas.

Grotesque and Kafkaesque, the film is constantly confusing but visually impressive. However, the film is more well known for what happened behind the scenes and the bitter battle between the director and producer that ended up in the cutting of the film. This, in turn, led to Gilliam using *Variety*, the industry's paper, to make fools out of the studio executives who'd meddled.

Memorable dialogue:

Mr Warren: What is this mess? An empty desk is an efficient desk.

Arresting Officer: This is your receipt for your husband... and this is my receipt for your receipt.

Bill, Department of Works: Mistakes? We don't make mistakes.

Charlie, Department of Works: Bloody typical, they've gone back to metric without telling us.

Kurtzmann: It's been confusion from the word go!

Jack Lint: It's not my fault that Buttle's heart condition didn't appear on Tuttle's file!

BRING ME THE HEAD OF ALFREDO GARCIA

1974 / 112 mins / USA / Mexico / (Not available)
Stars: Warren Oates, Isela Vega, Gig Young, Robert Webber,
Helmut Dantine, Emilio
Fernandez, Don Levy, Kris
Kristofferson, Jorge Russek
Director: Sam Peckinpah
Producer: Martin Baum
Script: Gordon Dawson, Sam Peckinpah
(from a story by Sam Peckinpah and Frank Kowalski)

El Jepe (Emilio Fernandez), a local wealthy landowner, discovers his daughter is pregnant having being seduced by one Alfredo Garcia. The wealthy Mexican rancher takes out a million-dollar contract with two homosexual hitmen (Gig Young and Robert Webber) and makes the pronouncement 'Bring me the head of Alfredo Garcia', attached to his body or otherwise!

The two hitmen enlist the help of sleazy local piano-player, Bernie (Warren Oates). Bernie's hooker girlfriend, Elita (Isela Vega), knows of Garcia's death and last resting place, so they all set off to find the head and receive a juicy reward.

On their journey across the countryside they encounter plenty of the trademark Peckinpah violence. Bernie is attacked while Elita is raped by a gang of Mexican Hell's Angels led by Pablo (Kris Kristofferson). Bernie manages to kill the bikers and retrieve the head, but a crazed Mexican gang kill Elita and steal the head.

Bernie has to re-enlist the help of the gay hitmen to help him kill the gang who've stolen the head, before knocking off the hitmen and returning the head (having lost everything) for a pay-off from El Jepe.

Shot in Mexico, it's another of Peckinpah's films examining death. Not surprisingly, it also features trademark Peckinpah slow-motion choreographed violence (no matter how much Tarantino tries to copy him, he'll never achieve the same effect).

Peckinpah always maintained this was the film he had most control over, with little interference from the studio. Well worth watching and one hell of a ride.

Memorable dialogue:

Bernie: Nobody loses all the time.

Bernie: Come on Al, we're going home.

THE BROOD

1979 / 91 mins / Canada / *DVD* / ▣ Video
Stars: Oliver Reed, Samantha Eggar, Art Hindle, Cindy Hinds, Henry Beckman, Nuala Fitzgerald, Susan Hogan, Michael Magee
Director: David Cronenberg
Producer: Claude Heroux
Script: David Cronenberg

Oliver Reed stars as eccentric psychiatrist Dr Raglan who runs the isolated Somafree clinic and uses innovative and theatrical techniques to breach the psychological blocks in his patients. He teaches patients how to manifest mental anguish in treatable boils and lesions on their skin – a practice that may be tied to a string of grisly murders committed by hooded, mallet-wielding dwarves.

Frank Carveth (Art Hindle) is an average man whose wife Nola (Samantha Eggar) is mentally unbalanced. Early on in the film, we discover that Nola is receiving treatment at Raglan's new-age psychiatric retreat. But rather than appearing as the usual strange lesions on the skin, Nola's anger not only manifests itself as bumps, it appears as these deformed, murderous children who slaughter anyone she's upset with. Frank has to protect himself and his daughter from Nola's psychotic brood.

Presenting a domestic drama, Cronenberg concentrates on the effects of divorce and broken marriages, child abuse and the power that cult gurus hold over their followers. Indeed, at the time of the making of *The Brood*, the director himself was going through a fairy messy divorce and custody battle.

A visionary horror film, *The Brood* is certainly one of David Cronenberg's most disturbing and provocative. It's haunting and completely terrifying and illustrates the central theme of his work: the body in revolt, mutating against our wishes and turning against us.

The film also has a great score by Cronenberg's regular composer, Howard Shore. A major contributor to the overall feel of Cronenberg's pictures, Shore has scored every one of the Canadian's features, save *The Dead Zone*. For this film, he came up with a score that includes a harrowing 12-minute suite called 'The Shape of Rage'.

Memorable dialogue:

    Juliana Kelly: Thirty seconds
    after you're born you have a past
    and 60 seconds after that you
    begin to lie to yourself about it.

BROOKS, MEL (MELVIN KAMINSKY)

Actor, director, writer
Born 28 June 1926, New York

Influenced by borscht-belt shtick, Mel Brooks began his career as a stand-up comic in the 40s, before working with Sid Caesar as one of the writers for his TV series *Your Show of Shows*. The programme and its follow-up, *Caesar's Hour*, boasted such other writers as Woody Allen, Neil Simon and co-star Carl Reiner. It also provided Brooks with a $5,000-a-week pay cheque. Brooks' first achievement in film was the Oscar-winning animated short, *The Critic* (1963). He scored a huge hit on TV by co-creating *Get Smart* (1965–69), which won him the backing, from Joseph E Levine, for his first feature film, *The Producers* (1968), which he wrote and directed. Gene Wilder's performance was perfect as the nervous accountant caught up in stage producer Zero Mostel's schemes to make money out of a flop. Brooks' all-too-Jewish humour remained in his cowboy-movie spoof *Blazing Saddles* (1974), also with Wilder, and in *Young Frankenstein* (1974), a hilarious horror parody. Later, he would parody Hitchcock in *High Anxiety* (1977) and *Star Wars* in *Spaceballs* (1987). During the 80s, his production company Brooksfilms produced some uncharacteristically straight films, including David Lynch's admirable *The Elephant Man* (1980), David Cronenberg's first Hollywood movie *The Fly* (1986) and the award-winning *84 Charing Cross Road* (1987). After rather limited success with a fairly straight comedy *Life Stinks* (1991), Brooks returned to parody for *Robin Hood: Men in Tights* (1993). See Filmography, p.238.

A BULLET FOR THE GENERAL (AKA: QUIEN SABE?)

1966 / 115 mins / Italy / (Not currently available)
Stars: Gian-Maria Volonté, Klaus Kinski,
Martine Beswick, Lou Castel, Andrea Checchi
Director: Damiano Damiani
Producer: Bianco Manini
Script: Salvatore Laurani, Franco Solinas

A Bullet for the General has achieved increasing cult success, admired by all fans of obscure Spaghetti Westerns. In fact, it ranks right up among the very best Italian Westerns, along with *Django Kill* (1967), *Once Upon a Time in the West* (1968) and *For a Few Dollars More* (1967). The film's original title is *Quien Sabe?* – 'Who Knows?'

Although he set it in revolutionary Mexico, Damiano Damiani shot the film entirely in Almeria, Spain. Damiani was a politically motivated director who saw his film as a comment on the effects of the US's intervention in Latin America. It's an outstanding piece of work, totally anti-Hollywood and a rejection of the romanticised views of mainstream American Western directors. The fast-moving plot was scripted by Salvatore Laurani and Franco Solinas.

A member of the Italian Communist Party, Solinas made sure most of his films were full of politics. He described *A Bullet for the General* as a more accessible version of his earlier film screenplay, a political thriller called *Battaglia di Algeri*, which was also released as *The Battle of Algiers* in 1965. A kind of pseudo-documentary, it charted the rise of Algerian nationalism and triumph over the colonial French forces.

The plot of *A Bullet for the General* concerns a Mexican revolutionary bandit known as El Chuncho who spends his time stealing arms to sell to General Elias. Chuncho is played by the great Spaghetti Western actor Gian-Maria Volonté, best known for his role as the bandit leader in the *Dollars* films. Volonte, a dedicated professional, was blacklisted during his early career for communist activities. Sergio Leone was the first director to offer him work again and he later appeared in more 'political' Westerns such as Sergio Sollinia's *Face to Face* (1967).

In *A Bullet for the General*, Chuncho's men are helped by a mysterious soldier of fortune – a gringo called Bill Tate, played by *Paranoia*'s Lou Castel. Tate brings a train to a standstill so Chuncho's bandits can steal all the rifles on board. The gringo is then allowed to join the group and

helps them to net bigger and better arsenals of weapons (including a much-coveted machine gun), which are sold to the rebels for a tidy profit. However, the gringo, who's nicknamed Nino by Chuncho, twists every situation to his favour and plays gang members against one another.

After discovering a machine gun has gone missing from San Miguel, Chuncho catches up with Nino in order to bring it back. But he's easily manipulated by the gringo and doesn't return to the vulnerable town. Interestingly, the film is completely open about the attraction between Chuncho and his nemesis. In one scene, when the beautiful Adelita (Martine Beswick) makes a play for Nino, he completely snubs her. 'The boy doesn't drink, doesn't smoke...and doesn't want women,' remarks El Chuncho. Nino's main interest is money and Chuncho's attraction to him could also therefore be seen as symbolic of the temptation of western capitalism. Nino's actions are a reference to the CIA's covert interventions in South America during the 60s, carried out in line with the US government's policy to 'Police Force the World', as stated in the controversial 'Monroe Doctrine'.

In Damiani's bold satire, Chuncho goes along with selling the weapons, only to be then told by the General that a raid was carried out on San Miguel, resulting in all inhabitants being killed because they had no arms. Chuncho orders his own death, but just as he walks out to face his execution, Nino's ruthless actions save his life but also force him to reassess his own morals.

Needless to say, in Damiani's film, the politics of the revolutionaries win through in the end, with a ringing call to arms: 'Don't buy bread, buy dynamite!'

Memorable dialogue:
The General: It was a massacre and you just earned yourself 5,000 pesos.

BURTON, TIM

Director
Born 25 August 1958, California

It took Tim Burton no time at all to become one of the hottest directors of his generation. His debut feature *Pee-Wee's Big Adventure* (1985), a surprise box-office hit, led to the supernatural comedy *Beetlejuice* (1988). Completely anarchic and grotesque, it was a comedy about a dead couple forced to call on the services of a repulsive spirit (Michael Keaton) to rid their house of obnoxious new tenants. *Beetlejuice* led to Burton being entrusted with the hugely expensive *Batman* (1989). Although his least personal film, it was one of the most successful films of all time. With his new-found power, Burton could easily have opted for a life of big-budget Hollywood blockbusters but instead he carried on as a maverick, making the surreal Christmas fable *Edward Scissorhands* (1990), full of mythic fairy-tale romance with deeply moving performances by Johnny Depp and Dianne West. *Batman Returns* (1992) was a far darker and quirkier film than the original, a reflection of how much creative freedom Burton had won (although Warner Brothers were reputedly unhappy with the final result). Burton's working relationship with Depp continued with *Ed Wood* (1994), his affectionate tribute to the life and work of the legendary Worst Director of All Time Edward D Wood Jr. It was a complete box-office failure but got Burton some of the best reviews of his career. Depp then featured in Burton's *Sleepy Hollow* (1999). Interestingly, Jack Nicholson, who headlined in *Batman*, also worked with Burton again in *Mars Attacks!* Burton has, up till now, always made the films that pleased him and not Hollywood financiers and it's this that pleases his faithful audience. See Filmography, p.238.

CARPENTER, JOHN

Director, writer
Born 16 January 1948, New York

John Carpenter was a self-confessed movie geek as a kid, a lover of low-budget thrillers from the 50s. His career began much like George Lucas' did, with his attending University of Southern California film school. His own full-length film-making debut was *Dark Star* (1974), which only cost $60,000, an extension of his student film. The ultimate cosmic comedy, it involves four astronauts in deep space, whose mission is to destroy unstable planets in star systems which are to be colonised. As the mission nears completion, they must cope with a runaway alien which resembles a beach-ball, faulty computer systems, and a 'smart bomb' that thinks it is God. Carpenter called his first movie 'One big optical *Waiting For Godot* in space.'

His second feature, *Assault on Precinct 13* (1976), was a homage to his idol, Howard Hawks, and basically updated that director's *Rio Bravo* in an urban LA setting. Carpenter's first big commercial success was the stylish *Halloween* (1978), the Hitchcockian film made for a mere $300,000. This cult horror flick is still the measuring rod against which all horror/slasher flicks are compared. Carpenter's masterful eye for composition and his use of shadows make for a particularly eerie atmosphere, intensified by his own piano score. One major plus point is that he uses basic scare tactics rather than gratuitous graphic violence (barely any blood is spilled during the film). It is also one of the few horror films that portrays its female characters as intelligent people and not bimbos. The movie ends with a real sense of foreboding and silent terror. Carpenter later wrote and produced (but did not direct) *Halloween II* (1981) and *Halloween III* (1982).

Later came the simple crowd-pleasing horror movie *The Fog* (1980) and *Escape from New York* (1982), in which Carpenter turned New York into a maximum security prison. *The Thing* (1982) was Carpenter's remake of the Howard Hawks' horror classic of the same name in which a group of scientists uncover an alien that has been buried in the Arctic ice for millions of years. When it thaws, it begins eliminating the men by taking over their bodies. This film is still frightening today with its paranoia among the men (a swipe at the McCarthyism and red scare of the 50s, from the original film) to a strangely predated AIDS parable. This film suffered the same fate as some of Carpenter's earlier work in that it was ignored on its release (a film called *ET* was released around the same time), but *The Thing* is now being re-evaluated as a classic.

However, Carpenter went on to make a few slip-ups. *They Live* (1988) was marred by extremely bad acting and an all-round weak script while the Chevy Chase comedy *Memoirs of an Invisible Man* (1992) was absolutely average. *In the Mouth of Madness* (1995) was a big improvement with Sam Neil as an insurance fraud investigator sent by a publishing company to find its prized horror writer, resulting in a wonderfully creepy climax.

It is strange to think that John Carpenter, having directed such well-known cult classics such as *Escape from New York*, *Halloween* and *The Thing* has remained one of the most under-appreciated directors in Hollywood. But like other mavericks, this is because he's ignored critics, stayed true to his vision and continued making movies that he would like to see. See Filmography, p.238.

CARRY ON . . .

From 1957 / UK / DVD / ▭ Video
Stars: Kenneth Williams, Sid James, Charles Hawtrey,
Frankie Howerd, Hattie Jacques, Peter Butterworth,
Joan Sims, Barbara Windsor, Jim Dale
Director: Gerald Thomas
Producer: Peter Rogers
Script: most by Talbot Rothwell

Carry On humour was born in 1957 when a low-budget Norman Huddis comedy was shot for £74,000 and was the third most popular film of 1958. The film was *Carry On Sergeant*, the first ever film in the highly successful Carry On comedy series – now an acclaimed British institution.

Forget sharp satire. The Carry On series began and continued with vulgar, but never crude, humour and jokes which could be seen a mile off. This predictability was and still is all part of the fun.

The early films were always suggestive and never explicit. Peter Rogers, producer of every film in the series, himself commented: 'We talk a lot about sex in our films. But nothing ever happens.'

Carry On actors soon became clichés of their own caricatures; Jim Dale, the nice young man; Charles Hawtrey, always sexually ambiguous; Hattie Jacques, matronly and in control; Kenneth Williams, the snobbish intellectual; Peter Butterworth, the frustrated old man and Sid James, with that unforgettable yak yak laugh.

Nobody was safe from ridicule: the army, the police force, the NHS and schools. Marion Jordan, in her essay 'Carry On... Follow That Stereotype', rightly points out that a great deal of the humour is derived from the contrast between the 'real' characters and these institutions that try to control them: 'Life, as the institution enforces it, would be, as the Sid James character puts it in one film, like having an itch and not being allowed to scratch.'

Some would argue that it isn't necessary to analyse the appeal of the Carry Ons, not because the series isn't worthy of analysis but because the humour, like seaside postcard humour, is so obvious. All in all, they're all just great fun. Today, there are an increasing number of Internet fan sites devoted to the Carry Ons and a whole new generation of devotees. All of the titles are constantly available on video and DVD.

Memorable dialogue:

Kenneth Williams: Stop messin' about!

Charles Hawtrey: Oh! Hello!

Kenneth Williams (as Julius Caesar): Infamy! Infamy! ... They've all got it in for me!

Sid James: Cor, blimey!

From Carry On Matron:
Hospital porter (Derek Francis): Are you expecting a baby or what?
Sid Carter (Sid James): Oh, definitely a baby - I don't like whats!

From Carry On Doctor:
Francis Bigger (Frankie Howerd): What is mind? No matter. What is matter? Never mind!

From Carry On At Your Convenience:
Hortence Withering (Patsy Rowands): I've heard shell fish do very strange things - in a sex way, I mean.
W C Boggs (Kenneth Williams): Ooh! Let's watch them for a bit then!

Sid James as Charlie Hawkins in Carry On Cabby *(1963)*

Left to right: Kenneth Connor, Joan Sims and Kenneth Williams in Carry On Abroad *(1972)*

CHEECH AND CHONG
(RICHARD MARIN AND THOMAS CHONG)

Actors, writers, directors
Born 13 July 1946, California and 24 May 1938, Canada

Two of the world's best-loved film-making hippies, Cheech and Chong honed their comedic personas in improvisational theatre in Vancouver. They may never have been nominated for an Oscar, but they did find favour with the 70s drug counter-culture and their movies were huge hits and undeniably funny. The key was the pair's way-out stoned humour – the whole point of their movies. Some memorable scenes include one hearty female party-goer snorting Ajax, thinking it was cocaine, and carrying on like a gorilla in the face of Stacey Keach, who brilliantly over-played an uptight DEA agent. The audiences for these movies knew what they were in for, as Cheech and Chong were making successful comedy albums long before movies. (Their biggest hit was 'Earache My Eye' backed with 'Sister Mary Elephant'.) Their most popular work is what's become known as the stoner's trilogy: *Up in Smoke* (1978), one of the highest-grossing films of that year. Several quasi-sequels followed: *Cheech & Chong's Nice Dreams* (1981) and *Still Smokin'* (1983). The two broke up the act in 1985, with Chong keeping a low profile, starring in and directing *Far Out Man* (1990) and Marin moving on to write and direct *Born in East LA* (1987), in which he starred as well. He has also appeared in *Ghostbusters II*, *Rude Awakening* (1989) and *The Shrimp on the Barbie* (1990). See Filmography, p.238.

CHILD'S PLAY

1988 / 83 mins / UK / _DVD_ / ▭ Video
Stars: Catherine Hicks, Brad Dourif, Chris Sarandon,
Alex Vincent
Director: Tom Holland
Producer: David Kirschner
Script: Don Mancini

When serial killer Charles Lee Ray is fatally wounded in a police shoot-out, he uses a voodoo spell to transfer his soul into Chucky, a 'Good Guys' doll. A cute kid called Andy receives the doll as a birthday present and Chucky soon resumes his killing spree, starting by throwing Andy's babysitter out of the fifth-floor window of their apartment.

However, Charles doesn't want to be trapped in the body of a doll for ever. His only escape would be to transfer into the first human he revealed his true identity to...which places Andy in mortal danger. One especially ape-like policeman takes the case, leading up to a crazy car-chase and Chucky's temporary destruction.

This cult horror flick spawned numerous sequels and immense controversy when it was linked to real-life copycat violence. Fans currently flock to www.chucky-online.com, a web site dedicated to Chucky, the star of the *Child's Play* movies. Within the web site there are picture galleries, sound files, movie clips, a forum (message board), Chucky's Chatroom and *Child's Play* reviews.

Memorable dialogue:

Chucky: We're friends 'til the end, remember?
Andy: This is the end, friend!

Andy: Chucky says Aunt Maggie was a bitch and got what she deserved.
Karen: Andy! How can you say such a thing?
Andy: I didn't say it, Chucky did.

Chucky: Hi, I'm Chucky. Wanna play?

CLERKS

1994 / 92 mins / USA / ⬛ Video
Stars: Brian O'Halloran, Jeff Anderson, Marilyn
Ghigliotti, Lisa Spoonhauer, Jason Mewes, Kevin
Smith, Scott Mosier, Scott Schiaffo
Director: Kevin Smith
Producers: Scott Mosier, Kevin Smith
Script: Kevin Smith

Shot in black and white on a budget of only £27,000, this off-beat slice-of-life comedy received a bevy of awards and earned first-time director Kevin Smith a contract with CAA. The story covers one eventful day in the life of Dante, a convenience store clerk (Brian O'Halloran) and his best mate Randal (Jeff Anderson) who works at the video shop next door.

While still in love with his high-school sweetheart Caitlin, he now has a serious relationship with long-suffering Veronica, who wants him to quit his job and begin college. The customers are a truly bizarre assortment of folk. This leads to some really funny bits, including the guy who gets his whole arm stuck in a Pringles tube as he desperately tries to reach the last few crisps.

This was one of the great film-making debuts. It's well written and well acted and far more entertaining than most of the more polished and slick Hollywood studio efforts from the 90s. *Clerks* is not just a film of crude banter (although there's lots of that) but also a film that features two main characters who, through a strange series of unlikely events, have to make choices that will affect the rest of their lives.

Memorable dialogue:

Silent Bob: You know, there's a million fine looking women in the world, dude. But they don't all bring you lasagne at work. Most of 'em just cheat on you.

Randal Graves: People say crazy shit during sex. One time I called this girl 'Mom'.

Randal Graves: I'm a firm believer in the philosophy of a ruling class. Especially since I rule.

Dante Hicks: Yeah, I mean aside from the cheating, we were a great couple. I mean that's what high school was about, algebra, bad lunch, and infidelity.

Randal Graves: Melodrama coming from you is about as natural as an oral bowel movement.

Randal Graves: Oh, hey Caitlin, break his heart again this time and I'll kill ya, nothing personal.

Jay Phat Buds: What's up, baby? What's up, sluts?

CLOCKWISE

1985 / 96 mins / UK / ▭ Video
Stars: John Cleese, Alison Steadman, Stephen Moore,
Sharon Maiden, Joan Hickson, Penelope Wilton
Director: Christopher Morahan
Producer: Michael Codron
Script: Michael Frayn

In the 80s, British film comedy was caught up in a strong parasitic relationship with television. Just as America's own *Saturday Night Live* team were providing a bunch of much-hyped stand-up comics for the movie business, in the UK a show called *The Comic Strip* allowed a group of very young and only slightly talented comedians to enter the film business with varied success. However, it was the BAFTA-award-winning television sketch show *Monty Python's Flying Circus* that provided the best group of new British film actors and directors.

Ex-Pythonites Terry Jones (*Personal Services*) and Terry Gilliam (*Time Bandits* and *Brazil*) flourished as directors. Michael Palin put in fine performances in the British-produced *A Private Function (1985)* and *The Missionary (1982)*. Meanwhile, John Cleese had already left the *Python* team to make a final series without him. He was busy writing the much revered BBC sitcom *Fawlty Towers* and later appeared with Peter Cook and Mel Smith in the 1986 film version of the British television series *Whoops Apocalypse*. After this solo success he took a starring role in the hilarious farce *Clockwise* in 1985.

In *Clockwise* Cleese stars as Brian Stimpson, a comprehensive school headmaster driven by punctuality, with an unenviable problem to solve. Having left his suburban home at 9am he must arrive at an important Headmasters' Conference by 5pm avoiding all the catastrophes that befall him on his way. One wrong move and a meticulously planned schedule goes completely out of the window for this compulsive clock-watcher. He crashes into a police car, gets stuck in the mud, is reported for vandalising a phone box and soon he's wanted by the police for kidnapping, theft and impersonating a monk –

and all because he missed his train! Cleese is a mix of British stiff upper lip and manic expressions as he quickly loses his composure after endless hitches on his trip to the conference. 'If you've ever been late', read the poster tagline, 'you'll know what this film is all about'.

The film is true laugh-out-loud British farce culminating in a hilarious climax of comic chaos. It features Sharon Maiden as the kidnapped schoolgirl and Penelope Wilton as Cleese's frantic former girlfriend who both end up a big part of his doomed journey. The original screenplay is by Michael Frayn, the prolific writer of adaptations, novels and stage plays such as *Noises Off* and *Benefactors*. *Clockwise* was directed by Chrisopher Morahan and was a big box-office success. This was mainly down to Cleese who once again had all the energy seen during his *Monty Python* years. He has a unique comic ability – a real talent for physical comedy. Cleese scored again two years later, with *A Fish Called Wanda* (1988) which he wrote, starred in, produced and co-directed.

Seen as quite mainstream in the UK, it is mainly in the US that *Clockwise* is developing cult status, as it was given a fairly limited release there. There are many Americans who have sought this movie, through internet auction sites and so on, having become fans of Cleese via *Monty Python*. However, thanks to US-based Anchor Bay Entertainment, a new video and DVD release is set to make the title more widely available outside the UK.

Memorable dialogue:

> Brian Stimpson: It's not the despair, Laura. I can take the despair. It's the hope.

A CLOCKWORK ORANGE

1971 / 137 mins / UK / DVD / Video
Stars: Malcolm McDowell, Patrick McGee, Michael Bates, Miriam Carlin, Adrienne Corri, Aubrey Morris
Director: Stanley Kubrick
Producer: Stanley Kubrick
Script: Stanley Kubrick

Modern society: gangs of punks run amok, peaceful citizens are imprisoned in their own homes and a political police government is no longer accountable to anyone or to any principles.

Based on Anthony Burgess' 1962 novel, Kubrick produced, wrote and directed this brilliant social satire, a stark and chilling film which sees Malcolm McDowell's finest performance ever as the young anti-hero Alex de Large, the leader of the teenage gang 'The Droogs'. Alex indulges in a reign of 'ultra-violence' as he describes it. The film is extraordinarily graphic and visually inventive. It is completely anti-Police and anti-Establishment with rapes, murders, disfigurements and testicle-crushing attacks. In one scene, to the sound of 'Singing in the Rain', Alex gives Patrick McGee a kicking, leaving him crippled. This sequence was directly emulated by Quentin Tarantino in his 1992 film *Reservoir Dogs*, in the scene when Mr Blonde tortures a police officer while dancing to rock music.

Alex is also a boy who's into Beethoven's Ninth and a bit of 'the old in-out, in-out'. But he soon finds himself at the mercy of the state and its brainwashing experiment designed to take violence off the streets and put it at the service of the government.

Kubrick's film is a brilliant celluloid celebration of adrenaline and testosterone. Subversive and shocking, even though only one character actually dies, *A Clockwork Orange* provides a strong argument for the preservation of respect for freedom of the individual, even freedom to do wrong. In the end, it's not totally clear if Alex has at last become the subdued 'Orange' that runs like 'Clockwork' or if human nature has begun to heal itself.

A Clockwork Orange, nominated for Best Picture in 1971, became the ultimate cult film throughout the world. Anthony Burgess' original book had already become a kind of dystopic cult novel and Burgess' own following undoubtedly helped ensure the film's cult reputation. Many young people identified with the Droogs' tribalism and style, their internal logic and loyalties. Bone-dry wit and dialogue played a major part in its cult status – in *Orange*, the gang use a strange mixture of Russian and English slang known as Nadsat, created for the novel by Burgess. Nadsat has now been appropriated by thousands of die-hard Kubrick and/or *Orange* enthusiasts, as seen on the vast number of internet chat-rooms devoted to the great man.

In the UK, until recently, Kubrick's film has been more of a mystery than a cult. Following the hysteria after its release here (it was blamed for countless real violent acts), Kubrick told Warner Brothers. he no longer wanted his masterpiece to be distributed in the UK. The withdrawal of *A Clockwork Orange* immediately lent it a desirable kudos. Only after Kubrick's death did the film get another UK theatrical release, in March 2000. It achieved tremendous acclaim from all sectors of the press, achieving a final box office of £2 million. Years of pent-up demand combined with a widespread reputation helped secure the further success of *A Clockwork Orange*. The recent theatrical release was followed by a video and DVD release (on Warner Home Video). And now, Malcolm McDowell's Beethoven-loving ultra-yobbo Alex is an icon all over again.

Memorable dialogue:

Alex: There was me, that is Alex, and my three droogs, that is Pete, Georgie and Dim, and we sat in the Korova milkbar trying to make up our rassoodocks what to do with the evening. The Korova milkbar sold milk-plus, milk plus vellocet or synthemesc or drencrom, which is what we were drinking. This would sharpen you up and make you ready for a bit of the old ultra-violence!

(from voice-over)

Being the adventures of a young man whose princjpal interests are rape, ultra-violence and Beethoven.

BEST FILM
BEST DIRECTOR
NEW YORK
FILM CRITICS

STANLEY KUBRICK'S

CLOCKWORK ORANGE

18

COCKFIGHTER

1974 / 84 mins / USA / (Not currently available)
Stars: Warren Oates, Richard B Skull,
Harry Dean Stanton, Patricia Pearcy, Millie Perkins
Director: Monte Hellman
Producers: Roger Corman
Script: Charles Willeford

Directed by Monte Hellman and produced by Roger Corman, *Cockfighter* is an offbeat and violent study of a man who trains roosters to fight in mostly illegal cockfights in the deep South. The screenplay was written by *Miami Blues* author Charles Willeford, an adaptation of his own novel. Interestingly, Quentin Tarantino cites Willeford's novels as a key influence in his movies.

Warren Oates plays Frank Masfield, the champion cockfighter who after losing his best bird to Harry Dean Stanton, undertakes a vow of silence, planning never to speak again until he wins the 'Cockfighter of the Year' medal. After losing everything – including his car, trailer and girlfriend – he begins his comeback. Oates is silent until the very end, although his thoughts are heard in voice-over narration.

Also known as *Born to Kill, Wild Drifter and Gamblin' Man*, Hellman's harrowing tale was banned by the censors in Britain because of the authenticity of the film's subject matter. A savagely accurate account of the violent world of cockfighting in Georgia, in which the viewer is shown footage of real fights, and in one scene, when the Oates character is trying to show his love for his girlfriend, he yanks a rooster's head off and jams it into her palm.

Oates was a regular actor in Hellman movies, appearing in *The Shooting* (1966), *Two-Lane Blacktop* (1971) and *China 9, Liberty 37* (1978). The toothy, balding, unshaven actor also played in classics such as Sam Peckinpah's *The Wild Bunch* (1969) and *Bring Me the Head of Alfredo Garcia* (1974). He was Peter Fonda's sidekick in the 1971 Western *The Hired Hand* and Sissy Spacek's disgruntled father in Terrence Malick's *Badlands* (1973). In *Film Comment* magazine, the noted critic David Thomson wrote: 'Oates was narrow in range, until you got into those narrows, and then you felt depths of humour, ferocity, foolishness, and honour.' The British film director Alex Cox commented, 'If you talk to a really good American actor who's working today – someone like Dennis Hopper, Harry Dean Stanton,

Ed Harris – and you ask who they think is the best American actor, living or dead, it is quite likely that they're not going to say Marlon Brando. They'll tell you it's Warren Oates.'

In the 70s the director of *Cockfighter* was one of the hottest around. Everyone wanted to know or work with Monte Hellman. His 1971 movie *Two-Lane Blacktop* had received rave reviews in the *New York Times*, *Time* magazine and *Newsweek*, and *Esquire* magazine even ran the screenplay as a cover story. However, Hellman found it very difficult working for studios in Hollywood and his career waned when political correctness seemed to put an end to gritty films about rough men. After the 1978 picture *China 9, Liberty 37*, Hellman didn't get to direct another film until another decade had passed. Unfortunately *Silent Night, Deadly Night 3: Better Watch Out* (1989) was a big disappointment. He was relegated to second unit director on *Robocop* (1987) and was left with an executive producer role when Quentin Tarantino took over on *Reservoir Dogs* (1992). Hellman had another comeback opportunity with the 1998 feature *Buffalo 66*, but star Vincent Gallo fired him and took over as director.

Hellman, like many great directors, feels he needs to make films with minimal crew and cameras rather than big-budget commercial projects. Although this attitude has kept him out of work for long periods, when he's managed to call the shots, it has usually been worth the battle. With *Cockfighter*, Hellman succeeded in making a thoroughly devastating portrayal of mankind in the worst possible circumstances. Controversial and distressing, with a curious morality, his film has a primitive quality that exerts an hypnotic fascination on the viewer.

Memorable dialogue:
Jack Burke (Stanton): You got two little faults, Frank. You drink too much and you talk too much.

COEN, ETHAN AND JOEL

Directors, producers, writers
Born 21 September 1957 and 29 November 1954,
Minnesota

Academy Award-winning Joel and Ethan Coen are the masters of originality and widely considered to be the most visionary and idiosyncratic film-makers of the late 20th century. Together, they create, write and plan every detail of each of their films through each stage of production, from storyboard stage to the edit room. It is Joel who normally directs while Ethan produces, although the siblings are involved extremely closely in every aspect of film-making.

During an average middle-class upbringing the pair made Super-8 films for fun, endlessly watched movies, and entered the industry doing all kinds of odd jobs. Joel even got to help out in the edit room for Sam Raimi's *The Evil Dead* (1982). Before long, the two brothers were writing their own murder and mystery scripts.

In 1984, they made their screen debut with *Blood Simple*, on a tiny budget with an unknown cast. Both of them wrote and edited the film (using the name Roderick Jaynes for the edit credit), for which Joel took directing credit and Ethan took producing credit. Critics everywhere loved it and praised the film for its black humour and complicated but dazzling plot in which a Texas bar-owner decides he's certain that his wife is cheating on him and hires a private detective to spy on her. *Blood Simple* won the Grand Jury Prize at the 1985 Sundance Film Festival.

Next came *Crimewave*, a film they wrote in 1985 that was directed by Sam Raimi. *Raising Arizona* (1987) was an off-the-wall comedy involving a Southern prison wardress (Holly Hunter) who runs away with an ex-con (Nicholas Cage) and steals a baby. After the success of their second film the brothers found themselves with a bigger budget – reportedly $9 million – for *Miller's Crossing* (1990), a stark gangster epic with a strong performance from John Turturro, whom the Coens would also use to great effect in their next film, *Barton Fink* (1991). *Fink* earned Joel a Best Director award and a Golden Palm at the 1991 Cannes Film Festival, as well as the Festival's Best Actor award for Turturro.

Although *The Hudsucker Proxy* (1994) failed to achieve the same critical and commercial success, it was still a film filled with the brothers' usual heavily stylised, post-modern irony. *Fargo* (1996) was yet another black comedy, similar to *Blood Simple* in its themes of greed, corruption and murder. The Coens received a Best Original Screenplay Oscar. Another Oscar, for Best Actress, went to Joel's wife, Frances McDormand.

After *Fargo*, the Coens went on to make *The Big Lebowski* in 1998, a warped crime comedy which won yet more awards and, more recently, *O Brother, Where Art Thou?* (2000) for which George Clooney won the prestigious Golden Globe award for his pivotal role as Everett Ulysses McGill, a garrulous, silver-tongued petty criminal having a hard time in Depression-era Mississippi. This film from the Coens is an inspired and unique modern-day spin on Homer's classic tale of *The Odyssey*. See Filmography, p.238.

THE COMPANY OF WOLVES

1984 / 95 mins / UK / (Not currently available)
Stars: Sarah Patterson, Angela Lansbury,
David Warner, Graham Crowden, Georgia Crowe,
Brian Glover, Kathryn
Pogson, Stephen Rea
Director: Neil Jordan
Producers: Chris Brown, Stephen Woolley
Script: Angela Carter, Neil Jordan

This movie is the allegorical story of a young girl's entry into womanhood, loosely based on the fairy tale *Little Red Riding Hood*. On ignoring the advice of her grandmother (Angela Lansbury) never to stray from the path through the woods, the girl (Sarah Patterson) encounters a man whose eyebrows meet in the middle and discovers a wolf in man's clothing.

Most of Jordan's film is the dream of Patterson and within her dream are other dreams and further strange, disturbing tales told by others. All of the stories tend to be about loss of innocence, coupled with a real need for pleasure and exploration of one's sexuality. The film itself deals with the end of childhood and the beginning of adolescence, with all its sexual connotations.

Visually the movie is amazing, thanks to Anton Furst's sensual and atmospheric forest settings, all based in the studio. Lovingly detailed sets and good effects (the werewolf metamorphosis scene is excellent) are integral parts in this exotic fairy-tale world, where the forest is always misty, the tall trees are sinister and the rural cottages come from gingerbread-land.

Memorable dialogue:

Granny: Never stray from the path, never eat a windfall apple and never trust a man whose eyebrows meet in the middle.

Granny: The worst kind of wolf is hairy on the inside.

CORMAN, ROGER

Director, producer
Born 5 April 1926, Detroit

The producer of over 500 films and director of around 50 others, the former 'king of the Drive-ins', Roger Corman has been a virtual one-man American Film Institute.

He will always be remembered for his ability to spot and foster other unique talent within the industry. Robert De Niro, Martin Scorsese, Jack Nicholson, Francis Ford Coppola, Peter Fonda, Bruce Dern, Diane Ladd, Talia Shire, Peter Bogdanovich, Sally Kirkland, Ron Howard, Charles Bronson, Joe Dante, Jonathan Demme, Gale Ann Hurd, James Cameron and many more owe a great deal to Corman. His influence on modern American cinema is therefore virtually incalculable.

Born in Detroit in 1926, Corman studied engineering at Stanford University. After a stint in the Navy, he took a job at 20th Century Fox and by 1949 was a story analyst at the studio. Never a fan of the workings of the American studio, he left and set off for England, where he did post-graduate work in modern English literature at Oxford's Balliol College. On his return to Hollywood Corman worked briefly as a literary agent but in 1953 he sold his first screenplay, *Highway Dragnet*, to Allied Artists and with the proceeds made the $18,000 flick *The Monster from the Ocean Floor*. Its relative success resulted in Corman getting to produce several low-budget features for American International Pictures – including Westerns, sci-fi flicks, rock 'n' roll movies and gangster films. In 1957 alone Corman churned out an incredible nine films, one of which was reportedly completed in two days! With unknown casts and tatty special effects, pictures such as *She Gods of Shark Reef* (1957), *Attack of the Crab Monsters* (1957) and *Teenage Caveman* (1958) grew to cult status and consolidated his reputation as 'King of the Z-movies'.

However, in the early 60s, Corman attained larger budgets and decided to go more upmarket with a string of Vincent Price/Edgar Allan Poe horror films which earned him international acclaim. When the French Film Institute honoured him with a retrospective in 1964, Roger Corman became the youngest producer/director ever to receive such an accolade.

Corman has also been credited with making the first 'biker' movie with *The Wild Angels* (1966) which starred Peter Fonda and Nancy Sinatra. Further trend-setting includes the 1967 film, *The Trip*, which was written by Jack Nicholson and began the 'psychedelic' film craze of the late 60s. Nicholson also had the lead role. Without these two movies, we'd never have seen *Easy Rider* (1969).

Occupying American International Pictures' top director spot, Corman helped build the company to success. But Corman was sick of executive interference and in 1970 he left to found his own production and distribution company, New World Pictures. New World's first year in operation astonished even Corman, as all eleven pictures proved very profitable. Hits included the cult film *Rock 'n' Roll High School* (1979). New World soon developed a reputation as a leading quality American film company with releases including Academy Award-winning films by Ingmar Bergman, Francois Truffaut, Federico Fellini, Akira Kurosawa, and Werner Herzog.

In 1983, Roger Corman sold New World Pictures and a day later announced the formation of his Concorde-New Horizons company. Through this, he released the teen sex school comedy *Screwballs* (1983), the sci-fi adventure *Space Raiders* (1984), the sword and sorcery *Deathstalker* (1984), the Jamie Curtis vehicle *Love Letters* (1984) and Penelope Spheeris' punk teen drama *Suburbia* (1984).

Concorde's more recent releases include Paul Anderson's *Shopping* (1994) and *Vampirella* (1996), with Roger Daltry as lead. Corman maintained he enjoyed going back to produce the kind of low-budget pictures with which he began his career, as nobody meddled with them. Having not directed a film since 1971's *The Red Baron*, he showed he could still tell a spooky tale once more in the 1990 atmospheric piece *Frankenstein Unbound*. See Filmography, p. 238.

COX, ALEX

Director
Born 15 December 1954, Liverpool, UK

Having debuted with the surreal and satirical film *Repo Man* (1984), Alex Cox went on to make the punk biopic *Sid and Nancy* (1986), experiencing both mainstream success and cult adulation, not to mention critical acclaim. With these films, Cox established himself as a highly rated cult auteur. Counter cultural hero Dennis Hopper described *Sid and Nancy* as 'an amazing film – a winner for all time. *Sid and Nancy* is a film that deals with a period of time and space that no other film has dealt with – a brilliant emotional experience. S&M, drugs, punk, rock 'n' roll, assassination of the senses. This film seems to self-destruct with Sid Vicious our protagonist. Brilliant! One of the important films of the century'.

Sid and Nancy got Alex Cox into Dennis Hopper's planned dream club of film directors, a company which was also to include David Lynch, Bigas Luna, Wim Wenders and Hopper himself. 'The dream was short lived because of financing', recalls Hopper.

After the success of *Sid and Nancy* Cox was offered a variety of Hollywood projects, including the awful comedy *The Three Amigos* (1987)! But he turned down the cheese in order to make *Straight to Hell* (1987), a Spaghetti Western homage with a cast that included the former lead singer of the Clash, Joe Strummer, rebellious punk outfit The Pogues, and the then-unknown Courtney Love. The film was completely grotesque and way ahead of its time, but did receive the Critics' Prize at the 1987 Madrid Film Festival.

Next came *Walker* (1987), Cox's most overtly political film. Cox's intention was to spend as many American dollars as possible in Nicaragua, in protest against the ongoing US-sponsored terrorist war against the FSLN and the Nicaraguan people. He made it clear that the film wasn't just an historical account of events that took place between 1853 and 1855, but was also about current events. With a limited theatrical release, the film failed to make an impact at the box office and Cox was immediately blacklisted by the American studios. Having been rejected by Hollywood, Cox spent a lot of time scraping together money for films that never happened. Most of his work came from scriptwriting jobs and a seven-year stint on BBC 2's *Moviedrome* series.

El Patrullero or *Highway Patrolman* (1991) was a Spanish-language feature which put Cox back on track. Described in *The Face* as 'a thrilling, gun-toting, whoring, car-chasing story', it's an entertaining, episodic account of the life of a Mexican highway cop, filmed in semi-documentary style and concentrating on the small happenings of an existence on the margins. For this film, Cox adopted a hand-held camera style with very few cuts (only 187 in the whole film) because he was simply sick of the formulaic editing style of the modern American or British film. Keeping with this new style, a film for the BBC followed – an adaptation of a short story by Jorge Luis Borges: *Death and the Compass*. It's an odd tale of conspiracy in which a series of murders may or may not be motivated by the occult. The cast includes Christopher Eccleston and Peter Boyle. The 55-minute BBC film was later turned into a full length theatrical film which premiered at the Tokyo Film Festival in 1996.

More recently, Cox was hired to direct and write the script for a new film version of *Fear and Loathing in Las Vegas* (1998). Cox soon walked from the project. His exit from the film was, in part, due to arguments with Hunter S Thompson but also to the fact that Universal Studios had become involved.

Virtually everything Cox does seems to be labelled cult, although he's not intending to go all out to secure a devoted audience: 'I think the word cult is one people often use when things just can't be categorised. Some things, such as *The Rocky Horror Show*, do have a demented following. I'm not so cultist as that. My films are all quite different. I sometimes think if you put them all end to end and watched them in a row, something would make sense'. See Filmography, p. 238–39

CRASH

1996 / 100 mins / Canada / _DVD_ / ▭ Video
Stars: James Spader, Holly Hunter, Elias Koteas, Deborah
Kara Unger, Rosanna Arquette
Director/Producer/Script: David Cronenberg

In his adaptation of JG Ballard's seminal 1973 novel, David Cronenberg ventures even further into territory mapped out in his previous films, exploring the extremes of behaviour, revealing how endlessly adaptable the human organism is, and how perverse.

The immediate subject matter of _Crash_ is the strange lure of the auto collision, provoking as it does the human fascination with death and the tendency to eroticise danger. Most motorists will slow down to stare at the scene of a collision; they may feel their pulses quickening and become exquisitely aware of the fragility of their own bodies. The characters of _Crash_ carry this awareness a step further, cherishing and nurturing it. For them, a car collision is a sexual turn-on, and a jolting life-force they come to crave.

Television commercial producer James Ballard (James Spader) and his wife Catherine (Deborah Kara Unger) have constructed a baroque marital sex life that is emotionally detached and relies heavily on their shared knowledge of each other's adulterous affairs. When Ballard is in a near-fatal car accident with Dr Helen Remington (Holly Hunter), he is drawn into an exploration of the links between danger, sex and death.

The Ballards and Dr Remington become involved with Vaughan (Elias Koteas), a renegade scientist obsessed with the erotic power of the crash, as witnessed by his head-to-toe scars. Vaughan introduces them to a strange crash-survivor subculture, a _de facto_ cult of which he is the high priest. In addition to watching test collision films, Vaughan and his cohorts stage re-enactments of famous collisions. Among Vaughan's acolytes is Gabrielle (Rosanna Arquette), who sports the physical mementoes of her accidents (scars, leg braces, a full-body support suit) like fetish gear. Dr Remington and the Ballards are steered toward a sexuality that gains potency and meaning from its head-on confrontation with mortality – and the knowledge that mortality must ultimately win.

Crash is a complex and frightening look at where the predictability and innovations of modern life have led us, at how dulled our over-sated senses have become. Like the book, the movie is a cautionary tale of how we might adapt to the sterile environment that we have ourselves created, and unfolds without moral judgement.

Cronenberg has said that he made _Crash_ to find out why he was making it. 'It's a dangerous film in many ways. It does violence to people's understanding of human relationships, it does violence to people's understanding of eroticism. If people find it disturbing, I think that's where the disturbing element is...But I think that's a primary function of art. To do violence to the little cocoon that we sometimes find ourselves enveloped in.'

Crash had its world premiere at the 1996 Cannes Film Festival, where it sparked considerable debate and ultimately received a Special Jury Prize 'For Originality, For Daring, and For Audacity'. _Crash_ has continued to be the subject of acclaim and controversy. It won five awards at the 1996 Genie Awards in Canada, including Best Director and Best Adapted Screenplay for David Cronenberg.

Memorable dialogue:

Vaughan: It's too clean.
Tattoo artist: Medical tattoos are supposed to be clean.
Vaughan: But this is not a medical tattoo. Prophecy is ragged and dirty...so make it ragged and dirty.

James Ballard: I'm beginning to feel like a potted plant.

Vaughan: The car crash is a fertilizing rather than a destructive event.

CREEPSHOW

1982 / 129 mins / USA / DVD / ▣ Video
Stars: Hal Holbrook, Adrienne Barbeau, Fritz Weaver, Leslie
Nielsen, Carrie Nye, EG Marshall
Director: George Romero
Producer: Richard Rubenstein
Script: Stephen King

The disposal of a young boy's comic is the catalyst for the blood-dripping pen of Stephen King to unfold five tales of terror contained in this horror omnibus. The stories are presented in the Gothic style of the old EC comics such as *Tales From The Crypt* and *The Haunt of Fear*.

Full of tongue-in-cheek humour, the first, entitled *Father's Day*, deals with a demented old man returning from the grave to collect the holiday cake his murdering daughter never gave him. The second, *The Lonesome Death of Jordy Verrill*, has King take on the title role of the dull farmer who discovers a meteor that turns everything into plant-life, including him. *Something to Tide You Over*, starring Leslie Neilsen, is about a vengeful husband burying his wife and her lover up to their necks on the beach. The fourth tale, *The Crate*, is about a malevolent creature that resides in a box from an Arctic expedition that's left under the steps of a college. The final story, *They're Creeping Up on You*, is about millionaire businessman EG Marshall who is literally bugged to death by hundreds of cockroaches bursting through his stomach. Ironic that he had an insect phobia.

Following the release of *Creepshow*, almost a dozen Stephen King-based adaptations came to the big screen, including Rob Reiner's touching *Stand by Me* (1986) based on *The Body From Different Seasons* and David Cronenberg's film adaptation of *The Dead Zone* (1983). But having distributed *Creepshow*, Warner Brothers. apparently lost interest in handling a sequel. Enter New World Pictures, who were keen to acquire the distribution rights.

Five years after the original fright-fest, the masters of the macabre, George Romero and Stephen King, came back with *Creepshow 2* (1987), which detailed three more tales of horror. Romero stepped down from the director's chair for the sequel and instead devoted his time to the screenplay, while long-time Romero cinematographer Michael Gornick (who shot the original *Creepshow*) made his directorial debut.

Memorable dialogue:
    Jordy Verrill: Meteor shit!

CRONENBERG, DAVID

Director, writer
Born 15 May 1943, Toronto

David Cronenberg started writing fantasy science fiction in college and while still there he became interested in film and produced two short movies. *Stereo* (1969) told the story of a group of youngsters involved in experiments which lead to an increase in their powers of telepathic communication. The second, *Crimes of the Future* (1970), was set in the Institute for Neo-Venereal Disease. It dealt with genetic mutilation, a topic associated with the Canadian director throughout his career. In fact, most of Cronenberg's films generally involve the horror caused by a mutation, a parasite or particular medical conditions: 'It's my conceit that perhaps some diseases perceived as diseases which destroy a well-functioning machine actually turn it into a new but still well-functioning machine with a different purpose...[you] see the movies from the disease's point of view. You can see why they would resist all attempts to destroy them. These are all cerebral games but they have emotional correlatives as well.'

From the word go, Cronenberg became one of the hottest properties in the film world, with incredible grosses for his early films. *Shivers/They Came From Within/The Parasite Murders* (1975) was co-produced by fellow Canadian Ivan Reitman. In its depiction of an artificially created parasite that passes from one tenant to another in a luxury block of apartments, Cronenberg provided an entertaining allegory on VD. Playing on the same theme, *Rabid* (1977) cleverly cast Marilyn Chambers, former Ivory Snow Girl and porn star, as the unfortunate victim of an operation that leaves her with a vampire appetite for blood. A deadly penile spike on her armpit infects anyone she embraces. These movies got the director dubbed 'The King of Venereal Horror'.

The Brood (1979), about a hate-ridden psychiatric patient who delivers a brood of murderous children, is said to be based on his own bitter divorce proceedings at the time of production. Next came *Scanners* (1981), about a group of social misfits imbued with telepathic powers.

Scanners has two of the most spectacular shock scenes ever filmed – one, the mind-blowing explosion in the opening moments, and the other, the classic cinematic display of scanner-power.

With *The Dead Zone* (1983) Cronenberg adapted the Stephen King novel about a man able to predict future events in people's lives simply by touching them. This marked Cronenberg's first outing as director only, without a hand in the screenplay. This movie has an excellent central performance by Christopher Walken who plays a man who emerges from an accident with psychic powers.

Videodrome (1983) was a brilliant satire about the effects of TV on its viewers and had James Woods as an opportunistic TV producer who grows obsessed with a sadistic-erotic pulp emanating from a mysterious pirate station. Cronenberg's remake of Kurt Neumann's sci-fi classic *The Fly* (1958) three years later was an even bigger success and was, arguably, his most polished horror film to date. The director added a much needed dose of dark humour to the camp classic and Jeff Goldblum turned in a quite remarkable if disgusting performance as the obsessed scientist tragically transforming into 'Brundlefly'.

Cronenberg followed up his biggest commercial success with *Dead Ringers* (1988) in which Jeremy Irons gives a disturbing, tour-de-force portrayal of twin brothers, both gynaecologists, whose lives fall apart when drugs, fame and a seductive patient break their lifelong bond. Based on a true case, this film is an unsettling masterpiece of graphic images and mounting instability.

Never one to shirk a challenge, Cronenberg then decided to film the 'unfilmable' William Burroughs novel *Naked Lunch* (1991). In 1993 he brought the challenging Broadway play *M Butterfly* to the screen. More recently, Cronenberg delivered the provocative and hyped *Crash* (1996) and the virtual-reality-based *eXistenZ* (1999), both of which fared well at the Cannes and Berlin Film Festivals. See Filmography, p. 239.

CUBE

1997 / 87 mins / Canada / *DVD* / ▭ Video
Stars: Nicole de Boer, Nicky Guadagni,
David Hewlett, Andrew Miller, Julian Richings,
Wayne Robson, Maurice Dean Wint
Director: Vincenzo Natali
Producers: Mehra Meh, Betty Orr
Script: Andre Bijelic, Graeme Manson,
Vincenzo Natali

Six people – a family man cop, a paranoid doctor, a pampered maths student, an autistic man, an escape artist and a man who's lost the will to live – wake from their daily lives and find they are imprisoned in a deadly maze which consists of metallic cube-like rooms. Doors in the centre of each surface lead to more rooms, some of which are filled with potentially fatal booby-traps. The purpose of the structure remains a mystery throughout. Those involved in the nightmare are Leaven (Nicole de Boer); Holloway (Nicky Guadagni); Worth (David Hewlett); Kazan (Andrew Miller); Rennes (Wayne Robson) and Quentin (Maurice Dean Wint). None of them know how they got into the Cube, and slowly they discover that each holds a key to unlocking this diabolical puzzle. Each prisoner has a talent that will help them figure out how to avoid booby-traps and ultimately how to escape. But factions begin to form and tensions build. They don't agree on the best course of action and there's also the fear that one of them may be a spy for whoever is in charge. As a mathematical formula for escape begins to reveal itself, the enemy rises from within themselves and survival is threatened by the same human weaknesses that created the Cube.

Cube features stunning digital special effects by C.O.R.E. Digital Pictures (1996's *Fly Away Home* and 1997's *Mimic*), prosthetic and physical effects by Emmy-nominated Caligari Studios (1990's *Jacob's Ladder* and 1994's *Natural Born Killers*) and was photographed by the talented Derek Rogers.

Natali's film is based around basic human fears: paranoia, isolation, the horrible feeling that we're being watched. Who put them in there? The government? Aliens? Is it a prison? A test? A rich psycho's entertainment? Like Patrick McGoohan's 1967 television cult classic *The Prisoner*, there are no easy answers and no happy endings. Many questions are left unanswered. There is no escape in the search for freedom. Within each of us, the most dangerous thing on Earth is what is within us. That is what the prisoners in *Cube* are trying to beat.

As Rennes says, 'Ya gotta save yourselves from yourselves'. You wouldn't wish this situation on your worst enemy. And who would that be? Yourself, of course.

Memorable dialogue:

Holloway: You've got a gift.
Leaven: It's not a gift. It's just a brain.

Quentin: For Christ's sake, Worth, what do you live for? Don't you have a wife or a girlfriend or something?
Worth: Nope. I've gotta pretty fine collection of pornography.

Worth: I have nothing to live for out there.
Leaven: What is out there?
Worth: Endless human stupidity.
Leaven: I can live with that.

Quentin: I'm not dying in a fucking rat maze!

Quentin: Is that your two cents worth, Worth?
Worth: For what it's worth.

Worth: There is no conspiracy. Nobody is in charge. It's a headless blunder operating under the illusion of a master plan.

Worth: Big Brother isn't watching you anymore.

DEAD OF NIGHT

1945 / 103 mins / UK / ▭ Video
Stars: Googie Withers, Michael Redgrave,
Sally Ann Howes, Mervyn Johns, Roland Culver,
Frederick Valk, Naunton Wayne, Basil Radford
Director: Alberto Cavalcanti, Basil Dearden,
Robert Hamer, Charles Crichton
Producer: Michael Balcon
Script: John V Baines, Angus MacPhail, TEB Clarke

Revered as the greatest piece of British ghost-story telling ever, this is a must-see for chiller addicts. An architect's recurring dream turns into a compendium of spine-chilling horror stories when he arrives to remodel a stately home and the other guests recall their own supernatural experiences. Inexplicably, he discovers the British estate and the group of people have all been part of his dreams.

The ultimate portmanteau horror movie, its pièce de résistance is the final story, a true suspense-rouser in which Michael Redgrave plays a ventriloquist whose dummy is imbued with a human brain and soul. It seems the pair are exchanging personalities and in the final scene, Redgrave delivers an extra special performance. In one of horror movies' most shattering climaxes, he is mesmerising as he's driven to 'kill' the demonic dummy.

So effective was this last tale that many have tried to remake it, most famously Richard Attenborough as *Magic* (1978) in which Anthony Hopkins is the ventriloquist dominated by his dummy. None of the remakes, including Attenborough's, has even been half as scary as the original.

No expense was spared in making this film. Obviously there was once a time when British directors making films in the UK didn't have to scrabble around for money from the Lottery or Government-sponsored film councils.

Memorable dialogue:

Craig: Everyone in this room is part of my dream.

Peter: The trouble's not in the mirror, it's in my mind.

Eliot: So we're all powerless in the grip of Craig's dreams. That's a solemn thought.

Craig: Hamlet was right doctor, there are more things in heaven and earth than are dreamed of in your philosophy.

THE DEVILS

1971 / 109 mins / UK / ▭ Video
Stars: Vanessa Redgrave, Oliver Reed,
Dudley Sutton, Max Adrian,
Gemma Jones, Murray Melvin
Director: Ken Russell
Producers: Robert H Solo, Ken Russell
Script: Ken Russell

In the 17th century, France is a country torn by religious wars and political intrigue. Louis XIII (Graham Armitage) sits on the throne but the policy of France is directed by Cardinal Richelieu (Christopher Logue), the King's chief minister, who asserts the power of the crown against all rivals. This policy brings Louis into unremitting conflict with the Protestants and Nobles of France.

The Huguenots are crushed by force and the feudal nobility lose their independence by an edict calling for the destruction of castles. It is to the walled town of Loudun that Laubardemont (Dudley Sutton), an agent of Richelieu, arrives to demolish the fortified walls. There he is stopped by Father Grandier (Oliver Reed). Urbain Grandier is a strikingly handsome priest of 35, a sensualist, an intellectual, a man born to be a leader were it not for a streak of cynicism which forever lurks behind his large, dreamy blue eyes. His vows of celibacy have not prevented him from bedding most of the pretty girls of Loudun. He performs an illicit marriage ceremony between himself and Madeleine (Gemma Jones), with whom he falls in love.

Within the walls of Loudun is the Convent of the Ursulines where a group of nuns are ruled strictly by their Mother Superior, Sister Jeanne of the Angels (Vanessa Redgrave). She is in her mid-20s, has a slightly humped back, but a truly angelic face. Sister Jeanne is sexually obsessed with Grandier, although they have never met. She often has visions of a sensual nature involving the priest.

When Jeanne hears of Grandier's illicit marriage to Madeleine, she is furious and falsely accuses the priest of lewdness and sorcery. Grandier's enemies recognise in this accusation the means with which to bring about his downfall and send for Father Barre (Michael Gothard), a professional exorcist.

It seems Sister Jeanne's lustful ravings have infected the other nuns in her convent and so begins a series of exorcisms. The methods that Father Barre and his helpers employ to extract the devils from the bodies of the nuns are the most erotic ever used. Circus-like public purges of the naked nuns are staged, which eventually result in Grandier's conviction, his torture and burning at the stake.

Russell's frantically paced film ends in the packed public square of Loudun as Grandier burns. The hysterical crowd rejoices at the public execution, oblivious to Laubardemont's demolition of the city walls behind them. Interestingly, the amazing sets were designed by Derek Jarman, himself a key cult director later in the 70s and 80s.

The Devils won Best Foreign Film at the 1971 Venice Film Festival. Although adapted from John Whiting's play of the same name, Russell claims his film's success was helped by him getting the rights to Aldous Huxley's *The Devils of Loudun*, which he says was 'a mind-blowing account of those fantastic events... which enabled me to not only "open them out", but turn them inside out and stand them on their head... His documentary novel is just about the trippiest version of a historical event it has ever been my good fortune to happen upon. It was also largely responsible for the original look of the film.'

Memorable dialogue:

Barre: Sin can be caught as easily as the plague.

Grandier: You have turned the house of the Lord into a circus and its people into clowns.

Grandier: Secluded women have given themselves to God, but something within them cries out to be given to man.

Peasant woman of Grandier: Now there's a man worth going to hell for.

65

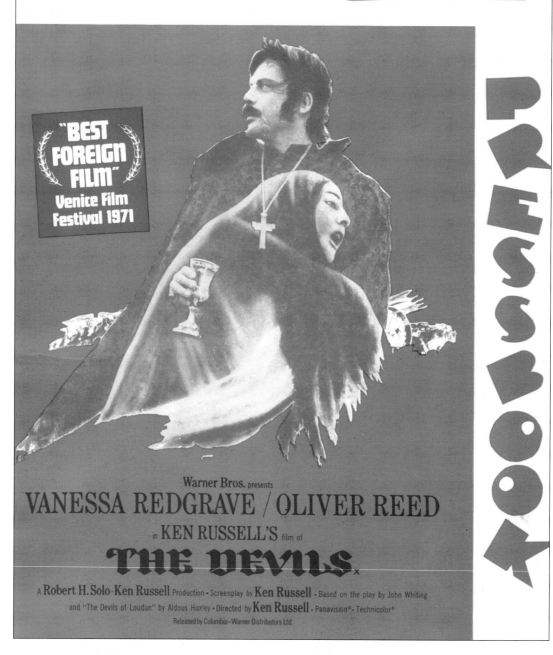

The original press campaign book for Ken Russell's 1971 film The Devils, *starring Oliver Reed*

"Divine madness, full of comedy, romance, opera and murder"
~Rolling Stone

DIVA

"Electrifying!"
~Roger Ebert,
Chicago Sun-Times

The spotlight's on soprano Wilhelmenia Wiggins-Fernandez as Cynthia Hawkins in the 1981 French thriller Diva

DIVA

1981 / 123 mins / France / ▭ Video
Stars: Frederic Andrei, Richard Bohringer, An Luu
Thuy, Wilhelmenia Wiggins-Fernandez
Director: Jean-Jacques Beineix
Producer: Irene Silberman
Script: Jean-Jacques Beineix, Jean Van Hamme
(based on the novel by Delacorta)

Jean-Jacques Beineix's high-tech debut feature *Diva* was an inspired succès d'estime, twisting the diverse styles of film noir, fairy-tale Gallic romance and New Wave with mad comedy and opera. Provoking gasps of admiration from critics, the film quickly became a cult favourite with audiences, as well as placing Beineix as one of France's most influential film-makers of the 80s.

Set in the neon lights of the highly stylised Parisian punk underground, *Diva* is an audaciously stylish dark thriller of romance, misunderstanding, prostitution and murder. The story revolves around an 18-year-old moped postal courier called Jules (Frederic Andrei). This young bohemian is obsessed with opera and its singers, especially the exquisite black soprano Cynthia Hawkins (Wilhelmenia Wiggins-Fernandez), whose work has never been recorded because she's notoriously protective of her own voice and simply refuses to make any records. But when Jules attends this super-Diva's first European concert at the Théâtre des Champs-Elysées, he manages to make a bootleg tape recording of his idol. Only the viewer sees that he is being observed by two sinister Taiwanese men.

Later, in a separate incident after the concert, two thugs follow a barefoot young woman through the streets of Paris. As she tries to get away she slips a cassette into Jules' bag. The thugs catch up with her, then murder her in the street. It turns out that this second tape features the name of a high-profile police commissioner as an accomplice in a seedy prostitution ring run by the mob. As a result, Jules finds himself being chased by both the rival Taiwanese record pirates, who are after the recording of the opera star, and crooked cops and hitmen (out to protect the police sergeant). Jules is helped along the way by a wild, idiosyncratic duo: Zen master Serge Gorodish (Richard Bohringer) and his partner and plaything Alba, a 13-year-old kleptomaniacal Vietnamese girl (An Luu Thuy).

Diva is based on the 1979 novel by Delacorta, the pen name of Daniel Odier, a Swiss novelist and screenwriter. As

a self-confessed auteur however, the film's director Jean-Jacques Beineix simply used Delacorta's novel as basic raw material, transforming it on film into an amalgam of traditional genres, mixing high art with pop culture imagery and alluding to popular movies such as *Some Like it Hot* (1959) and *The French Connection* (1971). A blend of modern TV images can be seen as well, mostly from the world of advertising. The film satirises our consumer culture in which only the best brands will do. For example, in *Diva*, a Rolls Royce and a Rolex watch symbolise perfection.

Diva has also been noted for its superb art direction and camera work. The art director in question is Hilton Macconnico who's offered up a glossy package of ultra-chic post-punk images and aesthetics, although beneath this flashy concoction lies an intriguing homage to the silent serials of Louis Feuillade. Vladmir Cosmas' background score, based mostly on Act 1 of Alfredo Catalani's glorious *La Wally*, is equally impressive

Diva was a big hit in France, the United States and the UK. After the success of his first feature, Jean-Jacques Beineix went on to direct the Oscar-nominated *Betty Blue* (1986) and the stunning road movie *IP5: The Island of the Pachyderms* (1992). However, for the rest of the 90s he gave up directing feature films, blaming a combination of a mid-life crisis plus some lack of inspiration, not to mention having to come to terms with the death of his mother. And then the death of his best friend. Nevertheless, by late 1999, Beineix was back on location in France and Germany, directing his comeback film, another exciting thriller based on his own screenplay, *Mortel Transfert* (2000).

Memorable dialogue:

Gorodish: Some get high on airplane glue … detergents … fancy gimmicks. My satori is this: Zen in the art of buttering bread!

DONT LOOK NOW

1973 / 110 mins / UK / Italy / ⊞ Video
Stars: Julie Christie, Donald Sutherland,
Hilary Mason, Celia Matania,
Massimo Serato, Renata Scarpa
Director: Nicolas Roeg
Producer: Peter Katz
Script: Allan Scott, Chris Bryant

In this gripping Daphne du Maurier occult thriller, John and Laura Baxter, the parents of a dead child, go to Venice where instead of solace, they find reminders of their tragedy. They meet a pair of elderly sisters, one of whom claims to be psychic. She insists that she sees the spirit of their daughter, who recently drowned. Laura is intrigued, but John resists the idea. He, however, seems to have his own psychic flashes, seeing their daughter walk the streets in her red cloak, as well as Laura and the sisters on a funeral gondola.

Donald Sutherland and Julie Christie star in this now-classic Gothic thriller as the grief-stricken parents. The film is often remembered for the steamy love scene between the two as well as a violent finale. The sex scene is often said to be a real one, the result of an off-screen love affair between the actors playing the two main characters. Out-takes from the scene, according to rumours, were being viewed in private Beverly Hills screening rooms. Roeg, however, remembers differently: 'I haven't seen them,' he says. 'We only cut nine frames. I think the rumour started because the censor thought he saw things that didn't happen. It's rather like prestidigitation: 'How many cards have I got in my hand? Five? No, there are four.''

Roeg filmed in the dead of winter which explains why the city's canals and ancient buildings are shrouded in fog and sinister mystery. The director's cross-cutting style adds to the disturbing nature of the film. It says a lot that after 25 years, *Don't Look Now* can still manage to frighten audiences. 'I'm glad it's had some relevance to people today – that it touches them in some way. It can still do its job,' says Roeg.

Once asked if he had pleasant memories of the making of *Don't Look Now*, he answered: 'Is memory pleasant? I don't know. It's sad and happy, and inevitably there are ups and downs.'

Memorable dialogue:

John: Seeing is believing. I
believe you.

DRILLER KILLER

1979 / 90 mins / USA / DVD / ▭ Video
Stars: Carolyn Marz, Jimmy Laine (Abel Ferrara),
Bob De Frank, Baybi Day, Peter Yellen
Director: Abel Ferrara
Producer: Rochelle Weisberg
Script: Nicholas St John

Abel Ferrara's *Driller Killer* provoked controversy when it was dubbed one of the original 'video nasties'. In fact, the film wasn't intended to be a run-of-the-mill slasher flick, but a study of urban alienation: a portrayal of insanity and fear in which viewers are invited inside the frustrations of a city dweller who finally decides enough is enough.

Reno, the psychotic New York artist in question, lives in a completely meaningless existence with his plain girlfriend Carol and her druggie pal Pamela. Life has not treated Reno with respect, for he, Carol and Pamela scrape to pay the monthly rent and high utility bills, and his art dealer, Dalton, is demanding that he complete his big canvas as promised. To make matters worse, a punk rock band named Tony Coca-Cola and the Roosters have moved into the loft downstairs and play loud music 24 hours a day which agitates Reno even more. It's no wonder that this, together with a combination of Reno's psychosexual fears and thoughts of ending up like his derelict father, means he gradually begins to lose his mind. When Dalton,

the dealer, laughs at his canvas he snaps and begins taking it out on the people responsible for his pain. He takes to the streets at night, armed with a power drill hooked up to a battery Port-O-Pack, and randomly kills homeless bums in a variety of gory ways.

Although giving the impression of a *Texas Chainsaw Massacre* rip-off, Ferrara's film is definitely not the video nasty British moral guardians feared, but more in line with Scorsese's *Taxi Driver*. Ferrara himself appears under the pseudonym Jimmy Laine, playing Reno.

Shot on a low budget on grainy 16mm-film blown up to 35mm, the poor lighting and sound is compensated for by some effective character development.

Memorable dialogue:

Gallery owner: The worst thing
that could happen to a painter has
happened to you. You've become
merely a technician.

DUEL

1971 / 88 mins / USA / ▭ Video
Stars: Dennis Weaver, Jacqueline Scott,
Eddie Firestone, Lou Frizell
Director: Steven Spielberg
Producer: George Eckstein
Script: Richard Matheson

Steven Spielberg's first feature (made for television) stars Dennis Weaver as David Mann, a salesman who tries to drive his rented car across California. During his routine drive, he attempts to pass a gas tanker. Big mistake. The driver of the huge truck takes offence and begins to play mind games. At first the unseen driver just annoys David by continually passing him and slowing down. Then he really starts the weird stuff, tempting him to pass the tanker, only to prevent him when he tries. The story is seen from David's point of view, with commentary as he thinks to himself.

This is a superb suspense film, from Richard Matheson's script. It originally played on television (the ABC network in the States at 73 minutes) but was later released theatrically in 1983 running at 88 minutes. While Spielberg went on to become Hollywood's most famous director, Duel's producer, George Eckstein – who had been co-producer and writer on the famous American TV series The Fugitive – went on to relatively little: just more TV movie producing credits and screenplay credits for the Perry Mason television films of the late 80s.

Spielberg is more associated with huge Hollywood blockbusters and crowd-pleasers but his work back in the 70s (1975's Jaws and 1977's Close Encounters...) was, without doubt, intense and gritty. Duel is a fine piece of work: the camera work is simple but effective, with lenses mounted low on the truck near the wheels to accentuate the sensation of speed, in the driver's footwell pointing up at a petrified Dennis Weaver and close-ups of the car's dashboard. This use of varying camera angles constantly builds up the tensions, from the very first shot up until the final confrontation. The whole ordeal plays like a long, drawn-out stalking scene from an 80s slasher flick. As Mann struggles with shock and reaction (laughing and crying simultaneously), Dennis Weaver shows himself to be an actor worth more than the McCloud television movies he's so famous for. The scene is touching and extremely well performed.

Spielberg originally wanted no dialogue at all in this film, but was over-ruled by the suits at ABC. It would have been most interesting to see Duel presented using only visuals and sound effects as the most effective sequences are those with no dialogue. The terrifying music is used sparingly and the opening credits have no music at all, just Mann's POV through the car windshield and the radio playing. When the action moves outside the car, we simply hear the frightening roar of the heavy diesel engine of the truck. The final credits (ascending in silence as the sun sets over the mountains) are equally masterful.

As with most cult films, devotees are constantly looking for deep meanings. Although a terrifying adventure, there's no doubt Duel examines that age-old theme of good against evil, but perhaps Spielberg's film can also be taken as another kind of allegory – representing man's relationship with technology. He's an ordinary Joe, an Everyman figure, with the odds stacked against him – until he finally snaps. The fact that Weaver's character is called Mann certainly asks us to examine the concept further.

Memorable dialogue:

Mechanic: Looks like you could use a new radiator.
David: Yeah? Where've I heard that one before?

David: He has to be crazy, but what do I do about it?

EASY RIDER

1969 / 94 mins / USA / DVD / ▭ Video
Stars: Peter Fonda, Dennis Hopper, Jack Nicholson,
Robert Walker Junior, Luana Anders, Phil Spector
Director: Dennis Hopper
Producer: Peter Fonda
Script: Peter Fonda, Dennis Hopper, Terry Southern

A seminal work of its day, devastating and original, Hopper's satire on gun-happy America electrified a generation. Fonda and Hopper saddle up as Wyatt and Billy, two hippie motorcyclists who make a pilgrimage across the south west in search of 'real America'.

They pull off a coke deal, hide the cash in Wyatt's petrol tank and head for New Orleans. They get high, get laid and get arrested. They also team up with Jack Nicholson, who turns in a great performance as George Hanson, a lawyer who gets them bail before joining them on their journey. In the course of one brilliant scene (where he smokes grass for the first time), Nicholson steals the whole film. The then-unknown B-movie actor replaced Bruce Dern at the last minute as the boozy lawyer desperate to escape from his middle-class lifestyle. In spite of having been around for 10 years, Nicholson suddenly became an instant star.

This ultimate youth/road movie cost less than $400,000 to make but was a huge box-office hit and scooped the Cannes Best Film Award. It was the start of a new cinema trend catering for a troubled generation and, of course, the film is now described as a 'cult classic'. *Easy Rider* has achieved this status through years of comment and discussion, underground opinion and criticism. The film has acquired an audience who are appreciative of its nuances. Principally, it's a cult among film students, academics and critics, not to mention fellow film-makers who have gradually made sense out of the film's mayhem and madness. The cult of *Easy Rider* also extends to a cult of Dennis Hopper and within the independent sector of the film industry, over the years, there have been many examples of up-and-coming young directors desperately trying to get to work with their hero. Luckily, as Hopper is still part of the whole counter cultural world of low-budget art-house and foreign films, many have succeeded.

Easy Rider's pounding acid rock soundtrack, including classics by The Byrds, The Band and Steppenwolf, adds extra lasting appeal.

Memorable dialogue:

George Hanson (to Wyatt and Billy): This used to be a hell of a country… They're not scared of you, they're scared of what you represent. What you represent to them is freedom.

Captain America: No, I mean it, you've got a nice place. It's not every man that can live off the land, you know. You do your own thing in your own time. You should be proud.

George Hanson: I mean, it's real hard to be free when you are bought and sold in the marketplace.

Billy: We did it, man. We did it, we did it. We're rich, man. We're retirin' in Florida now, mister.
Captain America: You know Billy, we blew it.

George Hanson: They'll talk to ya and talk to ya and talk to ya about individual freedom. But they see a free individual, it's gonna scare 'em.

George Hanson: What's 'dude'? Is that like 'dude ranch'?
Captain America: Dude means nice guy. Dude means a regular sort of person.

Dennis Hopper (left) with Peter Fonda in the seminal 1969 film Easy Rider

ELECTRA GLIDE IN BLUE

1973 / 106 mins / USA / (Not currently available)
Stars: Robert Blake, Billy 'Green' Bush, Mitch Ryan,
Jeannine Riley, Elisha Cook, Royal Dano
Director: James William Guercio
Producers: James William Guercio, Rupert Hitzig
Script: Robert Boris, Michael Butler

'Did you know that me and Alan Ladd were exactly the same height, down to the quarter inch?' Arizona motorcycle cop John Wintergreen (a very charismatic Robert Blake) is a small man with big dreams. He longs to get off his Harley and get into a suit and tie as a state police detective. In fact, it's his ambition to become a hard-boiled detective like Clint Eastwood's Dirty Harry.

Eventually, the brainy, pint-sized cop gets his wish and is promoted to Homicide following the mysterious murder of a hermit. After an old mountain man is found dead, it is Blake who makes the correct diagnosis of murder. But he is forced to confront his illusions about himself and those around him in order to solve the case, eventually returning to solitude in the desert.

This cult curiosity from the 70s was the cop's answer to *Easy Rider* (1969), set in the sacred Navaho Indian region of Monument Valley – the place directors now always use to shoot car commercials. *Electra Glide in Blue* is a very violent film with striking action sequences and good characterisations. The film's director, James William Guercio, was the manager of the rock band Chicago and producer of many their albums in the 70s. Conrad Hall's haunting photography of Monument Valley and the superb opening sequence, in which Blake's dedicated patrolman dons his uniform, sets a fine mythic tone. Guercio never made another film after *Electra Glide in Blue* and reportedly retired to a ranch in Colorado, never to be seen again. Conrad Hall, meanwhile, spent years shooting commercials in Monument Valley.

Watch out for Elisha Cook Jr as the raving desert lunatic Willie. Fans of US sitcom *Dharma and Greg* will recognise Mitch Ryan (Greg's uptight dad.) as a flamboyant, sadistic sheriff.

Incidentally, the film's title takes its name from the full-dress Harley Davidson motorcycle manufactured in the United States (the Electra Glide). Up until the mid-70s, all motorcycle cops used to ride Harleys.

Memorable dialogue:

John Wintergreen: I'm gonna do for you, in six weeks, what it took someone six months to do for me: nothin'.

... to a lineup of motor cops...
Sgt. Ryker: TEN-HUT! Good morning, you fascists. You pigs. You bigots. You PINKOS. You FAGS! You BASTARDS. Fuzz. This indoctrination of vocal harassment was compiled by our own Juvenile Division in preparation for the concert this weekend.

John Wintergreen: I need you to give me some information.'
Pig Man: 'I'll give you some information. You're standing in pigshit.

Harve Poole: Incompetence is the worst form of corruption.

ESCAPE FROM NEW YORK

1981 / 99 mins / USA / DVD / Video
Stars: Kurt Russell, Lee Van Cleef, Ernest Borgnine,
Donald Pleasence, Isaac Hayes, Harry Dean Stanton,
Adrienne Barbeau
Director: John Carpenter
Producers: Larry France, Debra Hill
Script: John Carpenter, Nick Castle

The year is 1997, and due to high crime rates the United States has turned its once great city of New York into a maximum-security prison, a kind of futuristic Alcatraz where hardened criminals are put for life. 'Breaking out is impossible. Breaking in is insane.'

All the bridges leading into the city are mined, a huge wall is built along the shoreline and a large police force army is based there to stop or kill any would-be escapees. En route to a conference, the President of the United States, on board Air Force One, is forced to eject in a pod when a terrorist brings down his plane. He's left stranded among the world's worst criminals. Snake Plissken (Russell), a condemned convict and former war hero is offered his freedom if he can rescue the President from this terrifying walled prison island of Manhattan and find a tape with important information for the conference. Snake accepts the offer but to ensure his co-operation he is injected with a small but powerful explosive that will be destroyed only if his mission is successful.

Budgeted in 1981 at $7 million, *Escape from New York* was Carpenter's most expensive film and was in some ways reminiscent of his earlier movie *Assault on Precinct 13* (1976), which was smaller and seemed to work better. There's somehow greater momentum behind *Assault on Precinct 13*, whereas *Escape from New York* lacks pace and never really gets off the ground. It's also not too difficult to notice that the film wasn't shot in New York. That the producers thought Century City, Los Angeles and St Louis could pass for Manhattan is beyond belief. As always, the music is composed and performed by the director.

Of interest to fans of this movie is a recent DVD extra called 'The Edit', which contains information about the 'missing' first reel (cut from the original film) in which Snake carries out a vicious bank robbery, thus explaining why he was imprisoned in the first place.

It was 15 years before a sequel emerged. *Escape From LA* (1996) re-employs the same director, the same star and more or less the same plot, except the second time around the venue is Los Angeles. Featuring cameos from Peter Fonda and Steve Buscemi, it's another good action movie but lacks the lean, mean spirit of the original.

Memorable dialogue:

Plissken: I don't give a fuck about your war... or your president.

President: God save me, and watch over you all.

Hauk: I'm not a fool, Plissken!
Plissken: Call me Snake.

Girl in Choc Full o' Nuts: You're a cop!
Plissken: I'm an asshole...

Brain: They're savages, Mr President.

Hauk: You going to kill me now, Snake?
Plissken: I'm too tired. Maybe later.

Hauk: We'd make one hell of a team, Snake!
Plissken: The name's Plissken!

The President: Good evening. Although I shall not be present at this historic summit meeting, I present this in the hope that our great nations may learn to live in peace...

THE EVIL DEAD

1982 / 85 mins / USA / DVD / ▭ Video
Stars: Bruce Campbell, Ellen Sandweiss, Betsy Baker,
Hal Delrich, Sarah York
Director: Sam Raimi
Producer: Robert Tapert
Script: Sam Raimi

Shot in Tennessee and Michigan, on 16mm at an initial cost of $85,000 in 1979, Sam Raimi's *The Evil Dead* was finished two years later. One of the great modern horror films, it's even more impressive when one considers its modest production values. One of Stephen King's favourite films, he dubbed it 'a black rainbow of horror.'

Five friends are spending the weekend in a remote cabin in the woods where they find unspeakable evil lurking in the forest. While investigating the cellar they discover the Necronomicon (The Book of the Dead), full of strange magic spells and formulas, and a taped translation of the text. The tape is played and it unleashes a powerful evil force from the forest, determined to destroy every last one of them. The people start turning into deadly zombies and the others soon learn from the tape that the only way to kill a person who is turned into a deadite is by total body dismemberment. People are dying all over the place and in one key sequence early on the film, a girl loses control and runs off into the woods, only to be raped and killed by the trees. Later, only one of the youngsters remains and it's up to him to survive the night and battle the evil dead.

An original and interesting use of lenses and lighting, not to mention the home-made Steadicam (the camera was fixed to a plank of wood carried by crew members), leads us to suspect a powerful force of demons lurking in the forest. The influence of the Three Stooges on its comical creative trio of director Raimi, producer Robert Tapert and lead actor Bruce Campbell gives the film a deceptively playful feel. This humour was mixed with gory scenes of flesh-eating rampages to create a genuinely suspenseful and nightmarish mood.

Raimi's sequel four years later had Campbell still besieged at the mountain cabin by vicious forest spirits, this time joined by the daughter of the professor who unleashed them.

Memorable dialogue:
Ash: We can't bury Sharyn. She's our friend.

THE EXORCIST

1973 / 121 mins / USA / DVD / Video
Stars: Ellen Burstyn, Max von Sydow, Lee J Cobb, Kitty
Winn, Jack MacGowran, Linda Blair
Director: William Friedkin
Producer: William Peter Blatty
Script: William Peter Blatty

This reviled but ground-breaking horror classic, effectively banned for many years, was recently given its UK television premiere, nearly 20 years after its initial release. An Oscar-winning dramatisation by William Peter Blatty of his own best-selling novel, this captivating chiller chronicles demonic possession of a young girl, Regan (Linda Blair) whose mother (Ellen Burstyn) has to seek divine intervention in a bid to stop her daughter's increasingly strange and obscene behaviour. In the end, it's up to Father Karras (Jason Miller) and Father Merrin (Max von Sydow) to perform the exorcism that could save Regan's soul.

Disturbing scenes, such as the possessed child's head spinning, coupled with opposition from religious leaders to the subject matter added to the movie's notoriety. Tales about the grim fates that met some of the production team added to the myth surrounding the film.

Ground-breaking special effects were so successful that reports emerged of cinema-goers fainting, vomiting and running from theatres when it was first released. But it was a huge success, taking more than $165 million in the US alone. *The Exorcist*, which won two Oscars, was re-released in 1998 in more than 250 UK cinemas, drawing in a massive audience for late-night showings. A year later the British Board of Film Classification gave the video an 18 certificate for the first time. It had been barred from home viewing in the early 80s because it was seen as a 'video nasty' that could cause emotional problems among young women (although it had already been available for three years before videos actually required certificates).

The Exorcist was inspired by real-life American events which occurred in 1949 in Mount Rainier, Maryland. Friedkin's film presents a contemporary twist to the age-old story of the battle between good and evil. According to the director: 'You take from *The Exorcist* what you bring to it. If you believe that the world is a dark and evil place, then *The Exorcist* will reaffirm that. But if you believe that there is a power for good in this world then that is what you will bring from *The Exorcist*.'

Back in 1974, the film won Oscars for best writing and sound. It also spawned countless imitations and spoofs, including *Repossessed* (1990), starring Leslie Nielsen and Linda Blair. Now married with two kids, Regan is repossessed by the devil while watching TV. But despite endless copies and parodies, *The Exorcist* has never been bettered. The recent cinema re-issue included 11 extra minutes of footage, including an expanded prologue, a theological debate between Karras and Merrin, and the infamous 'spider walk' sequence.

Memorable dialogue:

Regan: What an excellent day for an exorcism.

Regan: I'm not Regan.
Karras: Well, then let's introduce ourselves. I'm Damien Karras.
Regan: And I'm the Devil! Now kindly undo these straps!
Karras: If you're the Devil, why don't you make the straps disappear?
Regan: That's much too vulgar a display of power, Karras!

Regan: Let Jesus fuck you, let Jesus fuck you! Let him fuck you!

Karras: Take me! Come into me! God damn you! Take me! Take me!

Lt Kinderman: If certain British doctors never asked 'What is this fungus?' we wouldn't today have penicillin, correct?

EYE OF THE NEEDLE

1981 / 111 mins / UK / DVD / ▭ Video
Stars: Donald Sutherland, Kate Nelligan, Ian Bannen,
Christopher Cazenove
Director: Richard Marquand
Producer: Stephen Friedman
Script: Stanley Mann

Donald Sutherland plays a World War Two German super spy, 'The Needle', who, from his British base of operations, has infiltrated the military and is able to feed strategic information back to Germany. He discovers vital evidence about the Allies' D-Day invasion and makes for the Scottish coast to dash back to Germany with the details. But the murderous Nazi agent's boat is shipwrecked before being picked up and he is washed ashore on a remote island, inhabited by a bitter paraplegic and his lonely wife and child. A passionate affair develops between The Needle and Lucy (Kate Nelligan) which brings disaster in its wake. Both must decide between their love or country.

Based on the Ken Follett novel, *Eye of the Needle* is a tense thriller that takes its time to work the tension but then suddenly explodes during its frenzied conclusion. An interesting study of ruthlessness, it's spine-tingling to watch as Lucy slowly figures out what she's got herself into and it's terrifying viewing as she tries to protect herself and her son from the calculating killer.

During the making of *Eye of the Needle*, George Lucas selected Marquand to direct the third instalment of the *Star Wars* trilogy, *Return of the Jedi* (1983). After *Jedi*, Marquand went on to direct *Until September* (1984), *Jagged Edge* (1985) and his last film, *Hearts of Fire* (1987). He died of a heart attack in September 1987. He was 49. Five years after Marquand's death, one of his original stories became the feature film, *Nowhere to Run* (1992), starring Jean-Claude Van Damme.

Memorable dialogue:
The Needle: What else can one do?
One just can't stop.

DONALD SUTHERLAND   KATE NELLIGAN

EYE OF THE NEEDLE

15

FAHRENHEIT 451

1966 / 133 mins / UK / ▣ Video
Stars: Oskar Werner, Julie Christie, Cyril Cusack,
Anton Diffring, Jeremy Spenser, Bee Duffell
Director: Francois Truffaut
Producers: Lewis M Allen
Script: Francois Truffaut, Jean-Louis Richard

This is a good adaptation of author Ray Bradbury's story. The basic idea is this: books are illegal. Books make people unhappy. Firemen have the job of burning them. Fahrenheit 451, as explained in the film, is the temperature that paper will burst into flame. Oskar Werner plays Montag, an obedient and lawful fireman who carries out the burnings with efficiency and apparent enthusiasm. Julie Christie plays Montag's law-abiding wife who spends most of her time glued to the TV screen. Cyril Cusack is the dedicated fire station captain. 'Burn them all,' he says, throwing *Mein Kampf* on to the floor. If reading is a forbidden fruit, perhaps that's why Truffaut seems preoccupied with the use and misuse of apples throughout his film. Watch carefully.

When Montag is asked by his wife, 'Have you ever read any of the books you burn?' his whole life is changed. He becomes a secret 'book addict' and forms a cult with other reader-conspirators.

Parts of the film detail an interactive TV show called 'Family' whereby actors on the screen appear to communicate with individual viewers. An inspired touch, there are no written credits: they are narrated at the start of the film, along with close-ups of television antennas.

In a brilliant parody of social correctness, Francois Truffaut adds a few light touches to bring some much needed spots of relief from this excursion into a terrifying world. Bernard Herrmann contributes one of the best music scores of the 60s.

The movie is in English. Filmed at Pinewood, this was Truffaut's only English-language film. There is no indication where it all takes place.

Memorable dialogue:

A child to his mother: Is it true that once firemen used to put out fires and not burn books?

FEAR AND LOATHING IN LAS VEGAS

1998 / 128 mins / USA / ▣ Video
Stars: Johnny Depp, Benicio Del Toro, Tobey Maguire, Ellen
Barkin, Gary Busey, Christina Ricci, Mark Harmon, Cameron
Diaz, Lyle Lovett, Flea, Harry Dean Stanton
Director: Terry Gilliam
Producers: Laila Nabulsi, Patrick Cassavetti, Steve Nemeth
Script: Alex Cox, Tod Davies, Terry Gilliam, Tony Grisoni (from
the book by Hunter S Thompson)

Hunter S Thompson's 1971 counter-cultural book *Fear and Loathing in Las Vegas* has proven highly difficult to translate to the big screen. Portraying the self-described antics of the gonzo journalist would be a lot to ask of any writer–director. Terry Gilliam's version has entered the world of cult movie discussions and internet cult movie chat-rooms not because it's a great film but because of the reputation of the original Thompson novel. Most Thompson web pages list and discuss all attempts at bringing the book to the screen, analysing and re-assessing each sequence. Most net surfers are in agreement that although Gilliam's film is a cult curiosity, it doesn't live up to the impossibly high standards of the book.

Where the Buffalo Roam, starring Bill Murray as Thompson, opened in theatres in 1980 to universally bad reviews. It wasn't until more than a decade had passed that any firm new plans emerged for turning Thompson's book into a film. In 1992, producers Steve Nemeth and Harold Bronson decided they wanted to make it as the first film for the newly formed company Rhino Films.

Originally, Alex Cox was hired as writer/director but he walked out early on. His exit from the film was, in part, due to an argument with Hunter S Thompson but also to the fact Universal Studios had muscled in. Having befriended Hunter S Thompson, Johnny Depp (who'd already been cast) stayed. After all, Universal was about to spend more millions of dollars marketing him.

Terry Gilliam (*Brazil* [1985] and *Twelve Monkeys* [1995]) was brought in as the replacement director. Later on, Cox noticed how similar Gilliam's 'new' screenplay was to his own contribution and called in the WGA arbiters. The Writers' Guild of America (WGA) automatically arbitrates when a director claims screenwriting credit. The arbiters ruled in Cox and writing partner Tod Davies' favour, concluding that they should get sole credit. This upset Gilliam, who threatened to resign from the WGA, and also upset the studio. The producers had the arbitration re-opened and, after much lobbying, managed to get Gilliam and Grisoni's names added to the writing credits, with a bitter Gilliam claiming he'd had to fight with deranged egos.

In the end, the final movie stayed faithful to the book. The film details a wacky search for the 'American Dream', by Thompson and his crazed, Samoan lawyer. Fuelled by massive amount of drugs, they set out in the Red Shark. Encountering police, reporters, gamblers, racers and hitch-hikers, they search for some indefinable thing known only as the 'American Dream' but find only fear and loathing in the dementia of the modern American West.

This is a horrible mess of a movie, without shape, stylised, over-the-top and blatantly in-your-face. Gilliam's delivered a crass and vulgar trip devoid of subtleties and Depp simply can't seem to communicate the genius behind Thompson's madness. The dialogue he utters is, in parts, incomprehensible.

Interestingly, Gilliam's film was booed at its premiere in Cannes and was slaughtered by critics. Around the same time, Hunter S Thompson made clear his own feelings about Gilliam, telling him, 'You do not know me at all and you are not my friend. You are building a very distinguished enemies list, like Nixon.'

At the very least, the final production cost $20 million. Now, all the hype suggests the film cost a total of around $40 million. There is a certain disparity about this because the film was supposed to be a critique of consumer culture.

However, much of Thompson's brilliant dialogue is there untouched for all to hear. The only other plus point is that, hopefully, this may inspire those ignorant of the original cult novel to start reading what it was all really about.

Memorable dialogue:

Narrator: We were somewhere around Barstow, on the edge of the desert, when the drugs began to take hold.

Raoul Duke: There he goes. One of God's own prototypes. Some kind of high-powered mutant never even considered for mass production. Too weird to live and too rare to die.

Dr Gonzo: We've gotta get out of here. I have The Fear.

Raoul Duke: Wait! We can't stop here! This is BAT COUNTRY!

Raoul Duke: We had two bags of grass, seventy-five pellets of mescaline, five sheets of high-powered blotter acid, a salt shaker half-full of cocaine and a whole galaxy of multi-coloured uppers, downers, screamers, laughers also a quart of tequila, a quart of rum, a case of beer, a pint of raw ether, and two dozen amyls. But the only thing that worried me was the ether. There is nothing more irresponsible and depraved than a man in the depths of an ether binge, and I knew we would be getting into that rotten stuff sooner or later.

Raoul Duke: History is hard to know, because of all the hired bullshit, but even without being sure of 'history' it seems entirely reasonable to think that every now and then the energy of a whole generation comes to a head in a long fine flash, for reasons that nobody really understands at the time – and which never explain, in retrospect, what actually happened.

Raoul Duke: With a bit of luck, his life was ruined forever. Always thinking that just behind some narrow door in all of his favourite bars, men in red woollen shirts are getting incredible kicks from things he'll never know.

Raoul Duke: Look, there's two women fucking a polar bear!

Raoul Duke: If the pigs were gathering in Vegas, I felt the drug culture should be represented as well. And there was a certain bent appeal in the notion of running a savage burn in one Las Vegas, and then just wheeling across town and checking into another. Me and a thousand ranking cops from all over America. Why not? Move confidently into their midst.

Raoul Duke: Holy Jesus! What are these goddamn animals?

Hotel clerk: Can I call you a cab?
Police Chief: Sure, and I'll call you a cocksucker!

Opposite: The drugs don't work – Johnny Depp as Raoul Duke in Terry Gilliam's Fear and Loathing in Las Vegas (*1998*)

FEAR CITY

1984 / 96 mins / USA / *DVD* / ▭ Video
Stars: Tom Berenger, Billy Dee Williams, Jack Scalia,
Melanie Griffith, Rossano Brazzi, Rae Dawn Cheong
Director: Abel Ferrara
Producers: Bruce Cohn Curtis, Jerry Tokofsky
Script: Nicholas St John

This tough, nasty tale is another of Abel Ferrara's set on the wet city streets of Manhattan. Tom Berenger is Matt Rossi, a retired boxer who quit years ago when he killed an opponent in the ring. He's now the operator of a talent agency for the best strippers in town, among them his bisexual ex-girlfriend Loretta (Melanie Griffith).

But a psychopathic kung-fu fanatic is hell-bent on cleaning up the streets of New York and that includes getting rid of the girls. He launches a systematic genocidal assault on the strippers in the notorious back alleys of Times Square.

When it becomes clear that neither the homicide detective (Billy Dee Williams) or Mafia don Rossano Brazzi can clean up the situation, it's finally left to Rossi to confront his own violent past and end the methodical killings. So he returns to his murderous fighting methods to protect the strippers and stop the sadistic killer.

'I want this guy so bad I can taste his blood in my mouth', says Berenger. The movie itself seems to share this philosophy. The mutilation scenes are particularly gory and although we see it coming, the final, bloody showdown is an impressive big-league dose of trashy, violence-filled excitement.

Memorable dialogue:
Wheeler: I'll close your business down if you don't keep pussy off the bar.

Opposite: from left to right, Billy Dee Williams, Jack Scalia, Tom Berenger and Melanie Griffith in Abel Ferrara's Fear City *(1984)*

New York City... Open 24 Hours.

...where the night belongs to the girls. Everyone is watching them... but someone is waiting for them. Now everyone is living in...

FEAR CITY

BRUCE COHN CURTIS presents
TOM BERENGER BILLY DEE WILLIAMS JACK SCALIA MELANIE GRIFFITH and ROSSANO BRAZZI in FEAR CITY
Starring RAE DAWN CHONG JOE SANTOS MICHAEL V GAZZO and JAN MURRAY Co-Starring MARIA CONCHITA ALONSO OLA RAY
Music by RICHARD HALLIGAN Director of Photography JAMES LEMMO Edited by JACK HOLMES, ANTHONY REDMAN
Executive Producers STANLEY R. ZUPNIK and TOM CURTIS Co-Produced by JERRY TOKOFSKY
Written by NICHOLAS ST. JOHN Produced by BRUCE COHN CURTIS Directed by ABEL FERRARA
International Distribution through J&M Film Sales. Ltd. Copyright © 1984 Chevy Chase Films Limited Partnership. All Rights Reserved. A Zupnik-Curtis Enterprises, Inc. Presentation

FERRARA, ABEL

Director
Born 19 July 1951, New York

Nobody can present the streets of New York City like Abel Ferrara. Whether it's the graphic sleaze of *Bad Lieutenant* (1992) or the glossier *King of New York* (1990), he is cinema's most interesting chronicler of the Manhattan underbelly.

Himself a product of New York (born in the Bronx), his turbulent childhood there certainly led to a tendency to concentrate on the sleazy, brutal elements in the metropolis. For years, Ferrara made cheap Super-8 films in New York before he directed (and starred in) his first real commercial film, *Driller Killer* (1979), about a painter who goes on a killing spree. Notching up 13 extremely gory episodes, this film was quickly deemed *the* video nasty, disgusted many, but always brought Ferrara attention.

Next, *Ms. 45* (1981), also churned the stomach. It starred long-time associate Zoe Tamerlis as a mute woman who becomes a vigilante after being raped. *Fear City* (1984) led to offers to direct episodes of the flashy 80s television shows *Miami Vice* and *Crime Story*. In the end, Ferrara's two-hour pilot for *Crime Story* was given a theatrical release, albeit a fairy limited one.

Sticking with slick, low-budget cult efforts, *China Girl* (1987), a violent romantic thriller, was Ferrara's *West Side Story* take-off chronicling the inter-racial gang warfare ignited by the love affair between a Chinese girl and an Italian. A year later, he made *Cat Chaser* (1988), based on an Elmore Leonard novel, a torrid thriller directed in his usual *noir* style. In a sense, *Cat Chaser* was Ferrara's first foray into the world of mainstream movie-making and was set far away from the sleazy New York back streets in sunny Florida

King of New York, was even more stylised with a deliberately streamlined story. A glossy but overblown drama with Christopher Walken as a drug kingpin with a moral code, this was a new Ferrara. But in shunning his usual rough, tough underground style, he'd lost a lot of his unique power and vision. The follow-up to *King of New York* was the critically acclaimed *Bad Lieutenant* (1992), with Harvey Keitel as a depraved cop looking for salvation. Moving even closer to Hollywood's big budget mainstream, Ferrara then directed two turkeys, *Dangerous Game* (1993), which teamed Harvey Keitel and Madonna, and *Body Snatchers* (1993), the second remake of *Invasion of the Body Snatchers* (1956).

Certainly a cult figure, Ferrara is a man who (at least for most of his career) had a unique talent and vision. But he's also notoriously volatile. *Top Gun* (1986) heroine Kelly McGillis, huge in the 80s, has recently talked about a disastrous experience with Ferrara on *Cat Chaser*: 'It was the most hateful experience of my life. And I said, if this is what acting is going to be, I will not do it. On the last day of shooting, I said, "Are you done with me?" He said, "Yeah". I walked in my trailer and shaved my head. I said, "Screw you, I never want to act again". I got on a boat in the Caribbean and stayed for six months, in limbo. It took me six months of soul-searching, and nine months of pregnancy, and a couple of plays, to say, "I do love acting. I just don't want to work with assholes any more". See Filmography, p. 239.

THE FLY

1958 / 94 mins / USA / ▭ Video
Stars: Al Hedison, Patricia Owens, Vincent Price,
Herbert Marshall, Kathleen Freeman,
Betty Lou Gerson
Director: Kurt Neumann
Producer: Kurt Neumann
Script: James Clavell

Vincent Price, the star of Roger Corman's Edgar Allan Poe series, is a fine actor and well respected in the world of cult movies. His performance here is no exception.

Made in 1958, this original version of *The Fly* tells the story of a scientist experimenting with matter transference. Basically, it's another science gone wrong movie. There were a lot of these in the 50s, in the aftermath of the atom bomb. Films like *Forbidden Planet* (1956) and *Them!* (1954) dealt with the same subject – the perversion of science.

In this one, Hedison invents a machine that can disintegrate atoms and transport them to another that will then re-assemble the atoms. This he believes will allow humans to travel around the world within seconds.

In experimenting on himself, however, a fly gets trapped in the disintegration chamber with him and he emerges with the fly's head and one of its legs replacing one of his arms. This leaves the fly with his head and a rather useless human arm.

Tension builds as Hedison realises he has to find the fly so that he can try to reverse the damage. Meanwhile his 'other half' is trapped in a spider's web. This desperate 'double' struggle cleverly detracts from the cheap-looking effects and allows quite a dramatic and poignant story to develop on screen.

The plastic fly's head Hedison wears in the film took make-up artist Ben Nye 10 weeks to create. 'Trying to act in it though,' Hedison revealed, 'was like playing piano with boxing gloves.'

There were two sequels – *Return of the Fly* (1959, also with Vincent Price) and *Curse of the Fly* (1965) before the remake, by David Cronenberg, in 1986. In the updated version Jeff Goldblum added just the right touch of clinical curiosity as the scientist researching matter transportation.

Memorable dialogue:

Hedison: Help me ... help me!

THE FOG

1980 / 91 mins / USA / ▱ Video
Stars: Adrienne Barbeau, Hal Holbrook, Janet Leigh, Jamie Lee Curtis, John Houseman
Director: John Carpenter
Producer: Debra Hill
Script: John Carpenter, Debra Hill

Lock your doors. Bolt your windows. There's something in THE FOG!

John Carpenter's follow-up to *Halloween* (1978), this is a ghost story about a California coastal town cursed by a 100-year-old shipwreck.

The centenary of the small seaside town, Antonio Bay, is approaching. One hundred years earlier, a ship went down in the bay, lured to destruction in a dense fog by a false beacon. Legend has it that when the fog returns, so will the mariners, drawn from their watery grave to seek revenge.

As darkness falls and the townsfolk prepare to celebrate, a strange fog starts to move across the water towards the unsuspecting town. The victims of the crime that founded the town soon rise from the sea to claim retribution. Under cover of the fog, they carry out their vicious attacks, searching for what is rightly theirs.

The film is packed with horror-movie faces: Jamie Lee Curtis, her mother Janet Leigh, Adrienne Barbeau, John Houseman and Hal Holbrook. Even Annie from *Halloween* (Nancy Loomis) makes an appearance.

Memorable dialogue:

Stevie: Keep me turned on for a while, and I'll try my best to do the same for you.

Andy: First it was a gold coin, and then it turned into this neat piece of wood!

Dr Phibes: See, the water acts like ice.

Stevie: That driftwood you found – what was it doing?
Andy: I told you, first it was a gold coin, and then it turned into the wood.

FORBIDDEN PLANET

1956 / 98 mins / USA / (Not currently available)
Stars: Walter Pidgeon, Anne Francis, Leslie Nielsen,
Warren Stevens, Jack Kelly, Earl Holliman
Director: Fred McLeod Wilcox
Producer: Nicholas Nayfack
Script: Cyril Hume

A true landmark in sci-fi films, this ambitious 50s cult classic is basically a retelling of Shakespeare's *The Tempest*. Some of the special effects (revolutionary for its time) may look dodgy by today's standards but its intelligent storyline makes up for it.

The year is 2200 AD and mankind has figured out how to reach distant planets and one such colony on the planet Altair IV is due for a visit from Mother Earth. Leading the visiting mission on the US Planet Cruiser C5 7D is Commander JJ Adams (Leslie Neilsen). However, on approaching the planet he receives a frosty welcome from Dr Morbius (Walter Pidgeon) who warns the crew that he cannot be held responsible for the consequences if they land. But they do.

They are met on Altair IV by Robby the Robot, who has an English butler's voice and an electronic brain. He can also speak 187 languages. When he strides up to the spaceship with a huge load in his arms, he remarks casually, 'This is my morning's batch of Isotope 217. The whole thing barely comes to 10 tons'. Robby is described as 'a triumph of cybernetics only one step removed from total humanity'. He is supposed to be a kind of comedy relief, like the character Ariel in *The Tempest*. He can even create diamonds or emeralds with little more than a wave of his huge electronic hand.

Robby transports the crew at break-neck speed back to the doctor's home. There they meet Morbius' daughter Altaira (Anne Francis), and learn that her mother and the crew of their spaceship Bellerophon died when they crashed 20 years ago. Altaira and Dr Morbius are the only humans on the planet.

Morbius gives a tour of his home, built by a long-dead civilisation known as the Krell. This superior race has been wiped out. Soon, a destructive force, the projection of the Id of the Krell, begins to kill off Adams' crew one by one. Morbius, who wishes to protect his daughter, has unconsciously brought this 'Monster of the Id' back to life to save Altaira.

Full of camp humour and suspense, this instantly attracted a cult following and paved the way for countless other movies and TV shows.

Memorable dialogue:

Dr Edward Morbius: The fool, the meddling idiot! As though his ape's brain could contain the secrets of the Krell.

Dr Edward Morbius: Yes, a single machine, a cube 20 miles on each side.

Cookie: Another one of them new worlds. No beer, no women, no pool parlours, nothin'! Nothin' to do but throw rocks at tin cans, and we gotta bring our own tin cans.

Dr Edward Morbius: Monsters! Monsters from the id!

Robby: Quiet please. I am analysing.

Robby: Sorry miss, I was giving myself an oil-job.

Dr Edward Morbius: In times long past, this planet was the home of a mighty, noble race of beings who called themselves the Krell.

Dr Edward Morbius: My evil self is at the door, and I have no power to stop it.

The poster for the first Star Trek *film, undoubtedly inspired (like countless other movies and TV shows) by 1956's* Forbidden Planet

FOXY BROWN

1974 / 94 mins / USA / 🖵 Video
Stars: Pam Grier, Antonio Fargas, Peter Brown,
Terry Carter, Katheryn Loder,
Harry Holcombe, Sid Haig
Director: Jack Hill
Producer: Buzz Fietshans
Script: Jack Hill

After seeing Pam Grier in Quentin Tarantino's *Jackie Brown* (1997), a whole new generation have been delving into the world of the Blaxploitation films of the 70s. Suddenly, they're cool again.

Pam Grier delivered a knockout performance in the title role in *Foxy Brown*, a high-kickin', furniture throwin', good lovin', high-octane heroine in a one-woman war against the pusherman. Ya dig? She's a black belt in barstools and knows how to hold her own – preferably in a revealing halterneck.

But how the hell did she get in this mess? Well, when Foxy's federal agent boyfriend is gunned down, she sets out to fight for revenge and justice where the System has failed her. But there ain't no time for tears, 'cause we got fast cars, bitch fights and Willie Hutch's storming Motown soundtrack to keep us happy. Just wait till you see Foxy going undercover as Misty Cotton in crime boss Miss Katherine's harem – and I mean undercover!

The music is great and the opening sequence rivals those of the James Bond films. To top it all the inimitable Antonio Fargas (Huggy Bear from *Starsky and Hutch*) plays Foxy's brother. Possibly the sharpest dresser this side of Liberace, he gets involved with the bad dudes in town.

Coffy (1973), also directed by Jack Hill, was similar, with Grier as a nurse by day and an angel by night. It's another drug pusher/revenge plot with more car chasing, knock-down brawling, all-round shotgun shooting and lurid masterwork. In fact, Grier starred in loads of these movies, including *Scream Blacula Scream* (1973), *Black Mama, White Mama* (1972) and *Black Caesar* (1973). She's the Godmother of them all. The baddest one-chick hit-squad that ever hit town. So popular was she with today's cool kids in *Jackie Brown*, that all these titles were restored and recently released on video and DVD as the Soul Sisters Series. They include the original trailers and cover art. So now a new generation of funk fans are donning their zoot suits and checking out the soundtracks from Isaac Hayes, Edwin Starr and James Brown.

`Memorable dialogue:`

> Broad: Don't mess with me! I've
> got a black belt in crime!
> (Foxy knocks her down with a
> barstool.)
> Foxy Brown: I've got a black belt
> in barstools!

Opposite: Pam Grier, the Godmother of them all, pictured here in Coffy *(1973)*

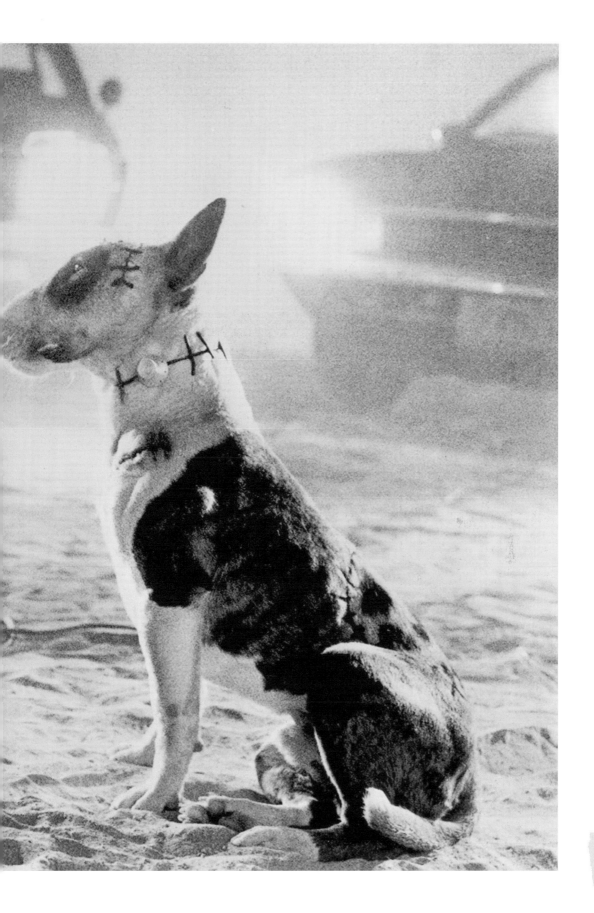

FRANKENWEENIE

1984 / 29 mins / USA / (Not currently available)
Stars: Shelley Duvall, Daniel Stern, Joseph Maher,
Barret Oliver, Roz Braverman, Paul Bartel
Director: Tim Burton
Producer: Julie Hickson
Script: Leonard Ripps

Frankenweenie is director Tim Burton's first live-action film. Normally, a short like this – one which was meant to be included simply as a 'special feature' to another of Burton's full-length movies – wouldn't warrant a full review. However, this stands up as its own movie.

Ten-year-old Victor Frankenstein is playing with his beloved dog Sparky, who unfortunately meets an untimely end. After seeing a dead frog move under electrical stimulation, he decides to reanimate his dog's corpse. His parents discover the new Sparky and, after a little hesitation, accept him. They try to defuse the neighbourhood rumours about a monster by having a party for Sparky, but their efforts go awry. The neighbours form a lynch mob and hunt the dog. The finale of the film takes place in a miniature golf course with a windmill (in a hilarious echo of the original film). When the mill is set afire, Sparky saves Victor and becomes a hero but dies in the conflagration. The neighbours, now united, get together and resurrect Sparky once more.

This is an ingenious replica of both James Whale's 1930 classic *Frankenstein* and its sequel *Bride of Frankenstein* (1933), with the same look in sets and lighting – but placed in the new setting of contemporary, middle-class America.

Previous page: a scene from Frankenweenie *(1984)*

FREE ENTERPRISE

1998 / 116 mins / USA / **DVD**
Stars: Eric McCormack, Audie England, Carl Bressler,
Thomas Hobson, Jennifer Sommerfield,
Rafer Weigel, William Shatner, Marilyn Kentz
Director: Robert Meyer Burnett
Producers: Mark A Altman, Dan Bates, Allan Kaufman
Script: Mark A Altman, Robert Meyer Burnett

Two young film-makers Rob and Mark (Rafer Weigel and Eric McCormack) have relied as children on the pretend advice from their invisible friend William Shatner. Here, they get to meet their screen idol, who, appearing as himself, pokes fun at the 'sad' Trekkie-types he's come to know and hate and also sends up his own image.

The two young nerds, who completely idolise him, are devastated at the reality of the middle-aged non-Captain Kirk type they end up meeting. (Shatner apparently insisted that he should play himself as a man with problems if he was going to do the film at all.)

Next, Rob meets Claire, a good-looking sci-fi geek, and falls head over heels in love. But Mark is scared he'll lose his best pal. At the same time, Shatner also starts to come between the two friends as they try to help him mount his dream project: a one-man show of *Julius Caesar* (with Shatner playing all the parts). Will the boys work with their hero? Will Rob settle down with Claire? And how can the two boys possibly live apart?

The movie culminates in a simply bizarre final scene, which puts a new twist on the Bard – a performance of Shakespeare's *Julius Ceasar*, rapped by Shatner.

Free Enterprise developed an instant cult following thanks to the endless science-fiction references, ranging from oft-quoted *Star Wars* (1977) dialogue to the more obscure *Logan's Run* (1976). Of course, Trekkers will recognise much of themselves in the two protagonists.

Incidentally, the music for this film was written by a man by the name of Scott Spock.

Memorable dialogue:

Young Mark: So you're saying I should engage my advanced-for-a-12-year-old intellect and use logic?
Imaginary William Shatner: Logic is the other guy's shtick, but yes.

Imaginary William Shatner: I'm not really here. I'm one of the top 10 imaginary friends kids have. Just behind John Travolta, Reggie Jackson and Farrah Fawcett-Majors.

Mark's Mom: Mark, Mark, what are you doing here? I thought you were supposed to go to that movie – that 'Star Track' movie.
Young Mark: Oh, Mom, how many times do I have to tell you? 'Track' is what a train goes on, okay? 'Trek' is what the Enterprise goes on, okay?
Mark's Mom: Yeah, and they say the pain of childbirth ends with labour.

Young Robert: He said that Han Solo was cooler than Captain Kirk.
Imaginary William Shatner: Kick the little fucker's ass.

Claire: Where are you going?
Robert: Looks like I'm going nowhere.
Claire: Don't you fucking quote *Star Wars* at me!

FRIDAY THE 13TH

1980 / 95 mins / USA / Video
Stars: Betsy Palmer, Adrienne King, Harry Crosby,
Laurie Bartram, Robbi Morgan
Director: Sean S Cunningham
Producer: Sean S Cunningham
Script: Victor Miller

Screenwriter Victor Miller's psychotic anti-hero Jason has featured in nine sequels, spanning nearly 20 years, and a popular television series. The films have achieved much notoriety and spawned a merchandising empire that includes comics, T-shirts and action figures.

The first film in the series is set in Camp Crystal Lake which has a bad history and no one has set foot there for 20 years – until now. In 1957, a young boy named Jason drowned at the camp and a year later the teenagers supposedly responsible were murdered by an unknown assailant. The camp closed, but in 1980 it is reopened by Steve Christie, who hires a group of teenagers to be councillors. However, its blood-drenched history has ensured that its reputation will live forever – unlike the luckless party of randy kids who arrive for a carefree vacation. One by one, they are despatched with a variety of crude weaponry, including knives, hatchets, spears and arrows. The killer is revealed to the lone survivor and the movie comes back with a surprise ending.

The film's success was in its ability to exploit the audience's fears and fantasies. It coupled the shock violence of nihilistic 70s gore-fests such as *Zombie Flesh Eaters* (1974) and *Driller Killer (1979),* with a good helping of teenage nudity.

Memorable dialogue:

Alice: The boy,... is he dead, too?

Tierney: Who?

Alice: The boy. Jason.

Tierney: Jason?

Alice: In the lake, the one,... the one who attacked me... the one who pulled me underneath the water.

Tierney: Ma'am, we didn't find any boy.

Alice: But... then he's still out there.

Opposite: Jason came back for more! Here, Dana Kimmell is pictured in Friday 13th Part III *(1982)*

FRIEDKIN, WILLIAM

Director
Born 29 August 1939, Chicago

William Friedkin went to work for WGN television in Chicago immediately after graduating from high school where he started making documentaries. In 1965, he moved to Hollywood and started directing TV shows, including an episode of the *Alfred Hitchcock Presents*. Hitchcock reportedly chastised him for not wearing a tie.

The Oscar-winning director of *The French Connection* (1971) and Oscar nominee for *The Exorcist* (1973) was once expected to become Hollywood's pre-eminent director, but his subsequent sporadic output and high percentage of box-office flops seem to have dispelled that notion.

His first work in film was *The People Vs Paul Crump*, a documentary about a man who spent eight years on death row in the Cook County Jail. With it, Friedkin won his first award, The Golden Gate Prize at the San Francisco Film Festival. More satisfying than the award was Crump's commuted sentence due to the attention the film garnered. The project so impressed station management that Friedkin was appointed head of a newly created documentary film unit.

His first feature film, *Good Times* (1967) also marked the screen debut of Sonny and Cher. It didn't receive too much attention but the word reached United Artists that Friedkin was the potential new hot young director of the moment. The studio gave him *The Night They Raided Minsky's* (1968) which turned out to be quite an authentic recreation of the vaudeville era. The two films that followed, *The Birthday Party* (1968) and *The Boys in the Band* (1970), didn't cause much of a stir.

During the late 60s and early 70s with the youth movement, Woodstock and the Vietnam War, using drugs became an integral part of the counterculture. *The French Connection*, a sharp, gritty exposé of the drug world, won Friedkin a Best Director Oscar and was voted Best Picture.

With its remarkable car chase below New York's elevated railway, the film set the tone for many cop movies and TV series that followed.

With *The Exorcist* (1973), Friedkin came up with one of the most horrifying pictures of all time. It received 10 Academy Award nominations. As with all moments that stand out in life, audiences still vividly remember the terror they felt watching the demonically possessed Linda Blair.

After *The Exorcist*, however, Friedkin lost ground. His next film, *Sorcerer* (1977), was an expensive remake of the French suspense classic *Wages of Fear*. Although one of modern cinema's great remakes, a truly inspired retelling, it failed to excite audiences. In fact, *The Brink's Job* (1978), *Cruising* (1980), *Deal of the Century* (1983), *To Live and Die in LA* (1985), *Stalking Danger* (1986) and *Rampage* (1988, release delayed until 1992) gave him a string of box-office losers. He also directed a couple of television movies, *CAT Squad* (1986) and *CAT Squad: Python Wolf* (1988). Later, *The Guardian* (1990) returned Friedkin to supernatural suspense.

Blue Chips (1994) put him back in the mainstream and finding himself back in favour, in early 1997, Friedkin directed a big budget Showtime/MGM television remake of the classic courtroom drama *12 Angry Men*, which included legendary stars such as Jack Lemmon, George C Scott, Armin Meuller-Stahl, Hume Cronyn and Ossie Davis. The DGA-nominated Friedkin for Outstanding Directorial Achievement for Best Dramatic Special. It was also nominated for six Emmy awards.

By the late 90s, Friedkin had completely ditched his humble beginnings and was directing big-budget thrillers such as *Rules of Engagement* (2000) starring Tommy Lee Jones and Samuel L Jackson. See Filmography, p. 239.

GALAXY QUEST

2000 / 97 mins / USA / *DVD* / ▭ Video
Stars: Tim Allen, Sigourney Weaver, Alan Rickman,
Tony Shalboub, Sam Rockwell
Director: Dean Parisot
Producers: Mark Johnson, Charles Newirth
Script: David Howard, Robert Gordon

Eighteen years after their sci-fi adventure TV show *Galaxy Quest* was cancelled, actors Jason Nesmith, Gwen DeMarco, Alexander Dane, Tommy Webber and Fred Kwan are begrudgingly still in costume and making appearances at sci-fi conventions and store openings.

They're wallowing in despair and at each other's throats until aliens known as Thermians arrive. The aliens have mistaken intercepted TV transmissions of *Galaxy Quest* for 'historical documents' and modelled their entire culture around it. So they whisk the actors into space to save them from the genocidal General Sarris and his armada.

With no script, no director and no clue about real interstellar travel, the make-believe crew of the *Protector* have to produce the performance of their lives to become the heroes the aliens believe them to be.

Poking fun at *Star Trek*, this movie is filled with some fantastic special effects from Stan Winston (*Jurassic Park*). One of the best spoofs from Hollywood in recent times, *Galaxy Quest* features a stellar cast, including Tim Allen, Sigourney Weaver and Alan Rickman.

Galaxy Quest could have been a bit too close to the mark for it to become treasured by cultists. However, although poking fun at Trekkie conventions in its opening reel, with obsessed fans knowing every bit of trivia about the show, the film is always affectionate in its spoofing. There's even a whole new language popped up on the internet, based on Thermian phrases used in the movie.

Aar, eeh, aar – it's a scream / Aaap – thank you / E-aap – you're welcome!

Memorable dialogue:

Commander Peter Quincy Taggart:
Never give up! Never surrender!

Gwen DeMarco: I mean, my *TV Guide* interview was six paragraphs about my BOOBS and how they fit into my suit!

Jason Nesmith: There is no 'quantum flux'! There's no 'auxiliary'! THERE'S NO GODDAMNED SHIP! You got it?!

Commander Peter Quincy Taggart: As long as there is injustice, whenever a Targathian baby cries out, wherever a distress signal sounds among the stars, we'll be there. This fine ship, this fine crew. Never give up... and never surrender.

Gwen DeMarco: Jason, we are actors, not astronauts!

Malthesar: We have enjoyed preparing many of your esoteric dishes. Your Monte Cristo sandwich is a current favourite among the adventurous.

Guy Fleegman: I'm not even supposed to be here. I'm just 'Crewman Number Six'. I'm expendable! I'm the guy in the episode who dies to prove how serious the situation is! I've gotta get outta here!

Dr Lazarus: By Grabthar's hammer, you shall be avenged!

GET CARTER

1971 / 111 mins / UK / DVD / Video
Stars: Michael Caine, Ian Hendry, Britt Ekland,
John Osborne, Tony Beckley, George Sewell
Director: Mike Hodges
Producer: Michael Klinger
Script: Mike Hodges

What happens when a professional killer violates the code? Get Carter!

Based on Ted Lewis' novel *Jack Returns*, *Get Carter* is both scripted and directed by Mike Hodges and is undoubtedly one of the greatest British gangster films ever made, a prime example of British film noir with decaying settings and tough street gangsters. An essential cult classic, Hodges' film is unprecedented in terms of style and visual inventiveness. It stars Michael Caine (his best film role to date) and features Britt Ekland, Brian Mosely and noted playwright John Osborne.

Caine is Jack Carter, a gangster who's made it big in London. He returns home to Newcastle to investigate and avenge the death of his brother, Frank. Carter is desperate to find out who killed him and sets out on a complex trail of lies, sleaze and murder through Newcastle's tawdry but vicious underworld. His relentless and brutal determination leads him to a sordid discovery that only adds to his anger and thirst for revenge.

Get Carter blows away the cosy myth of British criminals as tea-swigging wide boys, setting an unmatched standard that endures to this day. Forget *Lock, Stock*. This is how a British gangster film should be made. It is violent and uncompromising but always entertaining with a good dose of black humour. Hodges uses the locations of Newcastle – the city streets, the docks, the racetrack and bridges – to create an atmosphere of impending menace.

Get Carter was remade a year after its release with a black cast as *Hit Man (1972)* and, more recently, by Sylvester Stallone. Sly's dire version includes a cameo performance from Caine. The influence of *Get Carter* on British film-making can also be seen in *The Long Good Friday* (1980) and more recent Brit flicks such as *Face* (1997), *Gangster No. 1* (2000) and *Snatch* (2000). Nevertheless, Hodges' film has never been bettered. Carter set a precedent for the ultimate hard man but at the same time had room to be critical of machismo in a way recent gangster films have not. So it's no surprise to hear a negative response from Hodges on the adoption of Carter as an icon of 'lad culture' (the men's magazine *Loaded* recently serialised the film in cartoon form): 'I absolutely loathe it. I hate the whole lad culture. It's all a role. The horror is that this role is spreading like a virus. Do we really want to live in a world filled with male slobs? The gangster genre seems to have turned into something to laugh at. Before, people took film seriously. Now, it's pure entertainment.'

Remastered and released to buy on video and DVD, the new editions contain original trailers, exclusive commentaries (by Hodges and cinematographer Wolfgang Suschitzky) and Roy Budd's incredible music score.

Memorable dialogue:

Jack Carter: You know, I'd almost forgotten what your eyes looked like. Still the same. Pissholes in the snow.

Jack Carter: A pint of bitter… in a thin glass!

Jack Carter: You're a big man, but you're out of shape. With me it's a full-time job. Now behave yourself.

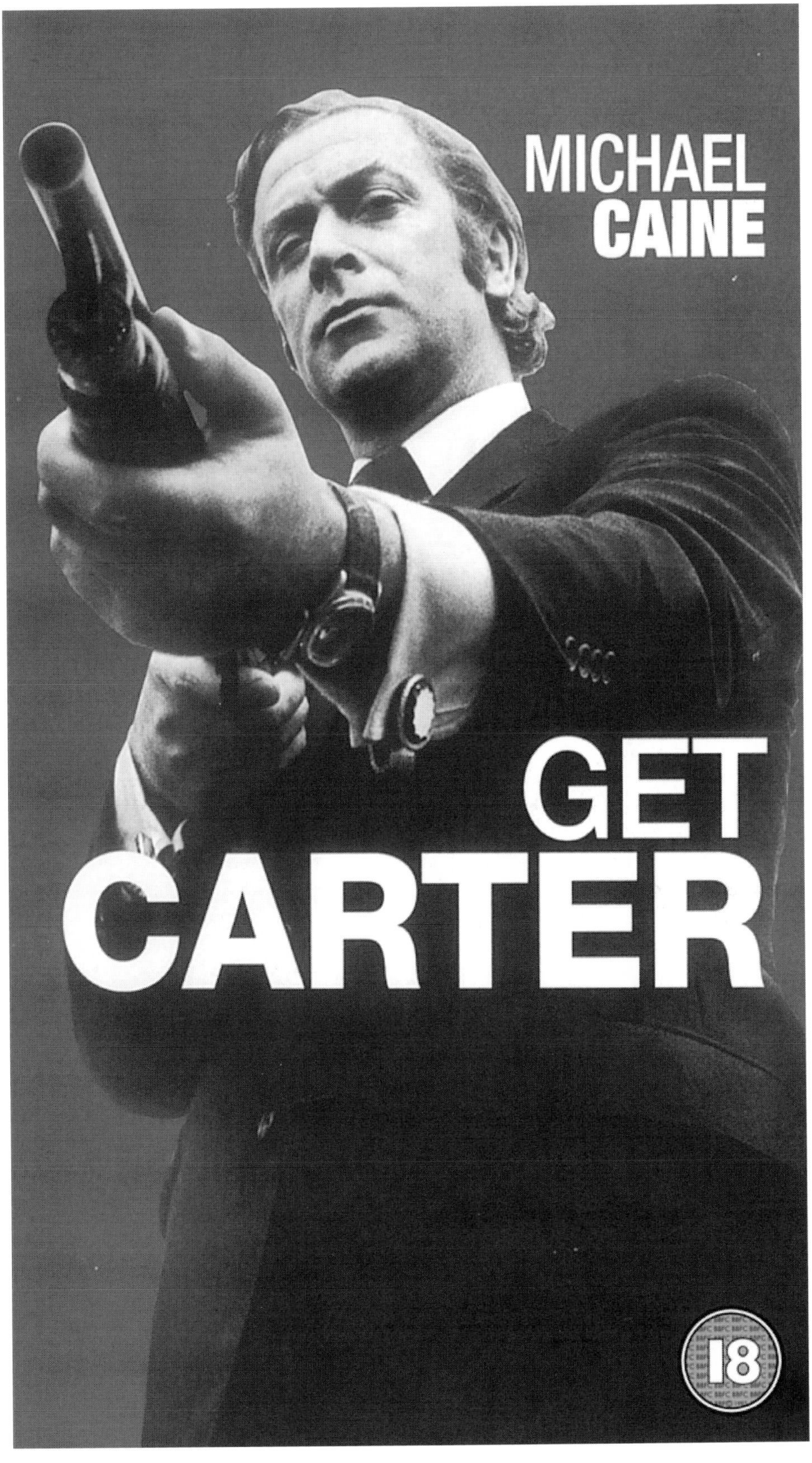
MICHAEL
CAINE
GET
CARTER
18

GILLIAM, TERRY

Director, writer, animator
Born 22 November 1940, Minnesota

As part of the *Monty Python* team on the BBC in the 70s, Gilliam was largely responsible for the surreal cartoon sequences. His directorial debut was *Jabberwocky* (1977), a piece of medieval madness about a humble apprentice who's mistaken for a prince and has to slay the obligatory dragon. He then helmed the sleeper hit *Time Bandits* (1981) and argued with studio heads over his futuristic satire *Brazil* (1985). This was his best film to date and earned him an Oscar nomination for co-writing the screenplay. Gilliam's spectacular, big-budget *The Adventures of Baron Munchausen* (1988) bombed, nearly bankrupting its Anglo-German producers, but three years later he returned with *The Fisher King* (1991). The commercial success of this movie was no surprise. Perhaps scared by the possibility of another box-office failure, Gilliam had opted to make a more optimistic and conventional movie with Robin Williams.

Having not directed a film since his version of *Fear and Loathing in Las Vegas* (1998), Gilliam is preparing to make *Good Omens* based on the novel by Terry Pratchett.

A lot of people like Terry Gilliam and there's no doubt his dark, comic-book-like voyages have found him a devoted audience. See Filmography p. 239.

The all-rounder: director, writer and animator, Terry Gilliam

GROSSE POINTE BLANK

1997 / 107 mins / USA / DVD / Video
Stars: John Cusack, Minnie Driver, Alan Arkin,
Dan Ackroyd, Joan Cusack, Hank Azaria
Director: George Armitage
Producers: Susan Arnold, Roger Birnbaum, John Cusack,
Steve Pink, Donna Roth
Script: Tom Jankiewicz, DV Devincentis,
Steve Pink, John Cusack

This smart black comedy comes with a big cult reputation. Hailed by both critics and audiences, John Cusack co-produced, co-wrote and starred in this.

A discontented freelance hitman, Martin Q Blank (Cusack) starts to develop a conscience, which causes him to botch a couple of routine assignments. On the advice of his secretary and his psychiatrist, he attends his 10th year High School reunion in Grosse Pointe, Michigan (a Detroit suburb where he's also contracted to kill someone). While he's there, he tries to rekindle an old relationship with Debi (Driver), the girl whom he once stood up on prom night. She's now a DJ. Cue loads of nostalgic 80s pop songs.

However, hot on his tail are a couple of over-enthusiastic federal agents, another assassin who wants to kill him and Grocer, an assassin who wants him to join an 'Assassins' Union'.

Countercultural hero Joe Strummer provides the music.

Memorable dialogue:

Martin: A BMW? In Detroit? That's sacrilege!

Debi: Some people say that you have to forgive and forget. I dunno; I say forget about forgiving and just accept.

Martin: If I show up at your door, chances are you did something to bring me there.

Bert Newberry: Ah, fuck it! Let's have a drink and forget the whole goddamned thing.

HACKERS

1995 / 105 mins / USA / *DVD* / 📼 Video
Stars: Johnny Lee Miller, Angelina Jolie, Fisher Stevens, Lorraine Bracco
Director: Iain Softley
Producers: Michael Peyser, Ralph Winter
Script: Rafael Moreau

A film about computer culture for internet-loving Nintendo kids, directed by Ian Softley (*Backbeat*). Fast becoming a cult movie thanks to a killer rave/techno type soundtrack (which has to date spawned no fewer than three CD albums). Some of the tracks include Prodigy songs years before they became popular.

The film's eccentric bunch of interesting characters have also helped stimulate a cult following. Matthew Lillard (*Scream*) is one, Johnny Lee Miller (*Trainspotting*) another. And the villain of the piece is very cool!

The story begins by showing us the early life of Dade Murphy or 'Crash Override' to his hacker buddies. When he was nine years old, Dade crashed computers all over the world. He was arrested by the Secret Service for hacking into a government computer and banned from using a computer until his 18th birthday. Years later, he and his new-found friends discover a plot to unleash a dangerous computer virus, but must use their computer skills to find the evidence while being pursued by the Secret Service and the evil computer genius behind the virus.

An inspired touch is that the screen-saver images that pop up on the screen from time to time are actually what they see in their minds – they are the pieces of a puzzle coming together.

Much more entertaining than the other computer flick *The Net* made the same year. *Hackers* is *War Games* for a new generation.

Memorable dialogue:

Dade Murphy: You look good in a dress.

Kate Libby: You would have looked better.

Kate Libby: Never send a boy to do a woman's job.

Cereal Killer: We have just gotten a wake-up call from the Nintendo Generation.

The Plague: Kid, don't threaten me. There are worse things than death, and uh, I can do all of them.

Kate Libby: I hope you don't screw like you type.

The Plague: There is no right and wrong. There's only fun and boring.

Kate Libby: God gave men brains larger than dogs' so they wouldn't hump women's legs at cocktail parties.

Cereal Killer: Spandex: it's a privilege, not a right.

Curtis: If it isn't Leopard Boy and the Decepticons.

Opposite page: The UK promo for Hackers *(1995), starring Johnny Lee Miller (bottom right)*

HITCHER

1986 / 97 mins / USA / ⬚ Video
Stars: Rutger Hauer, C Thomas Howell,
Jennifer Jason Leigh, Jeffrey DeMunn
Director: Robert Harmon
Producers: David Bombyk, Kip Ohman
Script: Eric Red

A direct descendant of Steven Spielberg's *Duel* (1971), *The Hitcher* is both a road movie and a battle between good and evil. Ignoring his mother's advice not to pick up strangers, Jim Halsey (Howell) picks up more than he bargained for when he stops to give a lift to a psychotic drifter called Ryder (Hauer), who will stop at nothing to play his evil mind games.

Ryder murders the drivers with whom he hitches lifts but when Jim decides to propel him from the car, his nightmare begins. Ryder goes on one big killing spree, murdering various helpless motorists, crimes for which Jim is eventually arrested and jailed. The police don't even believe the hitch-hiker existed.

The subtle soundtrack and sparse sound effects evoke the solitude of the open road and immediately put the viewer on edge. Howell is good as an average American teen and, surely, Rutger Hauer earns the title for one of the scariest and most charismatic men to walk the road.

Memorable dialogue:

Interrogation Sergeant: What's your name? Come on. What's your name? Do you have a name? Do you have a police record? Where are you from?
John Ryder: Disneyland.

[Picking up the hitch-hiker.]
Jim Halsey: My mother told me to never do this.

Jim: Why are you doing this to me?
John Ryder: You'll understand soon enough.

HOOPER, TOBE

Director
Born 25 January 1943, Austin, Texas

Tobe Hooper made his first film with his family's 8mm camera at the age of three and spent much of his early years in the cinema his father owned.

Hooper made his initial mark in the feature film industry by writing and directing the cult classic *The Texas Chainsaw Massacre* (1974). An amazing directorial debut, the film was honoured at the Cannes Film Festival and eventually inducted into the Horror Hall of Fame. It remains in the permanent collection of the New York Museum of Modern Art. This hugely successful film sparked three sequels and created a genre of extremely successful horror films dealing with the masked villain, spinning off such films as *Halloween* (1978) and *Friday the 13th* (1980). In a recent television special *The Anatomy of Horror*, Wes Craven credited Hooper with changing the horror genre forever.

The notoriety of the film may owe a lot to its original rejection by the British Board of Film Classification in 1975. However, it was recently passed for viewing in Europe, the USA, Australia and other countries and was most recently shown in central London in 1998 under a licence from Camden Council. There is, so far as the Board is aware, no evidence that harm has ever arisen as a consequence of viewing the film. For modern young adults, accustomed to the macabre shocks of horror films through the 80s and 90s, they say, *The Texas Chainsaw Massacre* is unlikely to be particularly challenging. Unlike more recent examples of the genre, violence in Hooper's film is implied rather than explicit.

After *Texas Chainsaw Massacre*, Hooper directed *Salem's Lot*, one of the first Stephen King movies developed into a television mini-series. This highly acclaimed four-hour mini-series featured James Mason and remains one of Stephen King's favourite film translations of his work. He also directed a Billy Idol music video *Dancing With Myself* (1983).

Hooper's black humour was to be seen in subsequent movies *The Funhouse* (1981), *Lifeforce* (1985) and *Invaders from Mars* (1986). But undoubtedly his most ambitious and commercial movie was the phenomenally successful *Poltergeist* (1982). Steven Spielberg enlisted Hooper to direct this effective haunted-house shocker which spurred two sequels and a television series.

In 1995 Tobe launched his first television series directing the pilot *Nowhere Man* for UPN. Akin to Patrick McGoohan's ground-breaking television allegory *The Prisoner* from the 60s, *Nowhere Man* is a psychological thriller which showcases Hooper's trademark visual style and tone. The following year he directed *Dark Skies* a two-hour pilot for NBC/Columbia dealing with the government agency Majestic and its cover-up of the Roswell incident. Set in Washington DC in the early 60s, the series eventually received an Emmy nomination.

Tobe Hooper has won numerous awards worldwide for his unique cinematic style. Most recently, he made a film entitled *The Apartment Complex* (1999) for Showtime and is currently developing projects for both film and television. See Filmography, p.239

HOPPER, DENNIS

Actor, director, writer
Born 17 May 1936, Dodge City, Kansas

'Like all artists I want to cheat death a little and contribute something to the next generation.'

Dennis Hopper is one of Tinseltown's most notorious stars. Married five times, this wild hellraiser was effectively excluded from Hollywood roles for eight years. An actor since his teens, in the 50s Hopper appeared twice with James Dean: in 1955's *Rebel Without a Cause* and 1956's *Giant.* Of that time Hopper says: 'In the 50s, when me and Natalie Wood and James Dean and Nick Adams and Tony Perkins suddenly arrived... God, it was a whole group of us that sort of felt like that earlier group – the John Barrymores, Errol Flynns, Sinatras, Clifts – were a little farther out than we were... So we tried to emulate that lifestyle. For instance, once Natalie and I decided we'd have an orgy. And Natalie says "OK, but we have to have a champagne bath." So we filled the bathtub full of champagne. Natalie takes off her clothes, sits down in the champagne, starts screaming. We take her to the emergency hospital. That was *our* orgy, you understand?'

Apart from a few supporting roles and guest-star slots in TV dramas in the 60s, the method actor was soon pegged as 'difficult' and it was the bizarre space vampire flick *Queen of Blood* (1966) which led Roger Corman, in 1967, to cast him in the acid spectacular *The Trip*, opposite Peter Fonda. Together the pair conceived, wrote and funded *Easy Rider* (1969) with Hopper directing.

Hopper went on to direct the daring and quite mad *The Last Movie* (1971), which alienated him from the Hollywood establishment. High on drugs and drink throughout the 70s, he spent much of that decade in low-budget art-house productions or in foreign films. Although he did put in good performances in both Francis Coppola's *Apocalypse Now* (1979) and Wim Wenders' *The American Friend* (1977). He

was equally as impressive as the father figure type to the Brat Pack cast of Coppola's *Rumble Fish* (1983) and soon got to direct his third feature. Having not been let in the director's chair since *The Last Movie*, Hopper came back with *Out of the Blue* (1980) a sinister thriller in which he also starred as the ex-convict father of a teenage girl obsessed by punk in small town America. Hopper was off the drugs and back on track.

After spending the early 80s getting himself cleaned up, he auditioned for *Blue Velvet* (1986) by telephoning director David Lynch and telling him 'I am Frank Booth.' So with the words, 'Don't you fuckin' look at me!' Hopper's career was reborn as the apotheosis of middle-American menace. In the same year he received his first Oscar nomination for *Hoosiers* (1986) and went on to make more than a dozen films within the three years that followed.

Hopper's next directing job was with Robert Duvall and Sean Penn in *Colors* (1988), a violent film about the intense gang warfare in LA. It was a serious, stark, unbiased look at a real-life problem, plumbing the depths sentimentality.

Backtrack which Hopper directed in 1989, was released in a cut and edited version called *Catchfire* and was attributed to, at Hopper's insistence, the pseudonym favoured by angry American directors who wish to disown a project: Alan Smithee.

Hopper, however, continues to win kudos for his fine starring turns in the cool movies of the moment. Over the decade or so, they've ranged from his brilliant portrayal of a tortured madman in *Paris Trout* (1991), his role as Christian Slater's father in *True Romance* (1993), to cameos in cult movies such as Alex Cox's Spaghetti Western *Straight to Hell* (1987) and lead roles in action movies such as 1994's *Speed.* See Filmography, p. 239.

I MARRIED A MONSTER FROM OUTER SPACE

1958 / 78 mins / USA / (Not currently available)
Stars: Tom Tryon, Gloria Talbott, Ken Lynch,
John Eldridge, Alan Dexter, Jean Carson
Director: Gene Fowler Jr
Producer: Gene Fowler Jr
Script: Louis Vittes

An interesting cult curiosity which has aliens slowly switching places with real humans; one of the first being a young man about to get married. Slowly, his new wife realises something is wrong. Her suspicions are confirmed when her husband's odd behaviour begins to show up in other townspeople.

Eventually she follows him out one night, only to discover him changing into his original form and boarding a spaceship. In a tense climax, the untouched townsfolk are drafted in by doctors to help break up the invasion in a final attack on the spaceship.

Gene Fowler Jr's movie ranks alongside other 50s sci-fi classics *The Invasion of the Body Snatchers* (1955), *The Day the Earth Stood Still* (1951) and *Them!* (1954).

Excellent acting, tight direction, believable dialogue and truly creepy aliens give this a black-and-white thumbs up. It was remade for TV recently in a faithful adaptation by Nancy Malone but this version remains the better bet to watch.

Memorable Dialogue

Marge: I know you're not Bill, you're some thing that crept into Bill's body.

Marge: Your race has no women, it can't have children, it will die out!

THE INCREDIBLE SHRINKING MAN

1957 / 81 mins / USA / (Not currently available)
Stars: Grant Williams, Randy Stuart, April Kent,
Paul Langton, Raymond Bailey, William Schallert,
Frank Scannell, Helene Marshall
Director: Jack Arnold
Producers: Albert Zugsmith
Script: Richard Matheson (from his own novel)

The 50s were pretty fructiferous for American sci-fi movies and Jack Arnold's *The Incredible Shrinking Man* is a particularly good one. Arnold made a number of camp classics, including *The Creature from the Black Lagoon* (1954) and *Tarantula* (1955).

Like most of the cult movies from the 50s sci-fi era, *The Incredible Shrinking Man* is really more than just a silly adventure. The style, narrative and dialogue to many of these 50s 'B' movies is always similar and they're really skirting around the theme of the atom bomb and mankind's vulnerability in the nuclear age. In *This Island Earth* (1955), an alien planet has been destroyed by years of nuclear war, while in *Them!* (1954), another nuclear age thriller, directed by Gordon Douglas, nuclear testing in the desert creates a race of giant ants. It's amazing to think that this handful of sci-fi thrillers could really tap into America's paranoia about the atomic age.

So, in *The Incredible Shrinking Man*, after an exposure to a strange radioactive mist, our hero, Scott Carey (Grant Williams) emerges from the atomic cloud and begins to shrink at the alarming rate of an inch a week. Doctors can do nothing and he ends up a 36-inch tall midget before shrinking even further and having to do battle with his angry cat. The fight between Carey and a spider remains a genuine chiller. In the end, he accidentally gets locked in the basement. His life then becomes a battle for survival, with only his wits to overcome the liability of his size.

The excellent special effects are by Clifford Stine and the imaginative art direction by Alexander Golitzen and Robert Clatworthy.

While leading man Grant Williams faded away like the shrinking man, original screenwriter Richard Matheson went on to write several screenplays for Roger Corman and wrote the novel *I Am Legend* which was adapted for the screen as *The Omega Man* (1971). He also wrote the screenplay for Steven Spielberg's first feature, the TV

movie *Duel* (1971). Unfortunately, Matheson came up with the script for the dire *Jaws* sequel, *Jaws 3D* (1983) and the sequel to this cult entry, *The Incredible Shrinking Woman* (1981) starring Lili Tomlin. Meanwhile, Peter Segal (who directed the third *Naked Gun* movie and the sequel to *The Nutty Professor*) is said to be in the process of remaking Arnold's movie with a top Hollywood cast.

Memorable dialogue:

Scott Carey: Easy enough to talk of soul and spirit and essential worth but not when you're three feet tall.

Scott Carey: I was continuing to shrink, to become — what? The infinitesimal? What was I? Still a human being? Or was I the man of the future? If there were other bursts of radiation, other clouds drifting across seas and continents, would other beings follow me into this vast new world? So close — the infinitesimal and the infinite. But suddenly, I knew they were really the two ends of the same concept. The unbelievably small and the unbelievably vast eventually meet — like the closing of a gigantic circle. I looked up, as if somehow I would grasp the heavens. The universe, worlds beyond number, God's silver tapestry spread across the night. And in that moment, I knew the answer to the riddle of the infinite.

INVADERS FROM MARS

1953 / 78 mins / USA / *DVD* / ⬛ Video
Stars: Jimmy Hunt, Helena Carter, Arthur Franz,
Morris Ankrum, Leif Erickson, Hillary Brooke
Director: William Cameron Menzies
Producer: Edward L Alperson
Script: John Tucker Battle, Richard Blake

Gone With the Wind (1939) designer William Cameron Menzies directed this 50s sci-fi tale of a Martian invasion with a distinctive visual flair which has made it a minor cult favourite. Having gained little sympathy with audiences at the time, *Invaders From Mars* has attained cult stature in recent years.

The story is told from the point of view of a young boy called David MacLean (Jimmy Hunt). All the adults in town begin acting strangely shortly after he notices odd lights settling behind a hill near his home. As more and more adults are affected, he must turn to the pretty Dr Blake for some kind of protection.

Back in 1953, the movie's amusing poster tagline read: 'From Three Hundred Million Miles Away They Come! Unusual... Unbelievable... Unimaginable... But It Could Happen Tomorrow... Don't Miss the Movie That's Packed With Thrills'.

Interestingly, Hunt made a special guest appearance in the 1986 remake, playing a police chief.

Memorable dialogue:

Colonel Fielding: Start digging!

Soldiers: Blast him!

INVASION OF THE BODY SNATCHERS

1978 / 115 mins / USA / DVD/ Video
Stars: Donald Sutherland, Brooke Adams,
Leonard Nimoy, Veronica Cartwright
Director: Philip Kaufman
Producer: Robert H Solo
Script: WD Richter

In Don Siegel's original *Invasion of the Body Snatchers* (1955), two lovers discovered the Earth had been invaded by alien monsters in the form of giant seed pods capable of draining humans of all emotion. The first remake of the paranoid infiltration classic moves the setting for the invasion from a small town to the city of San Francisco. Most remakes are bad and pointless. Kaufman's, however, was well worth it and possibly matches the original.

It begins with Matthew Bennell noticing that several of his friends are complaining that their close relatives are in some way different. When questioned later they themselves seem changed as they deny everything. As the invaders increase in number they become more open and Bennell, who has by now witnessed an attempted 'replacement' realises that he and his friends must escape or suffer the same fate. But who can he trust to help him and who has already been snatched? The psychiatrist turns out to be the ringleader of the replicants.

Whereas the 1955 original was the epitome of red menace propaganda, Kaufman hints at a bigger, unseen menace – a post-Watergate, post-Vietnam corporate power lurking everywhere. He shows us the mighty Transamerica Tower in several shots. Transamerica is also the huge corporation that owned the studio that made this film.

Kaufman's inspired use of lenses and warped mirrors gives this film a weird sense of distortion; strange camera angles tend to make you think you're in one place, until the camera quickly turns and you're somewhere else.

Kevin McCarthy and Don Siegel, star and director of the original film, have significant cameo roles and don't blink or you'll miss Robert Duvall. The eerie score is by Denny Zeitlin with Grateful Dead's Jerry Garcia on the banjo.

Memorable dialogue:

Elizabeth Driscoll: I have seen these flowers all over. They are growing like parasites on other plants. All of a sudden. Where are they coming from?
Nancy Bellicec: Outer space?
Jack Bellicec: What are you talking about? A space flower?
Nancy Bellicec: Well why not a space flower? Why do we always expect them to come in metal ships?

Matthew: Do you want to see my friend, he's a psychiatrist. He'd eliminate a lot of things – whether Geoffrey was having an affair, whether he had become gay, whether he had a social disease, whether he had become a Republican, all the alternatives that could have happened to him.

David (the psychiatrist): Don't be trapped by old concepts, Matthew, you're evolving into a new life form.

114

THE ITALIAN JOB

1969 / 117 mins / UK / ▭ Video
Stars: Michael Caine, Noel Coward, Benny Hill,
Raf Vallone, Tony Beckley, Rossano Brazzi, Maggie Blye,
Irene Handl, John Le Mesurier
Director: Peter Collinson
Producer: Michael Deeley
Script: Troy Kennedy Martin

The plot to this heist caper is a classic. A jailed criminal masterminds a daring gold bullion heist in Turin from his prison cell, aiming to create the world's biggest traffic jam as a diversion. The heist is funded by the ever patriotic inmate Mr Bridger (Noel Coward) and executed by ex-con Charlie Croker (Michael Caine).

All goes to plan and the team escape the police in a fleet of getaway Minis headed for Switzerland. But when their getaway coach careers off the road, it's Charlie who has to come up with another great idea.

The film was written by Troy Kennedy Martin (1986's *Edge of Darkness*) and produced by Michael Deeley (1976's *The Man Who Fell To Earth* and 1982's *Blade Runner*). The photography was by Douglas Slocombe (the *Indiana Jones* trilogy) and the soundtrack by Quincy Jones. Apparently, Robert Redford was the first choice for the Caine part.

The movie has enjoyed something of a renaissance in the last year with a Stereophonics pop promo and video re-release.

Memorable dialogue:

Charlie C: We're about to do a job, in Italy, and the only way we're gonna do it is by working together and that means doing everything I say.

Charlie C: Hang on lads, I've got a great idea.

Garage Manager: You must have shot an awful lot of tigers, sir.
Charlie C: Yes, I used a machine gun.

Charlie C: You're only supposed to blow the bloody doors off!

Peach: I like 'em big.

Next page: Caine and the gang in Peter Collinson's The Italian Job *(1969)*

JARMUSCH, JIM

Director, writer
Born 22 January 1953, Ohio

Jarmusch studied film-making at New York University. He worked as an assistant on Nicholas Ray and Wim Wenders' *Lightning Over Water* (1980) and his final student project, *Permanent Vacation* (1981), made for roughly $15,000, was seen overseas and greeted with much acclaim. His later film, *Stranger Than Paradise* (1984), was expanded from a 30-minute short made two years earlier and followed the marginally comic adventures of a young man, his best friend and his cousin from Budapest. It was a film he originally structured around the Screamin' Jay Hawkins' song, 'I Put A Spell On You', and eventually went on to win the Camera D'Or at the 1984 Cannes Film Festival and was named Best Picture of the year by the National Society of Film Critics.

Down by Law (1986) was a clever and funny film, largely thanks to a performance by the Italian comic Roberto Benigni as the outsider. It was photographed by Robby Muller, the Dutch cameraman responsible for most of Wim Wenders' movies as well as Alex Cox's *Repo Man* (1984) and William Friedkin's *To Live and Die in LA* (1985).

Mystery Train (1989), Jarmusch's first film in colour, offered a trio of stories about foreigners staying in a Memphis hotel. *Night on Earth* (1991), probably his most accessible film to date, is a five-part story set in five taxis in major cities around the world – New York, LA, Paris, Rome and Helsinki. In 1993 he won the Palme d'Or at Cannes for his short film *Coffee and Cigarettes (Somewhere in California)* which featured Tom Waits and Iggy Pop. He also directed the Waits video *It's All Right With Me*.

Jim Jarmusch's favourite director is the Finnish film-maker Aki Kaurismaki, responsible for *Hamlet Goes Business (1987)* and *Leningrad Cowboys Go America* (1993), in which Jarmusch plays a used-car salesman.
See Filmography, p.239

JOHNNY MNEMONIC

1995 / 98 mins / Canada / USA / 🖵 Video
Stars: **Keanu Reeves, Dina Meyer, Ice T, Takeshi Kitano,
Dennis Akayama, Dolph Lundgren, Henry Rollins**
Director: **Robert Longo**
Producer: **Don Carmody**
Script: **William Gibson**

Based on an original short story by acclaimed 'cyber-world' author and first-time screenwriter William Gibson, *Johnny Mnemonic* marks the feature-length directorial debut of celebrated artist Robert Longo.

In 2021, the whole world is connected by the gigantic internet and almost half of the population is suffering from the Nerve Attenuation Syndrome (NAS). Johnny (Reeves), a bio-enhanced, silicon chip-implanted mnemonic courier, is hired to carry 320 gigabytes of crucial information to safety from the Pharmacom corporation in Beijing to Newark. He is perfectly adapted to his 21st-century world, using his brain's computer-enhanced memory cells to transport valuable information loaded into his head via a wet-wire interface. While Pharmacom Industries supported by Yakuza tries to capture him to get the information back, the low-tech group led by J-Bone tries to break the missing code to download the cure for NAS, which Johnny carries. If he fails to deliver the data, he dies within 24 hours.

Johnny Mnemonic was filmed in 12 weeks on location in Toronto and Montreal, with sets constructed to represent Beijing, China and Newark, New Jersey in the 21st century. Production designer Nilo Rodis relied heavily on his degree in industrial design and his experience as an automotive designer to create the complex sets.

'The free city of Newark is like the Wild West', according to screenwriter Gibson. 'The government's gone bankrupt and the only law that's left is the Yakuza. It's not the Third World...it's the Fourth World. It's America's conceptual nightmare on the brink of a new century, a savage experiment in social Darwinism, where God seems to be a bored lab worker with his thumb permanently on technology's fast forward button.'

Memorable dialogue:

Johnny Mnemonic: I can carry nearly 80 gigs of data in my head.

Johnny Mnemonic: What the fuck is going on? What the FUCK is going on?! You know, all my life, I've been careful to stay in my own corner. Looking out for Number One – no complications. Now, suddenly, I'm responsible for the fate of the entire fucking world – and everybody and his mother is trying to kill me IF IF my head doesn't blow up first.

Johnny Mnemonic: I want the club sandwich. I want the cold Mexican beer. I want a $10,000-a-night hooker!! I want my shirts laundered like they do at the Imperial Hotel in Tokyo.

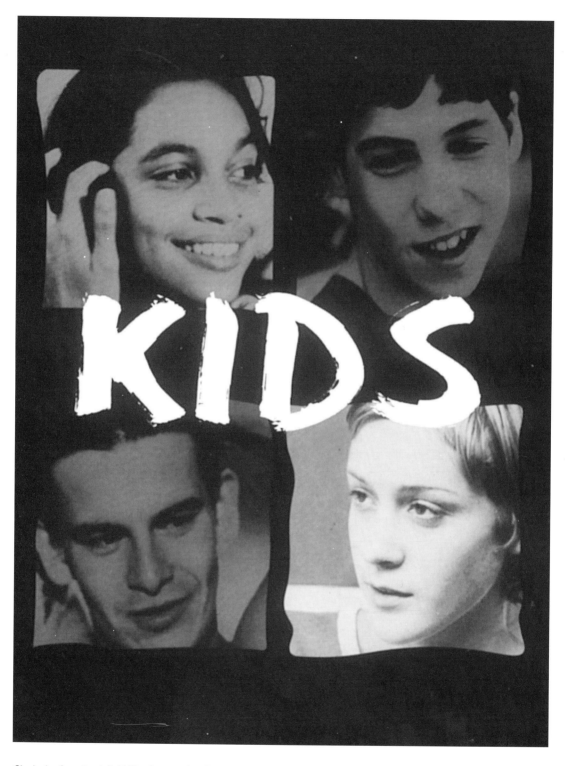

Clockwise from top left: Yakira Peguero, Leo Fitzpatrick, Chloe Sevigny and Justin Pierce in Larry Clark's controversial film Kids *(1995)*

KIDS

1995 / 91 mins / USA/ *DVD* / ▭ Video
Stars: Leo Fitzpatrick, Justin Pierce,
Chloe Sevigny, Yakira Peguero
Director: Larry Clark
Producers: Cary Woods
Script: Harmony Korine

Larry Clark, one of the most influential figures in American still photography, turned his uncompromising visual style to create a film that explores the motives and desires of Manhattan's teenage subculture.

Kids makes no apology in documenting the harsh world of two New York skateboarders, Telly (Leo Fitzpatrick) and his companion Casper (Justin Pierce), as they journey through adolescence, hanging out, shoplifting, fighting, taking drugs and seducing young girls.

The narrative spans 24 frantic hours. But as the two roam around the city streets care free, they are pursued across town, from Upper East Side to Washington Square Park and the bohemian East Village, by a desperate Jennie (Chloe Sevigny) who has news which will change their lives for ever.

The vision Clark exhibits in his photos of contemporary youth subculture is recreated in a film that travels to the heart of adolescent sexuality. This is certainly an explicit and disturbing film, the cause of much moral outrage on its original release. The picture that the movie paints may not be pleasant and it may not be typical, but it offers compelling food for thought. The kids at the core of the story are simply part of urban modern-day America. After all, HIV, date rape, drug-taking and promiscuity are as much a part of an average New York teenager's day as skateboarding and pool parties. But what's happening here could quite possibly happen anywhere. The film details one single day in which everything and yet nothing will change.

From observing kids, Clark said at the time: 'Their keys to survival are their peer group, their friends. They try to guide and protect each other. That's why I say today's kids aren't that much different than when I was a kid. I had great friends who had their own problems. They would get beat up, they had alcoholic parents, you name it. Even then, everything was out there. Now I think it's just much more in the open.'

Kids is scripted by 19-year-old skateboarder Harmony Korine, features extraordinary performances from a cast of non-professional actors and is filmed with a loose, hand-held intimacy by Eric Edwards, renowned for his work on Gus Van Sant's *My Own Private Idaho* (1991).

Memorable dialogue:

Telly: Fucking is what I love. Take that away, I have nothing.

Cabby: You look like the prom queen. I dated the prom queen when I was your age. She was the first girl I stuck my tongue in.

Casper: I love to fuck men, but you know what, I'm not gay. I just do it for the hell of it.

Kid at a rave: Didn't you know tricks are for kids?

Telly: Condoms don't work. They either break, or they slip off, or they make your dick shrink. Nah, but you still gotta use em, yo. At least I did once.

Telly: When you are young not much matters, when you find something you like that's all you got.

KINGS AND DESPERATE MEN

1981 / 118 mins / Canada / (Not currently available)
Stars: Patrick McGoohan, Alexis Kanner,
Andrea Marcovicci, Margaret Trudeau
Director: Alexis Kanner
Producer: Alexis Kanner
Script: Edmund Ward and Alexis Kanner

Alexis Kanner's little-seen movie has developed a cult reputation because of its link with the cultiest of all television series *The Prisoner* (1967). Following *The Prisoner*, Patrick McGoohan took on various roles in the 70s and hardly any in the 80s. *Kings and Desperate Men* is one of the more notable productions he has appeared in and seems to be similar in nature to *The Prisoner*, dealing with the same themes. It also suggests that the concept is still as important to McGoohan as ever. Not surprisingly, Kanner's film has been analysed and celebrated by the same group of people who devote their time to examining *The Prisoner*. Lengthy articles on *Kings and Desperate Men* have appeared in many of the quarterly magazines produced by 'Six of One', the official appreciation society for *The Prisoner*.

Alexis Kanner was himself in *The Prisoner* as 'the Kid' and wrote the lead role for McGoohan in *Kings*, that of John Kingsley, a radio talk-show host who's taken hostage in his penthouse broadcasting studio. History-teacher-turned-terrorist leader Lucas Miller (played by Kanner) is the man who forces Kingsley to host a strange trial over the airwaves.

Most of the film's main scenes were shot in December 1977, with some reshoots in 1978. It premiered at the Montreal Film Festival in 1981 and was released in Canada and the UK in 1984, although it wasn't until 1988 that *Kings* found a distributor in the USA.

The film begins with fragmented images of the gang of terrorists on their way to hijack Kingsley's radio show. These muddled pictures are coupled with an extraordinary array of voices, phones, loudspeakers, sirens, gun blasts and other strange noises and dialogue. This is all intercut with Kingsley interviewing a judge who's just passed a 15-year sentence on a man convicted of hitting and killing a policeman while driving a car. Miller and his followers believe there has been a gross miscarriage of justice and so take over the live show and let the people decide. Another group of Miller's gang hold Kingsley's wife and young son in their downtown apartment.

Back in 1967, McGoohan had been so impressed with Alexis Kanner's performance in the *Prisoner* episode *Fall Out*, he showed his appreciation by having his name 'boxed' in the closing title sequence. Ten years after being directed by McGoohan, the roles are reversed with Kanner in the director's chair: 'Actors are very vulnerable when they work, especially when they are out on a very long limb, playing a tremendously difficult part,' says Kanner. 'Patrick's part in *Kings and Desperate Men* required a tremendous commitment and trust from him, so he didn't have any of his producing, writing or directing hats on. He was very much dependent on what the guy standing next to the camera would tell him at the end of each take and before the next take. The role reversal never occurred to either of us but I suppose he must have listened to me as I listened to him all of those years ago doing *The Prisoner*'.

This film particularly merits attention because, like *The Prisoner*, it is ablaze with intelligence and thought-provoking themes. Billed as 'the Englishman's Englishman, the man you love to hate', Kingsley begins his radio show with a quote from John Donne: 'Thou art slave to fate, chance, kings and desperate men.' Later, the two men sing lines from 'God Rest Ye Merry Gentlemen', even though one is holding a gun and distorting people's lives. So on one level, *Kings and Desperate Men* becomes a modern-day morality play: 'It's a spiritual odyssey,' explains Kanner. 'Miller and Kingsley have had this date a long time. They're ready for it. Kingsley was always going to meet himself the other way one day. It was a date with destiny.'

Described by critics as 'mesmerising' (*LA Times*), 'fascinating to watch and every bit as compelling to listen to' (*Hollywood Reporter*) and 'innovative and compulsive' (*Time Out*), *Kings* is a brilliant tour-de-force that reunites two electrifying performers. FX Feeney of *LA Weekly* wrote: 'This is a remarkable film, one of the very best. Suspenseful,

Former Prisoner *star Patrick McGoohan as John Kingsley in Alexis Kanner's* Kings and Desperate Men *(1981)*

stylistically daring, wonderfully acted, its strengths are many – the photography and editing, the performances nothing short of splendid – it's wonderful to watch.'

Many critics have said that *Kings and Desperate Men* sees McGoohan's finest performance in a film role. 'Patrick was thrilled with the picture,' admits Kanner. 'I saw one article in the press in which Patrick actually said he could die happy, now that his grandchildren could see an example of what he was capable of in *Kings and Desperate Men*. We were both delighted with the end result. Of course, now Patrick is playing in *Braveheart* (1995) and *The Phantom* (1996) and *A Time to Kill* (1996) and suddenly it's a new lease of life!'

A few years after the release of his film, Alexis Kanner was asked to remake *Kings and Desperate Men* with another actor in Patrick's place. He turned down the offer instantly: 'A major studio, never mind which, wanted it remade with an American actor because they thought that the situation was really neat. I said no but later it was done anyway.' Indeed, many film critics noted the similarities between Alexis Kanner's film and the Bruce Willis action flick *Die Hard* (1988). The theme was the same – a tense hostage situation on the 30th floor of a city skyscraper on Christmas Eve. Even the dialogue that Alan Rickman speaks in *Die Hard*, playing Kanner's part, has distinct similarities. 'Now everybody's doing the hostage movie,' laughs Kanner. 'It's a really big franchise. In *Independence Day*, they take the whole Earth hostage!'

Memorable dialogue:

Kingsley: Aw, me name is Macnamara, I'm the failure of the band.

Miller: God!
Kingsley: Rest.
Miller: Ye.
Kingsley: Merry?
Miller: Gentle. Men.

KISS ME DEADLY

1955 / 101 mins / USA / ▭ Video
Stars: Ralph Meeker, Albert Dekker,
Paul Stewart, Juano Herandez,
Wesley Addy, Marion Carr
Director: Robert Aldrich
Producer: Robert Aldrich
Script: Al Bezzerides

Robert Aldrich's classic of late film noir, *Kiss Me Deadly* (1955), is a loose adaptation of one of Mickey Spillane's 'Mike Hammer' thrillers with Ralph Meeker as a sleazy Hammer, on the trail of 'the great whatsit' (a box filled with a radioactive substance).

One night Hammer picks up a desperate woman hitch-hiking. The woman – Cloris Leachman, in her first film role – alludes to a terrible secret. When she's killed soon afterwards, Hammer tries to find out why. 'This is something big,' he says.

Meeker is dead-on as Hammer, aficionado of flashy cars, fast women and clients who pay on the 1st. The case is a tough one to crack and he'll use violence to stop anyone who gets in his way. He's not Mr Nice Guy. He's alive. But many who got hold of the strange, glowing box central to the mystery aren't.

It's clear Aldrich is actually critiquing Spillane's macho style and the nuclear paranoia of 50s America and he creates a sense of anxiety about some sort of mysterious force at work in a civilisation on the edge of the apocalypse. Hammer's lack of principles is in keeping with the pessimistic view of the future of the human race in the nuclear age.

Intriguingly, the film's ending is now enhanced by the theatrical trailer presented on the most recent DVD releases. This extra includes an important shot of the hero's escape that Aldrich left out of the final cut.

Memorable dialogue:

Mike Hammer: So you're a fugitive from the laughing house.

Velda: Do me a favour, will you? Keep away from the windows. Somebody might... blow you a kiss.

Lily Carver: Kiss me, Mike. I want you to kiss me. Kiss me. The liar's kiss that says I love you and means something else.

Dr Soberin: Lot's wife was turned into a pillar of salt. Whoever opens this box will be turned into brimstone and ashes.

Dr Soberin: As the world becomes more primitive, its treasures become more fabulous.

Dr Soberin: The head of Medusa. That's what's in the box, and who looks on her will be changed not into stone but into brimstone and ashes. But of course you wouldn't believe me, you'd have to see for yourself, wouldn't you?

Dr Soberin: Listen to me, as if I were Cerberus barking with all his heads at the gates of hell. I will tell you where to take it, but don't don't open it!

KUBRICK, STANLEY

Director, writer
Born 26 July 1928, New York

Jack Kubrick's decision to give his son a camera for his 13th birthday was a wise move: Kubrick became an avid photographer and would often make trips around New York taking photographs to develop in a friend's darkroom. After selling an unsolicited photograph to *Look* magazine, Kubrick began to associate with their staff photographers and at the age of 17 was offered a job as an apprentice photographer. In the next few years, Kubrick took on regular assignments for the publication but was already focused on making movies.

In 1950 he pooled his savings to fund the documentaries *Day of the Fight* (1951) about a pugilist and *Flying Padre* (1951) about a priest. Next Kubrick was off to California to make *Fear and Desire* (1953) but shooting this movie was not a happy experience as his marriage to high-school sweetheart Toba Metz did not survive the filming.

Kubrick's *The Killing* (1956) brought him to the attention of Hollywood. This heist movie with a raw documentary edge was a clear inspiration to Tarantino for *Reservoir Dogs* (1991).

Paths of Glory (1957) was the first major salvo in the Kubrick anti-war campaign and even Winston Churchill applauded its authenticity. Kirk Douglas excels as the defender of three innocent privates who are court-martialled and subsequently executed. Douglas later called on Kubrick to take over the production of *Spartacus* (1960). Kubrick hated the experience so much that he forsook Hollywood altogether and moved to London, where was based up until his death.

Dr Strangelove (1963) was the director's darkest and funniest film with Peter Sellers in no less than three roles, an over-the-top George C Scott and a chilling Sterling Hayden. It earned Oscar nominations for Best Picture, Best Direction and Best Screenplay (by Kubrick, Terry Southern and Peter George).

Kubrick then spent four years working on the greatest science-fiction film of all time, *2001: A Space Odyssey* (1968). It was nominated for Best Direction and Screenplay, and earned Kubrick a Visual Effects Oscar.

A Clockwork Orange (1971), featured Malcolm McDowell as Alex, a Beethoven-loving thug who leads his vicious pack of 'Droogs' through a bleak, futuristic London. Kubrick vividly portrayed an establishment at pains to protect itself by destabilising and dehumanising a rebellious youth and was rewarded with nominations for Best Picture, Director and Screenplay.

Barry Lyndon (1975), adapted from a novel by William Thackeray, mesmerised many but for others it was far too slow and deliberate. Again, it received nominations for Best Picture, Director and Screenplay. Around this time Kubrick's reputation as an obsessive perfectionist began to filter through with reports that *Barry Lyndon* took a whole year to shoot. Similar reports came from the set of 1980's *The Shining*. Scatman Crothers reportedly had to do 75 takes of one scene – the slamming of a car door.

Kubrick's Vietnam war film *Full Metal Jacket* (1987) re-created the hellish environs of Vietnam within the gasworks of London. This received mixed reviews. In 1993 Kubrick began working on the futuristic, special-effects-oriented story *AI*. Although he didn't get to finish that project before his death, he did deliver *Eyes Wide Shut* (1999) with Tom Cruise and Nicole Kidman.

As far back as November 1996, Cruise and wife Nicole Kidman were spotted at the English studio locations for what would be Kubrick's last film, described in the original Warner Brothers press release as 'a story of jealousy and sexual obsession'. Eighteen months later, while Kubrick fans debated whether Cruise and Kidman were worthy of working with the greatest living film director, Hollywood's hottest couple were still being recalled for reshoots by the man who was notorious for his perfectionism. Cruise had come a long way from the teen flicks of the early 80s and working with the celebrated auteur can be seen as the high point of his career to date (the Oscar nomination probably a

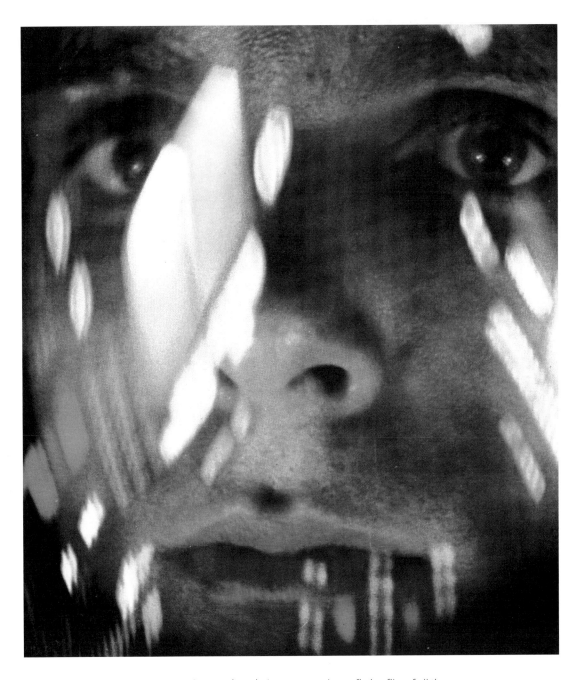

Keir Dullea in Kubrick's 2001: A Space Odyssey *(1968), the greatest science-fiction film of all time*

close second). Nevertheless, there is nothing particularly memorable about Cruise's performance. As the wealthy doctor Bill Harford, who is tormented by his wife's imagined infidelity, Cruise just seems to frown a lot. In fact, for Kubrick's last work, the film as a whole is disappointing and failed to live up to the hype. At two hours and 40 minutes, *Eyes Wide Shut* is simply too long and uninteresting and full of clumsy dialogue. Cruise has to take some of the blame. The character he plays is supposed to be in the grip of sexual jealousy, but Cruise is one of Hollywood's blandies with too much goodie-goodie history. Quite simply, he doesn't hold any interest. He's nice. Not surprisingly, rather than delivering a gripping or powerful performance, Cruise is dispassionate. See Filmography, p.239.

KURT AND COURTNEY

1998 / 93 mins / USA / UK / ▭ Video
Director: Nick Broomfield
Producers: Tine Van Den Brande, Michele D'Acosta

The most talked-about film at the 1998 Sundance Film Festival was the one they were afraid to show: Nick Broomfield's acclaimed documentary *Kurt and Courtney*.

Broomfield is the celebrated and subversive documentary director of *Heidi Fleiss – Hollywood Madam* (1995) and *Fetishes* (1996). Filmed in Seattle during 1997, *Kurt and Courtney* is a fascinating and searing account of the last days of grunge music icon Kurt Cobain and punk's bad girl turned movie star, Courtney Love.

Cobain's death in 1994 shocked his fans. As lead singer and songwriter for the seminal rock group Nirvana, he had touched the heart of a generation with his music. Despite its official ruling as a suicide, there have been a number of allegations since his death, insinuating that more sinister forces were at work.

Broomfield's film begins with a poignant portrait of Cobain's early years and continues on a voyage of discovery that brings the director in touch with some of the strangest characters imaginable – the people that featured in Cobain;s life. He meets Cobain's aunt who provides home movies and recordings, the estranged father of Cobain's widow Courtney Love, an LA private investigator who worked for Love, a nanny for Kurt and Courtney's child, friends and lovers of both, and many others.

Eventually, when he decides to question Courtney about her possible involvement in Cobain's death, the film becomes a startling commentary on modern celebrity and tabloid sensationalism.

The funniest parts of the film come when we see how Love has so obviously tried to stop it being made at all – the MTV suits suddenly pull their funds from the production (after a call from Courtney) and she freaks out when confronted by Broomfield. This is a woman who was once at home in the punk/grunge world (which Cobain always tried to stick with) but following praise for her performances in films such as Milos Forman's *The People vs. Larry Flynt* (1996), she's cleaned up her image, ditched the grunge look and now looks and acts more like a 'traditional' movie star. In interviews for various TV programmes, including the American *Today Show*, she refused to answer questions about drug use, even walking off set when the interviewer persisted. Instead, Love has taken part in carefully orchestrated profiles in glossy magazines like *Vogue*, and appeared, on her best behaviour, at the 1997 Academy Awards. Just two years earlier, at a 1995 Oscars party, a less polite Courtney Love bludgeoned the journalist Lynn Hirschberg with Quentin Tarantino's Oscar. Lynch had annoyed Love by writing an article for *Vanity Fair* that mentioned her use of heroin during pregnancy. Reminders of the old Courtney didn't fit in with the new way she wanted to be perceived. She had been hailed as a role model by the US magazine *Brandweek*, coming third in a list of Hollywood celebrities whose fashion sense was respected.

With *Kurt and Courtney*, Nick Broomfield powerfully reveals how the truth, like Kurt Cobain, may be a victim of our media-saturated times.

Opposite: Grunge music icon pictured in the poster for Nick Broomfield's Kurt and Courtney *(1998)*

THE LADYKILLERS

1955 / 97 mins / UK / 📼 Video
Stars: Alec Guinness, Alistair Sim, Katie Johnson,
Jack Warner, Peter Sellers, Herbert Lom, Danny Green
Director: Alexander Mackendrick
Producer: Michael Balcon
Script: William Rose

The Ladykillers is a delightful British comedy, shot in muted colours and almost grotesque in style. It's a film rooted in George Orwell's *English Murder* and the *Chamber of Horrors* and one that proves sometimes death *can* be funny. But a cult movie? Perhaps not in the UK but outside its country of origin, particularly in the US, the Ealing comedies have certainly attained a cult following.

After *Kind Hearts and Coronets* (1949), *The Ladykillers* is the blackest of Ealing comedies which centres around Mrs Wilberforce, a dotty little old landlady (Katie Johnson) who lives in a tumbledown Victorian house near St Pancras Station. She takes in a sinister lodger, supposedly a 'professor' (Alec Guinness in a role originally intended for Alistair Sim) who has four strange friends who visit regularly for the purpose, they claim, of playing chamber music. But behind the old lady's back, they are plotting a huge robbery and intend to use the house as their operation base. The group comprises Danny Green's loveable thug, Cecil Parker's bumbling ex-military-officer type, Peter Sellers' teddy boy crook and Herbert Lom's ruthless American gangster.

When Mrs Wilberforce gets suspicious of their comings and goings, the gang of bumbling bank robbers plot to kill her, but can't agree who should perform the deed. But their attempts to eliminate this middle-class pensioner fail and in the end, rather than wipe her out, they polish each other off instead. Mrs Wilberforce, finding herself in possession of bundles of used bank-notes, goes to the local police station to report it, but the friendly policeman (Jack Warner), who is by now used to her eccentricities, sends her on her way. As she walks home, wondering what to do with the money, she drops a pound note to a pavement artist who has drawn a portrait of Winston Churchill.

The screenplay was by Ealing's resident American writer, William Rose. His story is a triumph of morally secure mid-50s Victorianism over rebellious criminal tendencies, with most of the comedy deriving from the contrast between crooks and little old ladies. In *The Ladykillers*, Mrs Wilberforce reigns supreme with the gang of criminals forever helpless. At the strict Balmoral Private Hotel, the landlady is boss and guests must always wipe their feet. This is highlighted in the old ladies' tea party sequence in which they are forced to take part, simply standing around wondering what to do with themselves. The film captures Orwell's account of England as 'a family in which the young are generally thwarted, and most of the power is in the hands of irresponsible uncles and bedridden aunts.' In *The Ladykillers,* the frail old ladies still have the power. Perhaps the gang of crooks were being compared with the first post-war Labour government in Britain. Another theory is that they represented the money men at Ealing, with little old Mrs Wilberforce as Balcon.

This wickedly funny Ealing farce won an Oscar nomination and two 1955 BAFTA awards (Best Screenplay and Best British Actress). *The Ladykillers* was Mackendrick's last film for Ealing and when his work was done on the project he seized the moment and left for the bright lights of New York for his equally dark satire of *Sweet Smell of Success* (1957).

`Memorable` `dialogue:`
`Professor Marcus: It was all a`
`dream.`

THE LAVENDER HILL MOB

1955 / 78 mins / UK / ⬚ Video
Stars: Alec Guinness, Stanley Holloway, Sidney James,
Alfie Bass, Marjorie Fielding, Edie Martin,
Ronald Adam
Director: Charles Crichton
Producer: Michael Balcon
Script: TEB Clarke

Made at Balcon's studio, *The Lavender Hill Mob* can be seen as the quintessential Ealing comedy, a hilarious tongue-in-cheek crime caper. It was also one of Ealing's most successful pictures. This again is not a cult movie in its country of origin, the UK, but, to anglophiles everywhere, most notably in the US, where Ealing comedies are hard to find. Video search companies in the States list this particular film among their most wanted cult titles.

Alec Guinness stars as a timid, long-serving bank employee, Henry Holland, who plans and executes a bullion robbery. Stanley Holloway is the paperweight souvenir maker, Pendlebury, who inspires the plan. Together they team up with Sidney James and Alfie Bass as a pair of cockney crooks recruited to make the caper work.

Writing shortly before his death, Guinness fondly remembered his time spent on this Ealing classic: 'It was a good film, I think; well over 40 years old now and mercifully it only lasted an hour and a half. Stanley Holloway and I got on exceedingly well and became good friends. He was always genial, easy-going and meticulously professional.'

The Lavender Hill Mob is a story about what film writer Charles Barr calls 'the triumph of the innocent, the survival of the *un*fittest', a celebration of the ordinary man, the little man who rebels and triumphs. Opening with Holland enjoying the tropical climes in a Rio bar, the film cuts back to his drab past, 'when I was merely a non-entity among all those thousands who flock every morning into the City'.

'Most men who long to be rich', says Holland, 'know inwardly that they will never achieve their ambition'. But Holland seems to have been lucky. Don't blink during this opening sequence or you might miss a beautiful dark-haired girl. It's actually Audrey Hepburn, doing a couple of days bit-part work for the studio. She was not picked out by Ealing talent spotters, although they weren't always renowned for leading ladies!

In a film full of brilliant comic timing, we hear the millionaire-in-exile recount the saga behind his newly acquired fortune. Pendlebury's response to Holland's exciting plan for making off with the bullion is a comedy gem: 'By Jove, Holland! It's a good job we're both honest men'. Definitely not a moral tale, we see the group get away in an armoured car full of gold bullion and then melt it down before making it into cheap-looking models of the Eiffel Tower. This way, nobody suspects that the tourist souvenirs are actually real gold and the crooks get the entire consignment out of the country.

The Bank of England itself helped create the plan, after screenwriter TEB Clarke turned to them for advice on how to steal a million pounds' worth of gold. Clarke's Oscar-winning script is actually full of satirical swipes at the police, the press and the City but, amazingly, keen to help out, the Bank put together a special committee to work out a way in which the Bank could be robbed. It seems the Bank's executives cared more about working on a new movie than their own security. However, at the time, it was hoped the film's ending would deter any would-be real-life imitators.

The gold Eiffel Towers then get mixed up with genuine souvenirs on the sales stand of the landmark itself. A group of English schoolgirls buy them and Holland and Pendlebury have to chase them back to England. The final chase sequence is a parody of that in one of Ealing's own films, the police drama *The Blue Lamp* (1950), released a year earlier. The delightful twist is that back in the exotic Rio bar, the man to whom Holland has been telling his story is not a friend. The man stands up and so does Holland, his wrists handcuffed to the stranger – a Scotland Yard detective.

Memorable dialogue:

> Henry Holland: The saddest words
> in the world are 'it might have
> been'.

LISZTOMANIA

1975 / 104 mins / UK / (Not currently available)
Stars: Roger Daltrey, Sara Kestelman, Paul Nicholas,
Fiona Lewis, Veronica Quilligan, Ringo Starr
Director: Ken Russell
Producers: Roy Baird, David Puttnam
Script: Ken Russell

One of Ken Russell's most outlandish extravaganzas, *Lisztomania* is a wild and imaginative send-up of the bawdy life of Romantic composer and piano virtuoso Franz Liszt (played by The Who's Roger Daltrey). Russell uses ubiquitous phallic imagery and devotes a good portion of the film to Liszt's relationship with fellow composer Richard Wagner.

The film is set in 1830 and begins with an opening fantasy sequence. Franz Liszt (Daltrey), a handsome youth with shoulder-length blond hair, is in bed with the Countess Marie d'Agoult (Fiona Lewis), a proud, aristocratic young beauty. They are interrupted by the unexpected arrival of the Count d'Agoult (John Justin), Marie's husband, rapier in hand. Marie begs her husband to spare Liszt's life but the Count decrees they who deceive by the piano shall die by the piano. He orders them to be incarcerated together inside a grand piano and carried away to a railway line. An express train, puffing like the Wrath of God, bears down menacingly on its impotent victims.

The film dissolves to Liszt in his crowded dressing-room before a Beethoven concert. He's surrounded by bodyguards and groupies. Suddenly, a shabby young man bursts in. It's Richard Wagner (Paul Nicholas), a talented but penniless composer. He wants Liszt to buy the score for a new opera he's written about ancient Rome. Liszt says he's no impresario but will plug the composition that evening.

During his Beethoven Memorial Concert, he turns the spotlight on Wagner, then plays a fantasy on his themes to the delight of the crowd. Liszt also sees Princess Carolyne of St Petersburg and later, at her invitation, they elope. After their marriage is forbidden by the Pope (Ringo Starr), he embraces the monastic life. But this is just the beginning...

As in most Russell films, fantasy plays an important role. In *Lisztomania*, Richard Wagner portrayed as a Transylvanian vampire who gains musical inspiration by sucking the blood of Franz Liszt. Nothing too outlandish then.

At the time, as he's recently explained in his latest book *Directing Film*, Russell was riding on the success of *Tommy* (1975): 'I was able to set up *Lisztomania* by touting it as a film on a classical composer who was the Elton John of his day. No, I couldn't deliver Elton, but I could get Roger Daltrey, who starred in the title role of *Tommy*, and we all know how many millions that movie made. The fact that the treatment of the subject matter was symbolically and intellectually above the heads of the Daltrey fans was unfortunate, for the film was pure magic.'

Lisztomania is pure magic, each shot packed with more flair and creativity than a year's worth of Hollywood movies. It's pure 70s rock 'n' roll with a good dose of great classical music.

Memorable dialogue:

Cosima: I've polished your sword!
What do you want it for, to kill
the critics?
Liszt: Time kills critics, my
dear.

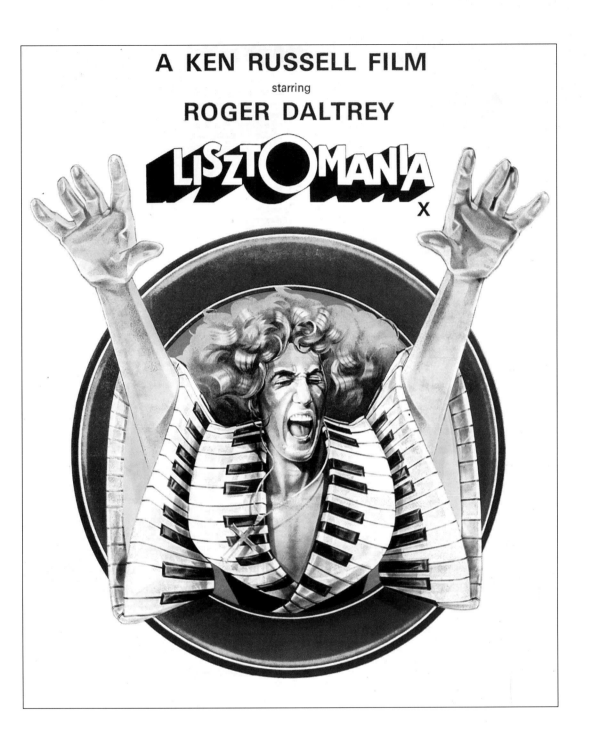

Roger Daltrey in the promotional poster for one of Ken Russell's most outlandish extravaganzas, Lisztomania *(1975)*

LYNCH, DAVID

Director, writer
Born 20 January 1946, Montana

Mel Brooks once described David Lynch as 'Jimmy Stewart from Mars'. His first feature, made almost single-handedly, set the tone for the master of bizarre. Set in a bleak cityscape, *Eraserhead* (1977) features John Nance and Charlotte Stewart as the parents of a mutant child. Nance, tormented by the child's cries, begins to retreat into more and more outlandish fantasies triggered by the apartment's hissing radiator.

A strong cult following for *Eraserhead* gave Lynch the clout to get backing to direct *The Elephant Man* (1980), the moving and uplifting story of John Merrick (John Hurt). Hideously deformed at birth, Merrick is forced to seek a living from travelling freak-shows until rescued by an eminent surgeon.

The enormous critical and commercial success of *Elephant Man* led to *Dune* (1984), a hugely expensive commercial disaster based on Frank Herbert's novel, although Lynch redeemed himself with *Blue Velvet* (1986), his most personal and original work since his debut. He subsequently won the top prize at the Cannes Film Festival with the dark, violent road movie *Wild at Heart* (1990), in which a drawling, Elvis-loving criminal (Nicholas Cage) and his girlfriend (Laura Dern) elope into the heart of America's Deep South, pursued by the henchman of the girl's mother.

Lynch achieved a huge cult following with his surreal TV series *Twin Peaks* (1990), which he adapted for the big screen, although his comedy series *On the Air* (1992) was less successful.

More recently, with the American ABC network having pulled the plug on his latest TV series *Mulholland Drive*, Lynch decided to turn it into a movie instead. Apparently, execs objected to an extreme close-up of dog turds! See Filmography, p.239.

MAD MAX

1979 / 90 mins / Australia / *DVD* / 📼 Video
Stars: Mel Gibson, Joanne Samuel, Hugh Keays-Byrne,
Steve Bisley, Roger Ward, Vince Gil
Director: George Miller
Producer: Byron Kennedy
Script: George Miller

A street fight that left the then-unknown Aussie actor Mel Gibson's face badly bruised for his audition with George Miller gave him the look that landed him the role of Max Rockatansky, a highway cop living in a desolate near-future world populated by murderous bikers and gangs of nomadic thugs. Following the senseless murder of his wife and children, Max leaps to murderous revenge. Exhilarating and unsettling, this action extravaganza catapulted Gibson to international stardom and spawned two sequels. In the US the Aussie accents were dubbed over and failed to impress but the film later found its audience in the wake of a successful sequel.

Mad Max was produced on a minute budget of $380,000. However, the instantly recognisable inexpensive pseudo-punk costumes and other low-budget elements are precisely what helped trigger its cult following. Also, around 60 per cent of the crew had never worked on a feature film, and most of the cast were unknown. This helped give the film a fresh look. Experimental editing and fast pace added to its appeal. As a result of its low budget, *Mad Max* has a visual style and pace that distinguishes it from all action films of that era. It also took more at the box office in Australia than *Star Wars* (1977) and found a place in the *Guinness Book of Records* as having obtained the highest cost-to-profit ratio of any feature film.

While American society, and film, portrays its cultural obsession with the gun, *Mad Max* highlights the violent nature of a car culture that kills far more people than guns do each year in the US. Like protagonists in a number of road movies and revenge tales, Max Rockatansky is a character who symbolises the normality within each of us which, when upset by one significant event, is transformed. Various 'psychological' Westerns, such as

Ford's *The Searchers* (1956), are alluded to, and Tobe Hooper's *Texas Chainsaw Massacre* (1974) is another strong influence, as is Hitchcock's *Psycho* (1960).

Mad Max takes its viewers on a wild ride through a variety of cinematic genres and styles in its formation of a chaotic future. It contains elements of the horror genre, as well as the cop movie, road movie and science-fiction work. These elements work together in the formation of a terrifying, dystopic world.

The 1981 sequel to *Mad Max*, originally titled *The Road Warrior*, is now simply known as *Mad Max 2* . Unusually, the sequel is as good as the original, also borrowing heavily from Westerns, road movies and punk fashion.

Memorable dialogue:

Roop: That scag and his floozie, they're gonna die!

Fifi: They say people don't believe in heroes anymore. Well, damn them! You and me, Max, we're gonna give em back their heroes!

Nightrider: I am the rocker, I am the roller, I am the out-of-controller!

Bubba Zanetti: We're here to meet a friend. Comin' on the train.
Station Master: Nothin' comin' on the train except a few crates and a...cuh-coffin!
Bubba Zanetti: Our friend.

MAGICAL MYSTERY TOUR

1967 / 55 mins / UK / ▭ Video
Stars: Paul McCartney, John Lennon, Ringo Starr,
George Harrison, Victor Spinetti, Neil Innes
Directors: The Beatles
Producers: The Beatles
Script: The Beatles

Originally the brainchild of Paul McCartney, this 55-minute film was The Beatles' first major project after *Sergeant Pepper* and the death of their original manager Brian Epstein. The 'psychedelic home movie' depicts a coach trip through the West Country which evolves into a magical mystery tour. It was entirely a product of the Liverpudlian band's own imagination.

Ringo Starr was in charge of photography while Paul, George and John collaborated on the final script editing (although much of the action was improvised). It was the first film following *Hard Day's Night* (1964) and *Help!* (1965), to be produced and directed entirely by The Beatles themselves (goodbye Dick Lester), although they reportedly wanted man of the moment Patrick McGoohan to direct (who made his own series *The Prisoner* in the same year).

An abstract, dream-like film light years ahead of its time, *Magical Mystery Tour* was an exhilarating visual creation which was originally watched on Boxing Day in 1967 by 15 million viewers on nationwide British television. Although the EP shot straight to number 2 and stayed in the charts for three months, it was prevented from topping the singles chart by one of The Beatles' biggest hits, 'Hello Goodbye'.

Composed of six songs (five of them specially written), the tracks include 'Fool on the Hill' (written by Paul and filmed by him in France), 'I Am The Walrus' (John Lennon's only, and highly surreal contribution, based on Lewis Carroll's 'Walrus and the Carpenter' piece from *Alice in Wonderland*) and 'Your Mother Should Know' (Paul's spectacular finale featuring girl guides and ballroom dancers filling the screen as The Beatles descend a white staircase, dressed in white evening suits).

In all, there were 43 passengers on the tour bus, mostly The Beatles' friends and acquaintances. They included four fan club secretaries, Paul's mini-skirted girlfriend, Spencer Davis of the Spencer Davis Group, a small party of dwarves and Alexis Mardas, the Apple electronics wizard.

In recent years, the film has been viewed by many as an advance raiding party for the avant-garde humour of Monty Python and a forerunner in style for many pop videos.

A few years ago, the film was restored and re-coloured to improve visual quality and digitally remastered and remixed in hi-fi stereo by Beatles producer, George Martin at Abbey Road Studios. It was released to coincide with the *Beatles Anthology* campaign in both the UK and North America. It will remain an essential collectors' item for Beatles fans everywhere but looks like appealing to a new generation of Beatles-inspired Oasis fans. Oasis still close their concerts by playing 'I Am the Walrus', confirming the track as the perfect Britpop anthem.

Memorable dialogue:

Buster Bloodvessel: (to Ringo's Aunt): I... love you.

Buster Bloodvessel: I am concerned for you to enjoy yourselves – within the limits of British decency. You know what I mean.

Ringo: I can't take it any more! I'm getting off!

Ringo's Aunt: Don't get historical!

Opposite: The Fab Four direct their own movie: 1967's Magical Mystery Tour

MALICK, TERRENCE

Director, writer
Born 30 November 1943, Waco, Texas

Terrence Malick made two of the great films of the 70s then disappeared for 20 years.

In 1973, film-goers discovered a new voice. In flat but evocative tones, *Badlands* tells the story of Kit and Holly (Martin Sheen and Sissy Spacek), adrift in a double fantasy of crime and punishment, a headlong flight from nowhere to nowhere. They're playing make-believe but the bullets are real. And the bloodshed is *very* real. Malick's debut was inspired by true events: the story is a provocative study of people numbingly alienated from everyday life. But fascinating to us. Although the pair model themselves on movie-star heroes, reality is soon shattered when Kit murders Holly's father. What ensues is a rebellious manic spree into the badlands of Montana, ending in a trail of bloodshed and murder. Co-starring Warren Oates (star of Sam Peckinpah's *The Wild Bunch* [1969], and *Bring Me the Head of Alfredo Garcia* [1974]), the film includes stunning photography of the South Dakota flatlands by award-winning cinematographer Tak Fujimoto (*Silence of the Lambs* [1991], *Philadelphia* [1993]).

It took Malick five years to bring out his next film, but when *Days of Heaven* (1978) arrived, it confirmed his promise. This time he played star maker to a young Richard Gere, one of a trio of drifters lost in the Texan wheat fields in 1916. It won Malick the Best Director award at Cannes; *Newsweek* called it 'hauntingly beautiful...unashamedly poetic, brimming with sweetness and bitterness, darkness and light'. *Variety* didn't mince its words: it was 'one of the greatest cinematic achievements of the last decade'.

Then Malick bailed out and stayed out of sight. He became known as the JD Salinger of cinema, his activities the cause of much speculation. He'd tired of the Hollywood game. Yet Malick has not been idle, making money by doing anonymous script rewrites on various Hollywood films such as 1989's *Great Balls of Fire*.

Malick's disappearance after his first two celebrated films turned him into a legendary recluse in the film industry but many welcomed his return in 1998 for the war film *The Thin Red Line*. His films are considered to be among the most poignant and richly photographed studies of the American Midwest to have been captured on celluloid but unfortunately his most recent work failed to live up to those impossibly high standards. See Filmography, p.239.

MALLRATS

1995 / 94 mins / USA / Video
Stars: Shannen Doherty, Jeremy London, Jason Lee,
Claire Forlani, Ben Affleck, Joey Lauren Adams,
Renee Humphrey, Jason Mewes
Director: Kevin Smith
Producers: Sean Daniel, James Jacks, Scott Mosier
Script: Kevin Smith

Not as brash and original as *Clerks* (1994), Smith's bigger-budget comedy still found a cult following. *Clerks* was made for just $25,000. Based on its success, Smith came up with *Mallrats* and was given a budget at least 100 times as large. Cue a glossier examination of some of the same material.

He stays in essentially the same world, with roughly the same demographic group – the young, the goofs and the randy – and the same time scheme, one long day. And he paints a world in which teenagers have no real concerns apart from hanging out, talking, scheming, fighting boredom and dealing with the demands of girlfriends.

TS Quint (Jeremy London) has made one of the biggest decisions a man can make...he's decided to ask his girlfriend, Brandi (Claire Forlani), to marry him. Brodie Bruce (Jason Lee) studiously avoids all adult responsibility. He's master of his comic book collection and slave to his video games.

His girlfriend, Rene (Shannen Doherty), has had enough. 'Hell hath no fury like a woman's scorn for Sega.' So Rene dumps Brodie because he spends too much time with his comic book collection and his Sega games. And Brandi splits with TS because he can't understand why she has to be a contestant on her dad's 'Truth or Date' TV game show. The two friends may have just lost their girlfriends, but Brodie and TS know what real men do when they need to regain their self-respect, their machismo, their standing in the community – they head for the mall.

Mallrats is a comedic and sometimes twisted adventure about boys who become men and women who are, well, still women. The characters are where the real entertainment lies – a topless psychic, an optically challenged slob who stares in mute frustration at Magic Eye 3-D posters and Smith himself, reprising his Jedi-in-leather Silent Bob. Plus, this film is the one where you'll learn the art of giving someone a stink hand.

Memorable dialogue:
Rene: I'm gonna fuck you up beyond repair!

Brodie: He must be halfway to Buy Me Toys by now.

Brodie: Listen, not a year goes by, not a year, that I don't hear about some escalator accident involving some bastard kid which could easily have been avoided had some parent – I don't care which one – but some parent conditioned him to fear and respect that escalator!

Jay Phat Buds: Where do you get these wonderful toys?

Silent Bob: Adventure, excitement...a Jedi craves not these things.

Brodie: My grandmother always said, 'Why buy the cow...when you get the sex for free.'

Brodie: You fuckers think just because a guy reads comics he can't start some shit!?

Rene: You wanna say something?
Brodie: Yeah! About a million things, but I can't express myself monosyllabically enough for you to understand it all.

Brodie: I love the smell of commerce in the morning!

MAN BITES DOG

1992 / 98 mins / Belgium / DVD / ▭ Video
Stars: Benoit Poelvoorde, Remy Belvaux, André Bozel
Directors: Rémy Belvaux, André Bozel, BenoitPoelvoorde
Producers: Rémy Belvaux, André Bozel,
Benoit Poelvoorde
Script: Rémy Belvaux, André Bozel, Benoit Poelvoorde,
Vincent Tavier

Benoit Poelvoorde plays an average guy with a slightly unusual hobby. He's an admirable yet seriously warped mass murderer who kills without motive. When a documentary film crew finds out about his pastime, rather than turn him in, they start making a film about him. The film becomes increasingly disturbing as the film crew develop a close relationship with the man and thus become implicated in his horrific crimes. If sometimes, for the sake of art, he needs a little help, well, they don't mind helping him out.

This spoof documentary from Belgium exceeds the furthest limits of black comedy. It is not short on violence but it asks very uncomfortable questions about the viewers' attitudes to watching it.

There are some very funny moments, if you can stomach some of the situations and the occasionally graphic gore (although it's all in grainy black and white). A satire on documentaries, as well as on slasher movies, prepare to be shocked, prepare to be outraged, maybe even to laugh.

Video box sets of this film have included the short film *Pas de C4 Pour Daniel.*

Memorable dialogue:
Ben: You can tan while you make love. When you're through you've got a brown ass.

THE MAN WHO FELL TO EARTH

1976 / 133 mins / UK / ▭ Video
Stars: David Bowie, Rip Torn, Candy Clark,
Buck Henry, Bernie Casie
Director: Nicolas Roeg
Producers: Michael Deeley, Barry Spikings
Script: Paul Mayersberg

Nicolas Roeg, the outrageously talented maverick co-director of *Performance* (1970) and *Don't Look Now* (1973), has crafted a gorgeously photographed, fabulously labyrinthine movie that tracks the rise and fall of Thomas Jerome Newton (David Bowie), a visitor from a doomed planet.

Arriving at a remote Kentucky town, he hires New York lawyer (Buck Henry of 1995's *To Die For*) to help him found a mysterious, world-spanning industrial empire using his centuries-advanced technological knowledge. As he takes on and beats every major US corporation, people can only guess at his true purpose: to find water for his arid home planet and save his dying world from agonising death by drought.

David Bowie's somewhat odd persona is perfect for the role of a man trapped where he doesn't want to be. He is ably supported by Candy Clark, Buck Henry and the brilliant Rip Torn, now known to many as producer Arty in *The Larry Sanders Show*.

One memorable scene has two assassins throwing Henry out of a window, but on the first attempt the glass doesn't break. So they apologise. 'Don't worry', says Henry. But they try again...

This was David Bowie's first acting role. The lead actor apparently became obsessed with the character he played, and Roeg's film sparked the singer's real-life spaceman-obsession and the creation of Ziggy Stardust.

The soundtrack consists of pop music of the time – Artie Shaw, Roy Orbison, Jim Reeves and so on – and this adds to the mixture of banality and surreality that characterises the world which Roeg portrays.

Above all, *The Man Who Fell to Earth* isn't as deep as *Performance* or *Don't Look Now*, but nevertheless a fascinating, hip, sexy trip with a strong cult following. Newton's fall from grace as he becomes prey to lust (with Candy Clark as the simple, devoted, eternally horny Mary Lou), alcohol, business rivals and finally, the US Government, makes Roeg's film not only a biting caustic indictment of the modern world, but also a poignant commentary on the loneliness of the outsider.

Memorable dialogue:
Newton: Get out of my mind – all of you!

MANHUNTER

1986 / 119 mins / USA / *DVD* / ▭ Video
Stars: William L Peterson, Kim Greist, Joan Allen,
Brian Cox, Dennis Farina, Tom Noonan
Director: Michael Mann
Producer: Richard Roth
Script: Michael Mann

FBI agent Will Graham (William Petersen of *CSI*) has an unusual ability. Graham can to immerse himself so deeply in his grisly investigations that he begins to think like the murderers he pursues. This 'gift' has enabled him to capture several famous serial killers, the most recent of which was Hannibal Lector (Brian Cox) – the infamous deranged psychiatrist, as featured in *The Silence of the Lambs* (1991). Although retired and recuperating from the physical and emotional scars inflicted by Lector, Graham is brought back by FBI head Jack Crawford (Dennis Farina of *Crime Story*) to help track a new serial killer, Francis Dolarhyde (Tom Noonan of *Robocop 2* [1987], *Heat* [1995]) with a frightening modus operandi: he slaughters entire suburban families and takes jagged bites out of the victims. The FBI is unable to track successfully the unpredictable killer who is nicknamed 'The Tooth Fairy' by the tabloids. In an effort to bring an end to 'The Tooth Fairy's' killing spree, Graham is forced to confront Hannibal Lector and the personal demons that threaten to push him over the brink of sanity. Can Graham successfully track Dolarhyde down without losing his mind?

Originally, *Manhunter* was to be titled *Red Dragon*, after Thomas Harris' novel. But when *Year of the Dragon* (1985) flopped a year earlier, the producer decided to avoid a 'Dragon' title. Many fans and critics alike consider *Manhunter* to be far superior to *The Silence of the Lambs* and *Hannibal* (2001), as well as one of the most unnerving serial killer movies ever made. Certainly, the films are very different. Mann's original was about style and mood, while Jonathan Demme's *Silence of the Lambs* was more Gothic and bloody. Mann's film investigated the clinical aspects of the subject, having Lector in a white cell. Anthony Hopkins, however, was put in a cage. With *Manhunter*, the violence was implied whereas in *Lambs* Hopkins went around biting ears.

Manhunter is one of those movies that people have found over the years and embraced, an effective thriller that works on a subliminal, subconscious level. However, with the recent release of *Hannibal*, and a well-timed DVD release (by Anchor Bay in the States), the first of the Hannibal Lector movies was propelled into the limelight.

'I am thrilled that Anchor Bay Entertainment is releasing *Manhunter* on DVD', commented Brian Cox. 'Years after its theatrical release, *Manhunter* continues to be an exciting project to be involved with. It is a film that really took on a life all its own.'

Memorable dialogue:

Lloyd Bowman: You're so sly... but so am I.

Doctor Hannibal Lector: You want the scent? Smell yourself!

Doctor Hannibal Lector: Have you ever seen blood in the moonlight, Will? It appears quite black.

Doctor Hannibal Lector: Save yourself, kill them all!

Doctor Hannibal Lector: If one does what God does enough times, one will become as God is.

Will Graham: I know that I'm not smarter than you.
Doctor Hannibal Lector: Then how did you catch me?
Will Graham: You had disadvantages.
Doctor Hannibal Lector: What disadvantages?
Will Graham: You're insane.

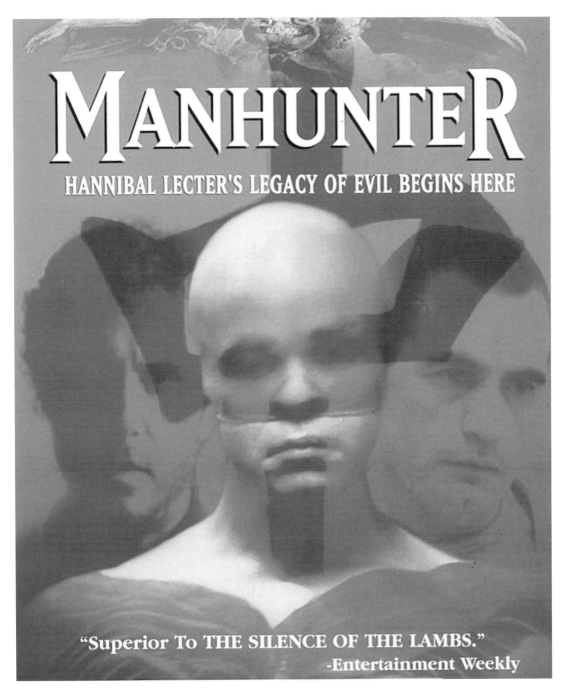

MANHUNTER

HANNIBAL LECTER'S LEGACY OF EVIL BEGINS HERE

"Superior To THE SILENCE OF THE LAMBS."
-Entertainment Weekly

Doctor Hannibal Lector: Dream much... Will?

Will Graham: It's just you and me now, sport.

Agent Crawford: You feel sorry for him.

Will Graham: As a child, my heart bleeds for him. Someone took a little boy and turned him into a monster. But as an adult... as an adult, he's irredeemable. He butchers whole families to fulfil some sick fantasy. As an adult, I think someone should blow the sick fuck out of his socks.

143

MARS ATTACKS

1996 / 106 mins / USA / DVD / Video
Stars: Jack Nicholson, Glenn Close, Annette Bening,
Pierce Brosnan, Danny Devito, Martin Short,
Rod Steiger, Tom Jones
Director: Tim Burton
Producers: Tim Burton, Larry Franco
Script: Jonathan Gems

Back in 1986, following the success of his first two films, *Repo Man* (1984) and *Sid and Nancy* (1986), Alex Cox was already in development with Tristar Pictures to make a film on the bubble gum card series *Mars Attacks*. He'd written two drafts of the screenplay, but after the hostile reaction to a film he'd made called *Walker* released in 1987, Tristar got cold feet. After all, he'd just got away with spending many millions of American dollars, belonging to a capitalist American studio, to make a pro-Communist film.

Tristar replaced Cox with another writer, novelist Martin Amis. He had never written a screenplay before and ended up delivering it very late. The studio didn't like what he'd submitted and Amis then wrote an article in the *New Yorker,* ridiculing the studio executives who had employed him. The entire project was cancelled.

Ten years later, it was back on again, this time a Warner Brothers. project with Tim Burton in the director's chair and Jonathan Gems (who adapted *1984* for the screen) in charge of the script. The result is very funny and even won the approval of the original sacked screenwriter–director: 'I like the Tim Burton movie,' admits Cox, 'I thought the Martians were just great with their Duck-like voices, and the fact that they have no plan at all! I just didn't like the human characters at all.'

Burton has the citizens of Earth facing their doom with gung-ho valour and brainless abandon as little green men from outer space gleefully terrorise the planet. Playing the Earthlings under intergalactic siege is a stellar cast of dazzlers unlike any assembled on the screen before. Jack Nicholson is the President of the United States James Dale, worried about the best suit to wear to greet the Martians; Glenn Close is the obsessive First Lady Marsha, not about to have those *things* in her house; and Natalie Portman is their daughter Taffy, bored with the whole hullabaloo. Rod Steiger is the 'blow-'em'- back-to-Mars' General Decker, who never met a war he didn't like; Paul Winfield is 'they come in peace' General Casey, who wants to drive the welcome wagon; Martin Short as the Oval Office's hormonally driven spin doctor, Press Secretary Jerry Ross; and Pierce Brosnan is Professor Donald Kessler, who wants to know what makes those big-brained fiends tick!

Blaxploitation fans, watch out for Pam Grier, who takes no guff – from her sons or from any ET – as Louise Williams. Even legendary showman Tom Jones pops up.

The film also features a horde of swollen-brained, blue-eyed Martians, not to mention a fleet of saucers sailing through space before unleashing their attack on Earth. The digital wizardry was provided by Industrial Light & Magic. All in all, *Mars Attacks!* is a great spoof of 50s alien-invasion movies and 50s attitudes with impressive effects and animation. The soundtrack boasts tracks from Slim Whitman, Tom Jones and the Bee Gees.

Memorable dialogue:

President Dale: Why can't we work out our differences? Why can't we work things out? Little people, why can't we all just get along?

Richie Norris: I want to thank my Grandma for always being so good to me, and, and for helping save the world and everything.

First Lady: I'm not allowing that thing in my house.
President: Sweetie, we may have to. The people expect me to meet with them.
First Lady: Well they're not going to eat off the Van Buren china.

Art Land: I'm not a crook. I'm
ambitious. There's a difference.

Richie Norris: Wow, he just made
the international sign of the
doughnut.

Gen. Decker: Intellectuals!
Liberals! Peacemongers! Idiots!

(Challenging a Martian to a fight)
Byron Williams: No weapons! No
tricks! Just you and me! Byron

Williams! The heavyweight champion
of the world!

The President: What do you think,
Marsha?
First Lady: Kick the crap out of
'em.

President: I want the people to
know that they still have two out
of three branches of the
government working for them, and
that ain't bad.

THE MATRIX

1999 / 136 mins / USA / DVD / Video
Stars: Keanu Reeves, Laurence Fishburne,
Carrie-Anne Moss, Hugo Weaving, Gloria Foster
Directors: Andy and Larry Wachowski
Producer: Joel Silver
Script: Andy and Larry Wachowski

Anecdotal, surreal, sexy and serious, *The Matrix* – directed by the Wachowski Brothers – is reminiscent of Philip K Dick's best novels. As in Dick's *Now Wait for Last Year!* our reality is an artificially constructed cover for an entirely different one. 'What is real?' asks Morpheus (played by Laurence Fishburne), 'How do you define real? If you're talking about what you can feel, what you can smell, what you can taste and see, the real is simply electrical signals interpreted by your brain.'

Poor old bemused Thomas Anderson (Keanu Reeves) has been living in a dream world and it's Morpheus who welcomes him into the desert of the real. Anderson (later Neo) is a computer hacker who comes to realise that his reality is an illusion created by computers that have taken over the world.

Sci-fi for the MTV generation, this fx-laden adventure if full to the brim with stunning visuals and terrific martial arts fights. Interesting ideas are certainly there to start with but, as with all commercially minded films, it ends with a shoot-out. This is a disappointment because up to this point, the film is very intriguing in its look into the nature of reality. To end with a sensational sequence in the way it did was just too safe. Been there, seen that (although rarely done this well).

Of course one added attraction for many will be the sight of Reeves being shaved naked and covered with slime, so if that tickles your fancy, here is your chance. Best performance though must go to the Australian actor Hugo Weaving (*The Adventures of Priscilla, Queen of the Desert* [1994]) who plays a *Men in Black*-style special agent. He plays it purely for laughs and has great fun in the process.

The Matrix was hugely successful not only in cinemas but on DVD, with no fewer than three supporting documentary features about the making of the film. Of course, in no way is *The Matrix* a cult movie because of difficulty of access. That will never be a problem! *The Matrix* is obviously part of modern mainstream film-making, one of the biggest-grossing pictures of the 90s. But take a look on the internet, as that is where the cult of *The Matrix* is developing. There is a devoted mass of people who have taken to debating and philosophising over the themes in this film, endlessly chatting on dedicated sites and message boards.

Memorable dialogue:

Morpheus: Throughout human history, we have been dependent on machines to survive. Fate, it seems, is not without a sense of irony.

Cypher: Good shit, huh? It's good for two things: degreasing engines and killing brain cells.

Spoon boy: Do not try and bend the spoon. That's impossible. Instead... only try to realise the truth.
Neo: What truth?
Spoon boy: There is no spoon.
Neo: There is no spoon?
Spoon boy: Then you'll see that it is not the spoon that bends, it is only yourself.

Agent Smith: Human beings are a disease, a cancer of this planet, you are a plague and we are the cure.

Morpheus: What you know you can't explain, but you feel it. You've felt it your entire life, that there's something wrong with the

Leather–clad Carrie-Anne Moss dressed for action in The Matrix (*1999*)

world. You don't know what it is,
but it's there, like a splinter in
your mind, driving you mad.

Morpheus: You have the look of a
man who accepts what he sees
because he is expecting to wake
up. Ironically, that's not far
from the truth.

Morpheus: I'm trying to free your

mind, Neo. But I can only show you
the door. You're the one that has
to walk through it.

Neo: Why do my eyes hurt?
Morpheus: You've never used them
before.

Morpheus: There is a difference
between knowing the path and
walking the path.

METROPOLIS

1927 / 120 mins / Germany / DVD / Video
Stars: Brigitte Helm, Alfred Abel, Gustav Frohlich,
Rudolph Klein-Rogge, Fritz Rasp, Theodor Loos
Director: Fritz Lang
Producer: Erich Pommer
Script: Fritz Lang, Thea von Harbous

Fritz Lang's vision of the future still stands as a monument to his genius and remains one of the most influential productions of its era. Shot in Germany in 1927, it is a silent movie with some of the best sets ever seen in a sci-fi film. The production design really is magnificent and has influenced a long list of post-modern architects. Consider London's MI6 building on the River Thames, for example, which appears to be an elaborate homage to the model buildings in Lang's futuristic film.

Lang conceived the idea for *Metropolis* one night in 1924. During his first trip to America, he was aboard a transatlantic liner docked on New York's West Side. Apart from a skeleton crew, he was one of only two passengers, the other being *Dr Caligari* (1920) producer Erich Pommer. 'The evening when we arrived, we were still "enemy aliens", so we were not allowed to leave the ship. From the deck where I stood I looked across to a magnificent sight: streets lit as though in full daylight; tall buildings; neon lights moving, turning and flashing...it was fantastic, all new and fairylike to a European like me. These powerful impressions gave me my first vision of a great city of the future.'

Metropolis is the tale of a mad genius, Rotwang (Rudolph Klein-Rogge) and a metal robot cast in the form of a girl, Maria (Brigitte Helm), who is given life. This strange city of the future, with its maze of skyscrapers built atop an underground world 10 stories down, is filled with robot workers. Humans are divided into two groups: the thinkers, up above, who make plans (but don't know how anything works), and the workers, down below, who achieve goals (but don't have the vision). Completely separate, neither group is complete, but together they make a whole. One man from the 'thinkers' dares to visit the underground where the workers toil, and is astonished by what he sees.

The film took nearly 18 months to complete and used eight leading actors, 1,500 supporting players and a crowd of 36,000 extras. Production costs all but bankrupted the giant German film studio UFA.

HG Wells saw *Metropolis* and called it 'the silliest film', whereas Adolf Hitler saw it and was so impressed, he made Lang an offer to work for the Nazi propaganda machine. His immediate response was to leave for Hollywood.

Memorable dialogue:

Freder: It was their hands that built this city of ours, Father. But where do the hands belong in your scheme?

Joh Frederson: In their proper place, the depths.

MEYER, RUSS

Director
Born 21 March 1931, California

The Fellini of the porn film industry began making home movies as a teenager. The son of a policeman and a nurse, he was already winning prizes at 15. He then spent the Second World War in Europe as a newsreel cameraman, and upon his return to the States he became a professional photographer, shooting some of the earliest *Playboy* centrefolds. He made his film debut in 1959 with *The Immoral Mr. Teas*, the first 'nudie' film to make a profit (over a million dollars). With this title, Meyer rejected the usual conventions of nudist films and served up a ribald storyline and amazingly endowed women. This led to a string of self-financed films that gradually became more bizarre, violent and cartoonish.

Titles included *Lorna* (1964), *Faster Pussycat! Kill! Kill!* (1965), *Cherry Harry and Raquel* (1969), *Supervixens* (1975), and *Up!* (1976). *Vixen* (1968) was one of the most critically acclaimed of these technically polished explicit dramas – about a girl who can't say no and proves it every seven minutes. She even finds time for her husband. Not only did this picture receive good reviews, it also caught the attention of 20th Century Fox executives, who signed Meyer to direct a sequel, *Beneath the Valley of the Ultra-Vixens* (1979), another enormous hit.

However, after the lukewarm reception of the uncharacteristically straight *The Seven Minutes* (1971), Meyer returned to the sex-and-violence films that made his name. The demise of the drive-in market and the emphasis on hardcore pornography (which Meyer always eschewed) effectively ended his directorial career, though he continues to promote and sell his product on video, mainly via the internet. He appeared as himself in a spoofy sequence of *Amazon Women on the Moon* (1987) and spent the rest of the 80s working on various autobiographies, both in film (*The Breast of Russ Meyer* [1986]) and in print (*A Clean Breast*).

Talking recently about his life and films, Meyer said: 'I made a ton of money. I'm sitting here, looking out at the marvellous hills of Palm Desert, overlooking an azure blue pool that's heated to the temperature I want. I have my editing facilities here. Tall, tall ceilings...I own a lot of water under Palm Desert...millions of gallons. So if people get mean to me, I can turn their water off! I refuse to stop fishing and womanising and having Epicurean meals and generally having a good time!' See Filmography, p.239–40.

THE NAKED GUN: THE FILES OF POLICE SQUAD

1988 / 85 mins / USA / *DVD* / 📼 Video
Stars: Leslie Neilsen, George Kennedy, Priscilla Presley,
Riccardo Montalban, OJ Simpson
Director: David Zucker
Producer: Robert K Weiss
Script: Jerry Zucker, David Zucker,
Jim Abrahams, Pat Proft

A huge hit from the makers of *Airplane!* (1980), this movie was adapted from the TV series *Police Squad*. Granite-jawed, rock-brained cop, Lt Frank Drebin, pride of the LAPD, creates even more mayhem than the villains when he tries to prevent an assassination on the Queen. Montalban's plans involve a plot to dispose of her at a Dodgers home game! Priscilla Presley, OJ Simpson, a stuffed beaver, two baseball teams and an odd assortment of others join the wacko goings-on and blow the laugh-o-meter to smithereens.

The visual gags come thick and fast and it's impossible to catch them all with one viewing. Famous walk-ons and cameos in the movie include not only Reggie Jackson but OJ Simpson and, in a very funny sequence, the late John Houseman plays a driving instructor who is unflappable in the face of disaster.

The Naked Gun is the work of Zucker, Abrahams and Zucker and the under-rated *Top Secret*. They're the same team behind the short-lived TV series *Police Squad*, which was dropped by the ABC network after six episodes. Allegedly, execs thought it too complicated for the average viewer. Because of its quick cancellation, the original series soon attained cult status on video, and *The Naked Gun*, in the same style of non-stop visual and spoken puns, attracted the same crowd.

The sequel *Naked Gun 2¹/₂: The Smell of Fear* (1991) had Drebin back, finding lost love Jane (Presley) and foiling a plot to sabotage a solar energy plant. A silly story of passion, intrigue and lobster salad! *Naked Gun 33¹/₃: The Final Insult* (1994) completed the trilogy.

Memorable dialogue:

Frank Drebin: It's true what they say: cops and women don't mix. It's like eating a spoonful of Drano, sure it'll clean you out, but it'll leave you hollow inside.

Frank Drebin: It's the same old story. Boy finds girl, boy loses girl, girl finds boy, boy forgets girl, boy remembers girl, girls dies in a tragic blimp accident over the Orange Bowl on New Year's Day.
Jane Spencer: Goodyear?
Frank Drebin: No, the worst.

Frank Drebin: When I see five weirdoes stabbing a guy in broad daylight, I shoot the bastards. That's my policy.
Mayor: That was a Shakespeare In The Park production, you moron! You killed five actors! Good ones!

Frank Drebin: Wilma, I promise you; whatever scum did this, not one man on this force will rest one minute until he's behind bars. Now, let's grab a bite to eat.

Jane climbs a ladder...
Frank Drebin: Nice beaver.
Jane Spencer (producing a stuffed beaver): Thanks. I just had it stuffed.

Frank Drebin: And I'll tell you one more thing: I faked every orgasm!

Jane Spencer: Would you like a night-cap?
Frank Drebin: No thank you, I don't wear them.

NATURAL BORN KILLERS

1994 / 119 mins / USA / *DVD* / Video
Stars: Woody Harrelson, Juliette Lewis, Robert Downey Jr,
Tommy Lee Jones, O-Lan Jones, Ed White, Richard Lineback
Director: Oliver Stone
Producers: Jane Hamsher, Don Murphy, Clayton Townsend
Script: Quentin Tarantino, David Veloz,
Richard Rotowski, Oliver Stone

An ultra-violent assessment of the degradation of the American family, *Natural Born Killers* chronicles the brutal killing spree of two mass murderers on a rampage across America. Stone's picture is not only a satirical look at the way the media controls the minds of the masses, but the ultimate testament of the proliferation of boredom in our culture, as shown by the public's willingness to wholeheartedly embrace anything or anyone that interrupts their monotonous, uneventful lives.

Mickey and Mallory Knox are pretty bored themselves. Bored with their families, bored with society, bored with America. So they have a little fun.

Written by Quentin Tarantino, during his days as a video rental shop assistant, *Natural Born Killers* is the story of two sexually abused teenagers, Mickey and Mallory Knox (Woody Harrelson and Juliette Lewis). They set off on a journey of mindless slaughter across America, killing anyone who ends up on their 'shit list' (leaving one person alive in each instance to tell their tale).

Mickey and Mallory are wanted by three people. A brutish detective and noted criminologist (Tom Sizemore) hopes to capture them and maybe write a bestseller about it. A tabloid-TV news reporter (Robert Downey Jr) thinks he can exploit their exploits, turning the two murderers into media darlings. And a crazed warden (Tommy Lee Jones) is determined to achieve fame as the man who put them to death. Jack Scagnetti (Tom Sizemore) is fascinated with the pair's antics but eventually becomes sexually obsessed with Mallory.

Not long after the film's cinematic release, Stone commented on how life had imitated art: 'When I started,' he said, 'this was a surreal piece. Now, thanks to Bobbitt and Menendez and Tonya Harding, it's become satire. By the time I'd finished, fact had caught up to fiction. OJ is the final blow-out.'

'The shoot was extraordinarily angst-ridden,' says Stone's superb cinematographer, Robert Richardson, 'because it was anarchy in style. It wasn't planned out in the traditional sense. It was more like throwing paint at the canvas – you don't know if you're making art. The only rule was that you could change your mind.'

With its intriguing range of visual styles, its odd camera gyrations, cartoon-style black comedy and dislocated music video editing, Stone's film turned out to be a stunning assault on the senses and on the polite conventions of the Hollywood status quo.

People who have seen *Natural Born Killers* can be divided up into two categories: those who believe the negative ought to be burned, and that Stone should be strangled, and those who believe it's a classic, a phenomenon, a masterpiece of the medium. Very few films inspire such passionate responses. Similarly, most of David Lynch's films are received this way, as are Tarantino's and Spike Lee's. This is one of the essential attributes of a cult film. They may be rough around the edges because of low budgets and other restraints (although *Killers* itself didn't have this problem), but they do have a certain fire that almost all mainstream films lack, and they cannot be ignored or dismissed.

Memorable dialogue:

Dr Emil; Reingold: Mickey and Mallory know the difference between right and wrong; they just don't give a damn.

Mallory: I do. Til you and I die, and die, and die again. Til death do us part.

Mickey: The media is like the weather, only it's man-made weather.

151

Mallory: How sexy am I now, huh? Flirty boy! How sexy am I now?

Mallory: You made my shit list!

Mickey: The whole world's comin' to an end, Mal!
Mallory: I see angels, Mickey. They're comin' down for us from heaven. And I see you ridin' a big red horse…

Wayne Gale: Repetition works, David. Repetition works, David.

(Two boys interviewed for TV)
Boy 1: Mickey and Mallory are the best thing to happen to mass murder since Manson.

Boy 2: Yeah! But… they're way cooler!

Reporter: Do you have anything to say to your fans?
Mickey: You ain't seen nothin' yet.

Mickey: We're not killing anybody on our wedding day.

Warden: Love makes the world go round, heh heh heh.

Mickey: I realised my true calling in life.
Wayne Gale: What's that?
Mickey: I'm a natural born killer.

Opposite page: Juliette Lewis and Woody Harrelson as two natural born killers

A NIGHTMARE ON ELM STREET

1984 / 91 mins / USA / DVD / ▭ Video
Stars: John Saxon, Ronee Blakely, Heather
Langenkamp, Amanda Wyss, Johnny Depp,
Robert Englund
Director: Wes Craven
Producer: Robert Shaye
Script: Wes Craven

Nancy Thompson is a teenage girl whose dreams are being plagued (and whose friends are being killed) by a hideous creature known as Freddy Krueger (Robert Englund). It turns out Freddy was a child killer acquitted on a technicality and roasted alive in his boiler room by a mob of irate parents. He's back and visiting the sins of the parents on the children.

Krueger always appears strangely dressed with knives on the fingers of his right hand. A group of four teenagers all begin to have the same strange dreams about Freddy until one of them is gruesomely murdered in her sleep. The survivors soon realise that if Freddy kills them in their dreams then they will die in real life too. Thus begins an ordeal of wakefulness as they try to find some way to stop Freddy.

This box-office smash led to a handful of sequels and a TV series, *Freddy's Nightmares*. It also made Robert Englund the first new horror-film star since Peter Cushing and Christopher Lee. Craven had built a solid cult reputation in the 70s with two unusual, graphically violent shockers, *The Last House on the Left* (1972) and *The Hills Have Eyes* (1978). But the cult of *A Nightmare on Elm Street* stems more from the cult of the film's main character, Freddy Krueger. Today, goths still dress in Freddy gear and at novelty shops around the globe kids can even buy the mask and glove with long razors protruding from the fingers. Nice.

Memorable dialogue:

Nancy: Whatever you do, don't fall asleep!

Doctor: Don't worry, you're not gonna turn into Bride of Frankenstein!

Nancy: What gave you the right to take the law into your own hands?
Marge: Because he took it into his hands to kill our kids.

Donald: What's happening?
Garcia: Well, if it were any more quiet, we could hear owls farting.

Children: One, two, Freddy's coming for you! / Three, four, better lock your door! / Five, six, grab your crucifix! / Seven, eight, better stay up late! / Nine, ten, never sleep again!

Rod Lane: I had a hard-on this morning and it had your name written on it.
Tina Gray: My name's four letters – there ain't enough room on your joint to fit it.

ONCE UPON A TIME IN THE WEST

1968 / 165 mins / Italy / *DVD* / ▭ Video
Stars: Henry Fonda, Claudia Cradinale, Jason Robards, Charles Bronson, Frank Wolff, Gabriele Ferzetti, Keenan Wynn
Director: Sergio Leone
Producers: Bino Cicogna, Fulvio Morsella
Script: Sergio Leone, Sergio Donati; Story by Dario Argento, Bernardo Bertolucci, Sergio Leone

There were three men in her life. One to take her...one to love her...and one to kill her.

Three men wait for a train on a deserted railway station, one cracks his knuckles, one studies a pesky fly, one catches drops of water in the brim of his hat. The train arrives, a passenger alights playing his harmonica. 'Where's Frank?' the stranger asks. In answer, one of the three pulls a gun but 'Harmonica' blows them all away. This 15-minute opening sequence sets the tone for the rest of the film; long, lingering, tension-filled set-pieces combining to create the best Western ever made.

The plot centres on crooked railroad boss Morton (Gabriele Ferzetti) who wants to build a railroad across the old West. Standing in his way is no-nonsense McBain (Frank Wolff). He has land needed by the railroad so Morton sends brutal killer Frank (Fonda) to bump him off.

When McBain's widow, Jill (Claudia Cardinale) inherits the property, the tangled web starts to unravel. It would be easy enough for Frank to kill her too, if it weren't for two other killers, Cheyenne (Jason Robards) and Harmonica (Charles Bronson), who are protecting her.

With a story co-written by Dario Argento and Bernardo Bertolucci, Leone could hardly go wrong. He is ably assisted by an excellent cast, notably blue-eyed Fonda cast against type as pure unadulterated evil and Bronson in Clint Eastwood's 'man with no name' role. The dialogue is superb, especially some of Fonda's now-classic lines: 'People scare easier when they're dyin'.' and 'How can you trust a man who wears both a belt and suspenders? The man can't even trust his own pants.'

The exteriors were filmed in Spain, not Arizona as most critics thought, while the interiors were completed in Rome. Ennio Morricone's superb score was recorded before the scenes were filmed, which lends an orchestrated feel to the set-pieces.

Memorable dialogue:

Frank: You're the one who makes appointments.
Harmonica: And you're the one who doesn't keep them.

Harmonica: Your friends have a high mortality rate, Frank.

Cheyenne: Hey, you could make thousands of dollars.... Hundreds of thousands of dollars.... Even thousands of thousands of dollars...
Harmonica: They call 'em millions.

Cheyenne: You know Jill, you remind me of my mother. She was the biggest whore in Alameda but the finest woman in the world. Whoever was my father for an hour or for a night... he must have been a happy man.

Harmonica: So you found out you're not a business man after all.
Frank: Just a man.

Frank: Keep your lovin' brother happy!

ORPHÉE

1950 / 112 mins / France / DVD / ⟐ Video
Stars: Jean Marais, Francois Perier,
Maria Casarès, Maria Dea
Director: Jean Cocteau
Producer: Andre Paulve
Script: Jean Cocteau

Jean Cocteau's film is based on the Greek legend of the poet Orpheus, who followed his wife Eurydice into the Underworld.

In a compelling cinematic allegory, set in modern times, Orphée is a poet who spends much of his time at a Paris café. When popular writer Cegiste (Edouard Dermithe) is knocked down and killed by a motorcyclist, outside the cafe, Orphée accompanies the mysterious Princess (Maria Casarès), as a witness, when she takes away the body in her car. The Princess moves Cegiste to her chalet, rather than the hospital, and appears to be in command of the motorcyclists who ran into him. Orphée becomes even more certain that this is all a strange dream when the Princess raises Cegiste from the dead and takes him through a mirror, into another world.

Orphée becomes obsessed with the Princess of Death. They fall in love. Orphée's wife, Eurydice, is killed by the Princess' henchmen and Orphée goes after her into the Underworld. Although they have become dangerously entangled, the Princess sends Orphée back out of the Underworld, to carry on his life with Eurydice.

More than 30 years after Cocteau's death, many are fascinated by his style. His lyrical way of looking at the world has been embraced by many. It's not uncommon to hear the phrase, 'Why, that's straight from Cocteau!' when someone's describing a magical cinematic experience. Cocteau believed that art should astound and astonish, and

that the cinema was a place of magic that enabled the artist to hypnotise an audience into dreaming the same dream.

Orphée is Cocteau's finest film, winning First Prize at the 1950 Venice Festival. It blends mythology and reality, colour and black and white, and is filmed with startling imagery and reverse photography. It forms part of Cocteau's Orpheus trilogy with *The Blood of the Poet* (1930) and *The Testament of Orpheus* (1960). *Orphée* was remade by Jacques Demy as *Parking* (1985).

Memorable dialogue:

The Man: Your trouble is knowing just how far to go too far.

The Princess: The role of the dreamer is to accept his dreams.

The Princess: What are you staring at, Cegiste? Did you expect a shroud and a scythe?

The Princess: Perhaps he sleeps and dreams us. We are his bad dreams.

Heurtebise: Mirrors are the doors by which death comes?

PANTHER

1995 / 124 mins / UK / USA (Not currently available)
Stars: Kadeem Hardison, Bokeem Woodbine,
Joe Don Baker, Courtney B Vance, Tyrin Turner,
Marcus Chong, Anthony Griffith
Director: Mario Van Peebles
Producers: Preston L Holmes, Mario Van Peebles, Melvin Van
Peebles, Robert de Niro (uncredited)
Script: Melvin van Peebles

The people called them heroes. The FBI called them Public Enemy Number One.

From the director of *New Jack City* (1991) and *Posse* (1993), comes the even more energetic *Panther*, his docudrama about the rise and fall of the Black Panther Party. Good editing, blustering rhetoric and non-stop gunplay, it intrigues and disturbs in equal measure. This is a film with, and about passion and politics. The Panthers are an integral part of a chapter in American history that desperately needed retelling.

The Panther organisation, founded in 1966 in an Oakland ghetto by Huey Newton and Bobby Seale, was a radical, armed, black community group dedicated to ending police brutality and beginning community self-help programmes. Their activities and the response of authorities led to violence, repression and a campaign by the FBI to eradicate them, including by illegal means.

Panther chronicles that history from its raw beginnings, when the Black Panther Party for Self-Defense was simply trying to get traffic lights installed at a dangerous intersection in their neighbourhood. From those humble beginnings, it turned into an international political action group with bombastic FBI boss J Edgar Hoover taking a personal interest.

Panther was produced and directed by Mario Van Peebles and produced and written by his father, Melvin Van Peebles, who used his own novel as the basis for this project. The story is told through the eyes of the fictional Judge (Kadeem Hardison). He is a highly educated, articulate young man who happens to be a Vietnam veteran, so he knows both social politics and guns. He is recruited by Newton to serve as a double agent and establish contacts with the FBI. More interesting are the real leaders of the Panthers, in particular Newton (Marcus Chong), Seale (Courtney B Vance) and firebrand Edridge Cleaver (Anthony Griffith). These are also among the film's finest performances, partly because they have the best, most dramatic material with which to work.

The film concludes by explaining that the FBI introduced cheap drugs into black neighbourhoods in order to discourage black activism and that's the reason drugs have so corroded our society. Many criticised the film, arguing it could open old wounds. However, a committee of black entertainers and athletes, including Danny Glover, Spike Lee and Magic Johnson, took out ads in *Daily Variety* to support the Van Peebleses: 'We laud their efforts and their courage for making a movie that sends a message of strength, dignity and empowerment to the African–American community, especially to our youth.' This was in response to an earlier ad, declaring *Panther* 'a two-hour lie,' that was placed in *Daily Variety* by David Horowitz's Center for the Study of Popular Culture, a neo-conservative outfit in LA. Horowitz, a reformed leftie who worked for the Panthers in the 70s, now believes that 'the overwhelming impact of the Panthers was negative.' He feared *Panther* would have a toxic effect: 'I fully expect that there will be people who will die because of this film.' Mario Van Peebles obviously disagreed: 'The kids don't see this movie as a call to arms but as a call to consciousness.'

`Memorable dialogue:`
```
Bobby Hutton: We ain't no
gangsters, we revolutionaries.
```

A FILM BY MELVIN & MARIO VAN PEEBLES

PANTHER

15

ALL POWER TO THE PEOPLE

PERFORMANCE

1970 / 106 mins / UK / *DVD* / 🖵 Video
Stars: Mick Jagger, James Fox, Anita Pallenberg,
Michele Breton, Johnny Shannon
Director: Nicolas Roeg, Donald Cammell
Producer: Donald Cammell
Script: Donald Cammell

The psychological melodrama *Performance* marked the directorial debut of cinematographer Nicolas Roeg. It was co-directed and written by Donald Cammell. However, Warner Bros promptly shelved the film for two years while they tried to agree with Cammell on the final edit. Seven different editors were drafted in to help. Disturbing, surreal and offbeat, it isn't for all tastes.

Set in 60s London, James Fox plays Chas Devlin, a flashy gangster on the run from his gangland colleagues. He eventually hides out in a house in Notting Hill run by a reclusive ex-pop star, Turner (Mick Jagger) who has two young ladies, Pherber (Anita Pallenberg) and Lucy (Michele Breton), in attendance. They begin to feed Chas drugs and break down his sense of identity. Out of his skull on mind-expanding drugs, Chas even begins cross-dressing. He then goes one stage further and admits Turner sexually attracts him. It's not long before mob boss Harry Flowers (Johnny Shannon) shows up for Chas, who is taken away on a final ride in the gangster's car, leaving behind Turner to experience one last head trip – a bullet in the head.

On the surface, *Performance* is about the dealings of a London crook. Deeper down, it's about identity and the revelation of the social constructions of identity under consciousness-altering drugs; it deals more successfully with this topic than any other cinematic attempt. The film addresses the concept of duality and personality switching. As Turner interacts with Fox's character, his whole perception of reality begins to change (with a little help from some hallucinogenic drugs) and their lives become intertwined, with one of the most startling, enigmatic and ambiguous endings of any recent film. When Chas shoots Turner in the forehead, the camera follows the bullet as it penetrates his brain, where, inexplicably, a portrait of Argentinian poet, essayist and short-story writer Jorge Luis Borges appears and is shattered.

According to Cammell: 'Nic and I had been friends for years. We both read the same books, which to my mind is more important than seeing the same films. Our initial inspiration came from Borges and Vladimir Nabokov's *Despair*, a story which makes a kind of ecstatic exploration of a character's fatal encounter with his double or alter ego, as in *Performance*. I was fascinated by the idea of murder which might also be suicide.'

Donald Cammell committed suicide in 1996. Completely disillusioned, his latest film, *Wild Side* (1995), had, he thought, been butchered by its producers. Copying the style used by Fox when he executed Jagger in *Performance*, he supposedly remained conscious for 45 minutes after the shooting but was in no pain. According to Cammell's widow, China Kong, the writer–director had been studying the art of suicide for some time, reading about where you should aim the bullet in order to obtain not just a painless death, but a pleasurable one. In her deposition, Kong recalled that Cammell asked for a pillow before he died, because he didn't want the carpet to be 'fucked up' by his blood. He also asked for a mirror in the hopes of observing his own death. Among the last things Cammell said was: 'Can you see the picture of Borges now?' For him, murder turned out to be truly a work of art.

Memorable dialogue:

Chas: I need a bohemian atmosphere!

Chas flicks his cigarette ash onto a rug...
Turner: That rug's over a 1000 years old.
Chas: Yeah, it looks it.

Turner: The only performance that makes it, that makes it all the way, is the one that achieves madness. Am I right? Eh?

PET SEMATARY

1989 / 102 mins / USA / ▭ Video
Stars: Dale Midkiff, Fred Gwynne, Denise Crosby,
Brad Greenquist, Michael Lombard
Director: Mary Lambert
Producer: Richard P Rubinstein
Script: Stephen King

There have been endless adaptations of Stephen King's novels over the years, from the dire (*Maximum Overdrive* [1986], *The Langoliers* [1995]) to the must-see (1990's *Misery*). In 1989, Mary Lambert gave us *Pet Sematary*, adapted from King's own script, about the Creed family and their hellish move into a new home.

The Creed family move to a quaint Maine country home and are charmed by the nearby pet cemetery created by the local children. Their neighbour Jud (Fred 'Herman Munster' Gwynne) Crandall, warns them about the grounds, past the children's pet cemetery in the local woods. Built on the site of an ancient Indian burial ground, the site has hidden powers which the Creeds discover to their cost.

Dale Midkiff turns in a subtle performance as Louis Creed, patriarch of a family that's about to go down the tubes. Fred Gwynne also gives one of his last and best screen turns. And watch out for King. He appears in a cameo as a minister presiding over a funeral.

Pet Sematary is the 'cultiest' Stephen King adaptation, atttracting most internet chat and discussion. This could be because it is probably the darkest King adaptation. with a weirder plot than the slightly more mainstream *Misery* and *Maximum Overdrive*. And, of course, there's also the cameo appearance by the King of Horror himself.

Memorable dialogue:

Victor Pascow: The soil in a man's
heart is stonier.

Jud Crandall: Sometimes dead is
better.

PINK FLAMINGOS

1972 / 95 mins / USA / (Not currently available)
Stars: Divine, David Lochary, Mink Stole,
Mary Vivian Pearce, Edith Massey, Danny Mills,
Channing Wilroy, Cookie Mueller
Director: John Waters
Producer: John Waters
Script: John Waters

If *A Clockwork Orange* (1971) was a deliberate exercise in ultra-violence, *Pink Flamingos* is a deliberate exercise in ultra-bad-taste. With no budget, grotesque images and the striking Divine, this movie soon attracted an endearing legion of admirers. It's still shown at select theatres and often at gay and lesbian festivals around the world with fans queuing to cheer for Babs and Cotton, hiss Connie and Raymond, quote endless lines and have a great time.

The plot of this seminal camp flick follows the adventures of Sleaze Queen Babs Johnson (Divine), a fat, style-obsessed criminal who lives in a trailer with her mentally ill 250-pound mother Edie (Edith Massey), her hippie son Crackers (Danny Mills) and her travelling companion Cotton (Mary Vivian Pearce). They're trying to rest quietly on their laurels as 'the filthiest people alive'. But competition is brewing in the form of Connie and Raymond Marble (David Lochary and Mink Stole), 'two jealous perverts' according to the script, who sell heroin to schoolchildren. Finally, they challenge Divine directly and battle commences.

Raymond and Connie try to seize Divine's title of 'filthiest person alive' by sending her a turd in the mail and burning down her trailer. The Marbles kidnap hitch-hiking women, have them impregnated by their servant Channing (Channing Wilroy) and then sell the babies to lesbian couples. As Raymond explains, they use the dykes' money to finance their porno shops and 'a network of dealers selling heroin in the inner-city elementary schools'.

Pink Flamingos has cult qualities in the same way the *Rocky Horror Picture Show* (1975) does, in that everyone in the film has something odd about them and both movies joyfully celebrate their uniqueness. Waters' film has endless memorable moments (who could forget?) – the shrimping scene with David's blue and Mink's orange pubic hair, Divine's infamous faeces snacking, brown teeth and all, sex with a chicken, eating people alive, incestuous fellatio and hardcore pornography. This commercial feature surely must be the first and only to end with the star eating dog shit.

Pink Flamingos is now 30 years old. Waters recently had the film blown up from 16 to 35mm and 'restored' ready for forthcoming video and DVD releases which feature a few never-before-seen out-takes, self-critical commentary by Waters ('You can see the bad continuity in this scene'), a new stereo soundtrack and the hilarious original trailer, which is made up only of shocked reactions from people who have just seen the picture.

Many won't enjoy either Crackers and Cookie's chicken-shagging scene or Babs' turd eating, but these sequences are what put the film on the map, brought Waters all the publicity, negative and otherwise, and gave *Pink Flamingos* a permanent place in cult film history.

Memorable dialogue:

Babs Johnson: Oh my God Almighty! Someone has sent me a bowel movement!

Babs Johnson: Kill everyone now! Condone first degree murder! Advocate cannibalism! Eat shit! Filth is my politics! Filth is my life!

Crackers: Do my balls, Mama.

Connie: There are two kinds of people, my kind and assholes.

QUADROPHENIA

1979 / 120 mins / UK / *DVD* / ▭ Video
Stars: Phil Daniels, Mark Wingett, Toyah Wilcox,
Sting, Leslie Ash
Director: Franc Roddam
Producers: Roy Baird, Bill Curbishley
Script: Dave Humphries, Martin Stellman,
Franc Roddham

Set in 1963, *Quadrophenia* perfectly captures the teenage need to belong and to identify with peers. Franc Roddam's 1979 film of The Who's rock opera has Phil Daniels playing Jimmy Cooper, a kid who divides his time between his Mod friends and slaving in the post-room of an advertising company. His job pays to keep his scooter on the road and for his bespoke suits. Jimmy explains to Kevin that he wants to be different, to stand apart from others. It's ironic then that the way he achieves this is by joining the herd of Parka-wearing, Lambretta-riding Mods. His friends Dave (Mark Wingett), Chalky (Philip Davis) and Spider (Gary Shail) are all part of the same gang, also into scooters, music, drugs and chatting up Steph (Leslie Ash) and Monkey (Toyah Wilcox).

One Bank Holiday weekend, the gang go down to Brighton, all looking for trouble. On the first night out, Jimmy gets kicked out of the club and spends the early hours staring into the sea. The next day, after a small punch-up in a café develops into an all-out nasty riot on the seafront, Jimmy is arrested along with Ace (Sting), the leader of the Mods.

While the action on the screen has dissolved into chaos, director Franc Roddam keeps a firm hand on the proceedings, orchestrating the violence with just the right amount of restraint. Roddam's greatest achievement, however, is the film's authenticity, from the smart uniforms to the way in which the Who-influenced soundtrack complements Jimmy's actions and feelings.

After returning to London, Jimmy jacks in his job, is kicked out of home by his Mum and disowned by his girlfriend Steph. He goes on a drink-and-drugs-binge train journey down to Brighton again, only to discover his hero Ace working as a hotel bell-boy.

This is a cult movie about youth cults and the shallowness of image and style. By the end, Jimmy's world is shattered by Ace. His loss of identity results in him stealing Ace's scooter and riding it down to the cliffs. Jimmy's frustrations have ultimately led to self-destruction as we see the bike speed towards the edge of a cliff.

Memorable dialogue:

Jimmy: What's normal then?

Jimmy: Nothing seems right apart from Brighton.

Jimmy: You've killed me scooter!

Steph: You going to be one of the faces?
Jimmy: What do you mean going to be? I AM one of the faces!

Jimmy: I don't wanna be the same as everyone else. That's why I'm a Mod, see?

[On Kev's leather jacket]
Jimmy: Ere, I never realised.
Kev: Never realised what?
Jimmy: You's a rocker.
Kev: What, am I black or something?
Jimmy: Well you ain't exactly white in that sort of get up, are you?

Previous page: Phil Daniels (left) and Leslie Ash in a scene from Quadrophenia *(1979)*

RAIMI, SAM

Director, writer
Born 23 October 1959, Michigan

As a teenager, Sam Raimi directed Super-8 films. Some years later, he left Michigan State University to form Renaissance Pictures with Robert Tapert and long-time friend and actor Bruce Campbell. Out of this association came the trio's first feature film, the cult favourite *The Evil Dead* (1982). Written and directed by Raimi, produced by Tapert and starring Campbell, this low-budget horror picture became an immediate cult hit at the Cannes Film Festival. It also became a theatrical and video phenomenon in the UK, mainland Europe and the Far East. *The Evil Dead* was soon followed by Raimi's equally impressive sequel, *The Evil Dead II: Dead By Dawn* (1987).

Raimi's first studio film was the mainstream fantasy thriller *Darkman* (1990), starring Academy Award nominee Liam Neeson and Frances McDormand, which Raimi co-wrote and produced. He directed and co-wrote *Army of Darkness* (1993), an outrageously comic sword-and-sorcery fantasy starring Bruce Campbell; executive produced the feature films *Hard Target* (1993) and *Timecop* (1994), both starring Jean-Claude Van Damme; co-wrote the feature film *The Hudsucker Proxy* (1994), starring Paul Newman, Tim Robbins and Jennifer Jason Leigh; and directed the action-Western *The Quick and the Dead* (1995), starring Leonardo DiCaprio, Sharon Stone, Russell Crowe and Gene Hackman.

Raimi's television credits include the two-hour series pilot *MANTIS* (1994), which he co-wrote and executive produced. Along with Robert Tapert, his business partner for over 20 years, Raimi has also executive produced TV's *Hercules: The Legendary Journeys* (1995) which recently concluded its enormously successful six-season run; the hit series *Xena: Warrior Princess* (1995), and the nationally syndicated *Cleopatra 2525* (2000) and *Jack of All Trades* (2000).

Most recent directing credits include the suspense thriller *A Simple Plan* (1998), starring Bill Paxton, Billy Bob Thornton and Bridget Fonda, for which Thornton received an Academy Award nomination as Best Supporting Actor, and *For Love of the Game* (1999), starring Kevin Costner, Kelly Preston and John C Reilly.

Can all this mainstream work – TV adventure series, vehicles for DiCaprio and Costner – come from the man responsible for *The Evil Dead?* What happened? Does Sam Raimi really enjoy churning out fodder for the studios? In films such as *The Evil Dead II* and *Darkman,* Raimi used an array of flashy camera tricks and special effects to shock and thrill audiences. Now, it's all become rather pointless.

He did, however, come back in 2000 with the Billy Bob Thornton-scripted *The Gift* starring Cate Blanchett as a woman with extrasensory perception who's asked to help find a missing young woman. This was an improvement but still annoyingly predictable with stereotypical characters and some really boring run-of-the-mill courtroom scenes. Raimi has the talent to be coming up with the innovative movies of our time but instead he's making copies, cashing in on *Sixth Sense* (1999), *The Blair Witch Project* (1999) and so on. See Filmography, p.240.

REPO MAN

1984 / 92 mins / USA / 📼 Video
Stars: Emilio Estevez, Harry Dean Stanton,
Sy Richardson, Tracey Walter, Olivier Barash,
Dick Rude
Director: Alex Cox
Producers: Peter McCarthy, Jonathan Wacks
Script: Alex Cox

Repo Man is the story of a disaffected young punk called Otto (Estevez) who, after quitting his nine-to-five supermarket job, meets Bud (Harry Dean Stanton) who tricks him into repossessing a car. After the initial disgust at what he's just done, Otto takes a full-time job as a car repossessor in this seedy LA underworld. He becomes the protégé of Bud who has his own unique philosophy: 'Ordinary people. I hate 'em'. After teaching him the ropes, Otto soon learns enough to challenge his mentor for the $20,000 1964 Chevy Malibu together with the sinister contents of its trunk.

The offbeat nature of the film concerns the race for the Chevy and the prize money. But as well as Otto and Bud, there are other pursuers: government agents, amateur UFO investigators and the infamous Rodriguez Brothers. None of them realises the glowing contents of the trunk could change the course of civilisation overnight.

Cox's world of urban chaos and absurdist behaviour is similar in style, narrative and dialogue to many of the 50s and 60s 'B' movies. It has obvious allusions to Robert Aldrich's classic of late film noir, *Kiss Me Deadly* (1955) and captures the same sense of anxiety about some sort of mysterious force at work in a civilisation on the edge of the apocalypse.

With its rebellious nature and killer West Coast punk soundtrack, *Repo Man* was a real hit with punk audiences. This is not to say he went out intentionally to make a 'cult' film: 'At first, I found the idea of *Repo Man* gaining this cult audience quite odd and I really hadn't expected that to happen. Having analysed it, I think in a certain way it's a compendium of weird ephemera. The film does have a lot of modern myths in it such as the idea that people can self-combust, that they can spontaneously explode while sitting in an armchair and the idea of all this stolen nuclear material and weird poison drifting around. Not to mention the pop culture aspects of punk rock. I think the monologues of Sy and Tracey Walter also added to it.'

Repo Man undoubtedly found an audience because the punk movement was still alive at the time of its release. The film is infused with the spirit of punk. Bands like Black Flag, Suicidal Tendencies, Fear and The Circle Jerks dominate the soundtrack and the incidental music is provided by two members of The Plugz, Tito Larriva and Steven Hufsteter. They are responsible for the extraordinary Morriconeesque final track.

Understandably, punks and others sympathetic to the punk culture got behind the film because it had that anti-establishment flavour.

Memorable dialogue:

Miller: I don't want no commies in my car. No Christians either!

Miller: A repo man spends his life getting into tense situations.

Miller: The life of a repo man is always intense.

Miller: The more you drive, the less intelligent you are.

Agent Rodgers: It happens sometimes. People just explode. Natural causes.

Miller: John Wayne was a fag.
All: The hell he was!

RESERVOIR DOGS

1992 / 99 mins / USA / *DVD* / ▭ Video
Stars: Harvey Keitel, Tim Roth, Michael Madsen,
Chris Penn, Steve Buscemi, Lawrence Tierney,
Randy Brooks, Kirk Baltz
Director: Quentin Tarantino
Producer: Lawrence Bender
Script: Quentin Tarantino

Reservoir Dogs, the supremely confident debut feature by writer and director Quentin Tarantino, shocking, perversely funny and extremely stylish, quickly earned itself a reputation as a violent picture and provided a convenient platform for some hysterical media reaction. As always, viewing reveals a different truth. Much of the violence is suggested. Tarantino cranks up the tension but then cuts away at the climax, as in the infamous ear-severing scene.

The plot details a robbery that has gone wrong. Tarantino uses flashbacks to build to a conclusion and mixes in separate scenes to be showcased as individual vignettes that the cast exploit to the full. It's a very well-made exploration of violence, mayhem and paranoia, focusing on men who perpetuate crime for very selfish motives.

The opening scene with the black-suited guys enjoying a power breakfast is a perfect hook. But most of the film takes place in an abandoned warehouse. The gang return there individually, their pre-arranged getaway rendezvous. Within these claustrophobic confines the paranoid hoods recount their own version of events in a bid to determine just who might be the rat in the house responsible for tipping off the cops.

A strong ensemble cast, for reasons of security known to each other by their colour-coded names, principally Mr White (Keitel), Mr Pink (Buscemi), Mr Blonde (Madsen) and Mr Orange (Roth), each with his own story, prefaced by the character's name, flashed up on the screen in chapter-like fashion.

The film boasts a great soundtrack with some terrific songs, along with amusing running commentary by an unseen disc jockey, voiced by comic Steven Wright.

Tarantino, a self-confessed movie geek, has filled *Reservoir Dogs* with references to his favourite films, including *Straight Time* (1977), *Ocean's Eleven* (1960), *The Killing* (1955) and *White Heat* (1949), and dedicated it to his heroes, Jean-Luc Godard, Jean-Pierre Melville, Chow Yun-Fat and Roger Corman. Originally, executive producer Monte Hellmen (himself a cult film-maker) considered coming out of retirement to direct the picture.

Memorable dialogue:

Nice Guy Eddie: Okay, first things fuckin' last!

Joe Cabot: You don't need proof when you have instinct.

Mr Blonde: I don't give a good fuck what you know or don't know, I'm going to torture you anyway.

Mr White: If you shoot this man, you die next. Repeat. If you shoot this man, you die next.

Mr Pink: Somebody's shoved a red-hot poker up our ass, and I want to know whose name is on the handle!

Mr Blonde: If you're talking like a bitch, I'm gonna slap you like a bitch!

Mr Blonde: Are you gonna bark all day, little doggy, or are you gonna bite?

Mr Blonde: Gee, that was really exciting. I bet you're a big Lee Marvin fan, aren't you?

Mr White: You shoot me in a dream, you'd better wake up and apologise.

167

THE ROCKY HORROR PICTURE SHOW

1975 / 100 mins / UK / _DVD_ / ⊑ Video
Stars: Tim Curry, Susan Sarandon, Barry Bostwick,
Richard O'Brien, Jonathan Adams, Nell Campbell
Director: Jim Sharman
Producer: Michael White
Script: Jim Sharman, Richard O'Brien

Richard O'Brien's wacky stage show was turned into the definitive cult movie thanks mainly to Tim Curry's camp Dr Frank-N-Furter, Meat Loaf in a deep freeze, that all-singing-all-dancing toe-tapping 'Timewarp' finale and a script full of kitsch appeal.

The Rocky Horror Picture Show is an outrageous assemblage of the most stereotyped science-fiction movies, Marvel comics, Frankie Avalon and Anette Funicello outings. Running through the story is the sexual confusion of two American 'Ike Age' kids confronted by the complications of the decadent morality of the 70s, represented by mad 'doctor' Frank-N-Furter, a transvestite from the planet Transexual in the galaxy of Transylvania.

O'Brien, who wrote the book, music and lyrics and calls it 'something any 10-year-old could enjoy'. The original play opened in London at the Royal Court's experimental Theatre Upstairs as a six-week workshop project in June 1973. It was named Best Musical of 1973 in the _London Evening Standard_'s annual poll of drama critics. Lou Adler, who was in London, saw _The Rocky Horror Show_ and promptly sewed up the American theatrical rights to the play within 36 hours.

Filming of _The Rocky Horror Picture Show_ began a year later at Bray Studios, England's famous House of Horror, and at a 19th-century chateau which once served as the wartime refuge of General Charles de Gaulle.

The film version retains many members of the original Theatre Upstairs company. Repeating the roles they created in the theatre are Richard O'Brien (Riff Raff), Patricia Quinn (Magenta), Little Nell (Columbia) and Jonathan Adams (who played the Narrator on stage and in the film appears as Dr Scott). The result (co-written by O'Brien) is a faithful adaptation of the original.

On the way to visit an old college professor, two clean cut kids, Brad Majors (Barry Bostwick) and his fiancée Janet Weiss (Susan Sarandon), run into car trouble and seek help at the Frankenstein place, where Dr Frank-N-

Furter (Tim Curry) is in the midst of one of his maniacal experiments. He's created the perfect man, a rippling piece of beefcake christened Rocky Horror (Peter Hinwood) and intends to put him to good use (his own) in his kinky household retinue, presided over by a hunchback henchman named Riff Raff (Richard O'Brien) and his incestuous sister Magenta (Patricia Quinn) and assisted by a tap dancing groupie-in-residence, Columbia (Little Nell).

Meanwhile, an oafish biker, unwed Eddie (Meatloaf), ploughs through the laboratory wall, wailing on a saxophone. Frank puts a permanent end to this musical interruption. The old professor whom Brad and Janet set out to visit, Dr Scott (Jonathan Adams), then turns up at the castle in search of his missing nephew (who is in fact Eddie). He knows that Frank-N-Furter is an alien spy from another galaxy and sets out to turn him in, but Frank moves too fast, seducing first Janet, then Brad into his lascivious clutches. Overwhelmed by a new-found libido, Janet hotly attacks the stud Rocky Horror while Brad is under the covers with Frank.

Before Dr Scott can bring justice and morality into this topsy-turvy Transylvanian orgy, Frank-N-Furter has turned his captives to stone, in preparation for a new 'experiment'. Riff Raff and Magenta reappear in Transylvanian space togs to wrest control of the mission from Frank-N-Furter, whose lifestyle is too extreme even for his fellow space travellers. Frank-N-Furter tries to escape, only to be gunned down by Riff Raff and Magenta's power ray guns. Rock rushes to save his creator, but he, too, is blasted to outer space by the militants.

Brad, Janet and Dr Scott are left in a fog, incapable of readjusting to the normality of the life they've left behind in Denton, now that they've tasted the forbidden fruits of the Time Warp.

Richard O'Brien's cross-dressing sensation will forever be an acquired taste but elicits a fiery passion in devoted fans. Like many cult movies, it was rejected by most viewers on its initial release. But after late-night screenings took place in New York, the cult began to develop. Devoted fans started to arrive at theatres in costume ready to join in the musical madness! One of the few movies that consistently inspires dancing in the aisles, the film's audience recite the dialogue simultaneously with the characters on screen, many even mocking the characters or coming up with improvised quips aimed at the actors involved. Water pistols are squirted, toilet rolls thrown and playing cards tossed at the screen. Each of these sorts of screenings become major advertised events.

This camp classic always deserves another look and was perfect for DVD. The various discs include an amazing line-up of essential extras for *Rocky* fans. Extras include commentaries by O'Brien and other cast members, the deleted musical sequence Superheroes, which has been edited back into the film, 'The theatrical experience' – a branching function that gives you an in-theatre experience viewing option to allow DVD owners to see the crowd's reaction or the performers on stage at certain points as they watch the film, the engrossing documentary Rocky Horror Double Feature, deleted scenes, out-takes including 11 alternate takes on key scenes in the film, excerpts from VH-1's *Behind-the-Music* and *Where Are They Now?*, featuring interviews with Susan Sarandon, Barry Bostwick, Richard O'Brien, Patricia Quinn and Meatloaf, two lively sing-along songs, two theatrical trailers and loads of photo galleries.

Memorable dialogue:

Frank: A mental mind fuck can be nice.

The Criminologist: I would like if I may to take you on a strange journey.

Dr Frank-N-Furter: Give yourself over to absolute pleasure. Swim the warm waters of sins of the flesh – erotic nightmares beyond any measure, and sensual daydreams to treasure forever. Can't you just see it? Don't dream it, be it.

The Criminologist: And crawling on this planet's face, some insects called the human race. Lost in time. And lost in space and meaning.

Janet: What have you done to Brad!
Frank: Nothing. Why, do you think I should?

Magenta: I ask for nothing!
Dr Frank-N-Furter: And you shall receive it, in abundance!

Dr Scott: Janet!
Janet: Dr Scott!
Brad: Janet!
Janet: Brad!
Dr Frank-N-Furter: Rocky!

Dr Frank-N-Furter: In just seven days, I can make you a man. Dig it if you can.

Riff Raff: Say good-bye to all of this. And say hello to oblivion.

ROEG, NICOLAS

Director
Born 15 August 1928, London

Starting as a clapper boy in the 50s for MGM in Britain, Roeg worked his way up to cinematographer by 1959 and photographed such diverse films as Corman's *The Masque of The Red Death* (1964), Truffaut's *Fahrenheit 451* (1966), Richard Lester's *Petulia* (1968) and John Schlesinger's *Far From the Madding Crowd* (1967).

His directorial debut (with Donald Cammell) was *Performance* (released 1970), immediately shelved by Warner Brothers who were so horrified by this multi-layered kaleidoscope of sex, violence and questions of identity that they handed it over to seven different editors to chop it up and make it more 'understandable'. This delayed its release for two years. Roeg went to Australia for his solo debut *Walkabout* (1970), a stimulating adventure with disturbing social overtones, based on a story of two white Australian children stranded in the Outback.

Throughout the 70s, Roeg produced an excellent body of work that revealed his uniquely off-kilter view of the world, expressed through fragmented, dislocated images and a highly original yet strangely accessible approach to narrative. In *Don't Look Now* (1973), his stylistically beautiful thriller about psychic phenomena, Donald Sutherland and Julie Christie play the parents of a dead child who go to Venice where, instead of solace, they find reminders of their tragedy.

Roeg found a niche in the cult pantheon by directing rock star David Bowie in the peculiar, paranoid science-fiction drama *The Man Who Fell to Earth* (1976) but his more recent films have been erratic, to say the least. Several of them – including *Bad Timing: A Sensual Obsession* (1980), *Eureka* (1982), and *Insignificance* (1985) – have been severely restricted due to problems with the films' distributors.

Roeg refuses to discuss the suicide of Donald Cammell, who co-directed the 1970 Mick Jagger vehicle *Performance* with him, and is as enigmatic as ever when asked how *Don't Look Now* compares with the rest of his films: 'It's something of one's life. All movies . . . are the sum total of one's thoughts and values and relationships at the time.'

Separated from Theresa Russell, the American actress whom he married in 1982 and directed in several films (*Eureka, Insignificance, Bad Timing*), Roeg says it's a jinx to talk about current projects: 'If I do, it goes down the drain.' But he does admit he's more interested in the making of a film than its financial result. 'It's quite odd,' he says. 'People just say, "Did it do well?" now. I was talking to a producer a little while ago at a party. I said, "I saw your movie and I loved it." He said, 'Really? It didn't do any business.' And that was the end of the conversation. He didn't say, 'Hey, I liked it, too.' See Filmography, p.240.

ROMERO, GEORGE A

Writer, director
Born 4 February 1940, New York

Mad on movies as a kid, Romero made 8mm shorts and his first short feature, *The Man From the Meteor,* in 1954. After college, he and some friends formed The Latent Image, a production company responsible for a variety of TV commercials and industrial shorts.

Soon, enough funds were raised to finance a full-length feature, *Night of the Living Dead* (1968). Shot in Pittsburg, this unnerving low-budget chiller about zombies prowling the streets devouring human flesh became a cult hit and its lean, mean, no-nonsense approach to horror influenced many future directors of the genre.

Although Romero's next few films went relatively unnoticed, he returned in 1978 with *Martin,* starring John Amplas as a teenager capable of making love only to women he's sedated. This is no run-of-the-mill psychotic kid flick though, as we discover that the kid might be a 100-year-old heir to a family tradition of vampirism.

Rather than move to the dead end streets of Hollywood, or even New York, Romero decided to remain in Pittsburgh and continued to make films on the edge of the mainstream, often drawing on local talent, including actors from prestigious Carnegie-Mellon University. *Dawn of the Dead* (1979), a gory, satiric sequel to *Night of the Living Dead,* had four survivors of a zombie plague trapped in a huge shopping centre.

Two years later, *Knightriders* (1981) – with Ed Harris in an early lead role – followed a gang of bikers living under Arthurian codes. This was an amusing way to bring 60s counterculture movies into contemporary terms. Romero then returned to his roots for *Creepshow* (1982), a film which also marked his first collaboration with Stephen King.

Day of the Dead (1985) was the third in the trilogy but fared less well than the previous two. In 1984 he fronted the long-running TV anthology series *Tales From the Darkside,* as well as taking the role of executive producer. Romero scripted 1987's *Creepshow 2* and executive produced the 1990 remake of *Night of the Living Dead* directed by long-time collaborator Tom Savini. More recently, he returned to King territory, adapting and directing the author's *The Dark Half* (1993).

Romero tries to avoid any serious discussion of the art of his films, preferring to keep interviews light-hearted: 'Just because I'm showing somebody being disembowelled doesn't mean that I have to get heavy and put a message behind it!' Nevertheless, the shooting script for *Dawn of the Dead* (1979) suggests he secretly agrees his films are not without deeper meanings: 'Stores of every type offer gaudy displays of consumer items...at either end of the concourse, like the main altars at each end of a cathedral, stand the mammoth two-storey department stores, great symbols of a consumer society... They appear as an archaeological discovery, revealing the gods and customs of a civilisation now gone.'

Romero is currently said to be writing a fourth *Dead* film under the working title *Dusk of the Dead.* See Filmography, p.240.

RUMBLE FISH

1983 / 94 mins / USA / ▭ Video
Stars: Matt Dillon, Mickey Rourke, Diane Lane,
Dennis Hopper, Diana Scarwid, Vincent Spano
Director: Francis Ford Coppola
Producers: Fred Roos, Doug Claybourne
Script: Francis Ford Coppola, SE Hinton

Rumble Fish (1983) was shot in Tulsa by Francis Ford Coppola, made back-to-back with his other movie *The Outsiders*. Both are based on novels by SE Hinton. Filmed in monochrome with intermittent use of colour, *Rumble Fish* is darker and more atmospheric than *The Outsiders*, with a great moody look, full of clouds, clocks and shadows.

Matt Dillon is Rusty James, a young punk who idolises his older brother, the ageing 'Motorcycle Boy' gang leader, played by Mickey Rourke. But, like the Siamese fighting fish of the title, the brothers cannot exist together. For one to survive, the other must die. The two brothers struggle to break out of the urban jungle, resulting in a new beginning for one but death for the other. A hero not just to his brother but to a whole neighbourhood, Rourke's idol character is completely hip. In fact, Coppola's seminal film has an impressive line-up of American teenage stars acting their hearts out like there was no tomorrow. Unfortunately, for Rourke, there wasn't – he has never bettered his role as the eccentric Motorcycle Boy.

Coppola's stunning adaptation was shot by Stephen Burum and has a musical score by ex-Police drummer Stewart Copeland. However, perhaps because it was black and white, or perhaps because of Dillon's out-of-body experience, the studio sabotaged *Rumble Fish*. Universal released the film at just two cinemas in the United States, before sending it straight to video. Coppola's film suffered a similar fate to Alex Cox's *Repo Man* (1984), another Universal picture made around the same time. Cox blames the failure of both pictures on a regime change: 'The head of the studio Bob Rehme was ousted from his post and a new boss came in. The new guy at Universal had to make the person who previously held his chair look bad. So all the films Universal had made were doomed at that point. Some of them, like *Streets of Fire*, which cost $20 million, did get a release in an attempt to recoup. But cheaper films like *Repo Man* and *Rumble Fish* had to be dumped because they pissed off the executives.'

Despite the failure of *Rumble Fish* at the box office, the film was much talked about and became something of a cult classic.

Memorable dialogue:

Steve: I don't know why someone
hasn't taken a gun to your head
and blown it off.
Motorcycle Boy: Even the most
primitive of societies have an
innate respect for the insane.

THE RUNNING MAN

1987 / 101 mins / USA / (Not currently available)
Stars: Arnold Schwarzenegger, Maria Conchita Alonso,
Richard Dawson, Yaphet Kotto, Jim Brown,
Jesse Ventura
Director: Paul Michael Glaser
Producers: Tim Zinnemann, George Linder
Script: Stephen E de Souza

This sci-fi tale, based on the novel by Stephen King (written under the pseudonym Richard Bachman), provided the perfect early role for Arnold Schwarzenegger and the violent view of an American police state city of 2019 is fairly imaginative.

A futuristic game show offers convicts the chance to go free if they survive a brutal chase through the Los Angeles wasteland. Arnie plays Ben Richards, an innocent man framed for murder, who seizes his one shot at freedom by taking part in the bloodthirsty challenge. And he's determined to win at any cost. Maria Conchita Alonso, Yaphet Kotto and wrestler-turned-politician Jesse Ventura co-star.

The villains have great names. They're called Fireball, Captain Freedom, Dynamo, Buzzsaw and Subzero. One after another, they go into battle and are destroyed. One inspired choice in the casting of this movie was to get the real-life veteran television game-show star Richard Dawson to play himself, hosting the fictional show *The Running Man*. His role forms the basis of a huge industry in-joke. Dawson looks as though he's always had a few to drink, chain-smokes his way through backstage planning sessions, and then appears in front of the cameras as a polite, all-round nice American Mr Sincere. And the audience adore him. In essence, he's exactly like most genuine game show hosts.

Memorable dialogue:

Amber: They're running men. Last season's winners.
Fireball: No. Last season's losers.

Damon Killian: This is television, that's all it is. It has nothing to do with people, it's to do with ratings! For 50 years, we've told them what to eat, what to drink, what to wear... for Christ's sake, Ben, don't you understand? Americans love television. They wean their kids on it. Listen. They love game shows, they love wrestling, they love sports and violence. So what do we do? We give 'em what they want! We're number one, Ben, that's all that counts, believe me. I've been in the business for 30 years.

Ben Richards: I'm not into politics. I'm into survival.

Damon Killian: Hello, this is Killian. Give me the Justice Department, Entertainment Division.

Ben Richards: Killian! I'll be back!
Damon Killian: Only in a rerun.

Damon Killian: You bastard! Drop dead!
Ben Richards: I don't do requests.

RUSSELL, KEN

Director, writer
Born 3 July 1927, Hampshire, UK

As a child, Russell's closest relationship was with his mother, who frequently took him to the cinema after school. At age 10, Russell was given a film projector and his love of movies intensified. Later on, he found a store that rented films by the likes of Fritz Lang and Leni Riefenstahl who were highly influential in developing Russell's dramatic visual flair as a director.

Aged 15, he was sent to Pangborne Nautical College, but would sneak out on weekends to attend the local cinema. A taste of things to come, Russell produced the school's annual concert, replete with cadets in drag and the sounds of big band jazz.

Russell joined the Merchant Navy as sixth officer on a cargo ship bound for the Pacific. However, after World War Two, Russell, now in his early 20s, soon found himself attending dance school. With little success in this he found photography, working as a freelancer for various British magazines. At the same time, he started to make some black and white silent films, one of which called *Amelia* he took to the BBC who were impressed by it. Russell soon landed a job on the BBC arts programme *Monitor* and his film on the British composer Elgar became one of the most popular shows in British television history. After delivering 32 films for *Monitor* and *Omnibus*, he made his first films for theatrical release, *French Dressing* (1963) and *Billion Dollar Brain* (1967). Both received little attention but Russell soon shot to fame with *Women in Love* (1969). Oliver Reed pointed out, 'When I worked with Ken on *Women in Love*, he was starting to go crazy. But in the days when we made TV movies about composers and writers, he was a sane, likeable, television director. Now he's an insane, likeable, film director.'

Ken Russell's best-known film is probably *Women in Love*. But it's not the best, a fact with which the director agrees. He argues it was the film that critics could just about cope with: 'It was literal and had just the right amount of violence and erotic things in it. But I don't think it was as good as the others.'

Russell has often been referred to as 'The enfant terrible of films'. The sexual and religious audacity of movies such as *The Devils* (1971) and *Valentino* (1977) – and the unparalleled irreverence of his biographical accounts of such musical giants as Tchaikovsky, Liszt and Mahler – rarely find favour with the critics. Russell's musicals, *The Boy Friend* (1971) and *Tommy* (1975) found more critical approval than his fact-based movies, but by the early 80s, things got difficult for this feared director and it looked as though he could end up wasting his visual style working for studios as a director-for-hire on projects such as *Crimes of Passion* (1984).

However, thanks to the barrow-full of video cash around in the mid-80s, Russell came back with a variety of cool films. This new way of financing projects allowed Russell toi deliver a variety of weird and interesting films to take our minds off standard 80s fare, including *Gothic* (1986), *Salome's Last Dance* (1988), *The Lair of the White Worm* (1988), *The Rainbow* (1989) and *Whore* (1991). Again, not all won praise from the critics but then Russell wasn't making acceptable movies for the conventional scene.

So who cares if some of Russell's films have been panned as giant turkeys? If they are turkeys, they're the best I've ever tasted. Watching a Ken Russell movie removes the need for mind-altering drugs. Seeing one is a trip in itself. See Filmography, p.240.

A true British maverick: Ken Russell behind the camera

SCANNERS

1981 / 103 mins / Canada / DVD / Video
Stars: Jennifer O'Neill, Stephen Lack, Patrick McGoohan,
Lawrence Dane, Michael Ironside, Charles Shamata,
Adam Ludwig
Director: David Cronenberg
Producer: Claude Heroux
Script: David Cronenberg

In a strange scientific experiment, two men confront each other on a bare stage. They stare intently into space, channelling and focusing their mental energies. The tension mounts. Then it snaps, in an explosion of violence as frightening and spectacular as anything audiences had seen. *Scanners* has begun and the destructive potential of the human mind imaginatively unleashed.

In this fascinating concept from the imagination of David Cronenberg, 'Scanners' are a unique breed of people with one extraordinary talent: they can bend, twist, mutilate and explode other human beings, using only the power of their minds.

For some, the talent remains untapped. They know only that they are 'different'. But one 'Scanner', who calls himself Revok, has set out to band his fellow mutants together through mental murder and intends to use their power to control the world.

Parapsychologist Paul Ruth knows that to stop Revok, he must find a 'Scanner' whose brain waves are equally powerful. He seeks out Cameron Vale, a young derelict desperately roaming the streets of the city, trying to escape strange thoughts and voices that assault him.

Soon, Vale will learn the terrifying depths of his talent. He will send bodies hurling through the air – watch his enemies erupt in flame – and become a mental link in a vast computer network. Finally, he will face Revok in a climactic meeting of master minds that ranks among the movies' all-time shock scenes.

Scanners was budgeted at $4.5 million and was far and away the most expensive film Cronenberg had directed at that point in his career. This allowed him to hire the talents of New York's top special effects people as well as an excellent cast. Conceptually, *Scanners* is also in a different league from his other movies, in that the menace emanates from an intellectual approach.

The special effects in *Scanners* are sensational. What make-up genius Dick Smith achieved in the art of prosthetics had never been done before – or even attempted. In a final key scene, a phone booth – short-circuited from a distant computerised control room – melts and blows up, causing a nearby car and gasoline station to catch fire and explode across a half-mile of countryside. Credit for this, and other stunning special effects, goes to Gary Zeller, whose wizardry created effects for such films as *Dawn of the Dead* (1979) and *The Wiz* (1978). The final scene of *Scanners* looks as real as any war scene, with many of the techniques and devices as those used in *Apocalypse Now* (1979). Howard Shore's pre-synthesiser electronic score is one of his best for Cronenberg, a disquieting low drone repeated in an electronic loop, building up gradually in layers in a crescendo to a screaming cacophony to represent the chaos of the mind.

Back in 1981, both in the UK and North America, *Scanners* benefited from a very clever publicity and promotions campaign. There were special midnight screenings of the film, dubbed 'Midnight Scannings' along with endless 'psychic competition tie-ins' on television and radio. Unfortunately, Cronenberg's mind-blowing trip was followed by a number of dire sequels (1994's *Scanner Cop* and so on).

Memorable dialogue:

Cameron Vale: I'm one of you.
Benjamin Pierce: You're one of me?
You're one of me?

Paul Ruth: Freak of nature born
with a certain form of ESP;
derangement of the synapses which
we call telepathy.

Darryl Revok: We're gonna do this
the Scanner way. I'm gonna suck
your brain dry!

Left to right: Patrick McGoohan, Lawrence Dane and Stephen Lack in David Cronenberg's cerebral thriller Scanners *(1981)*

SCROOGED

1988 / 97 mins / USA / _DVD_ / ▭ Video
Stars: Bill Murray, Karen Allen, John Forsythe,
Bobcat Goldthwait, Carol Kane, Robert Mitchum,
Michael J Pollard, Alfre Woodard
Director: Richard Donner
Producers: Richard Donner, Art Linson
Script: Mitch Glazer, Michael O'Donoghue

Bill Murray stars as Frank Cross, the boss of an American TV station which is planning a live adaptation of Dickens' _Christmas Carol_. Cross hates the Christmas season though and has cut himself off from everybody who loves him. He leads a lonely life, sitting in his high-rise office, watching TV and pouring down the vodka. His idea of an effective promotional ad is one that scares viewers into watching. One viewer (to his delight) actually has a heart attack.

During preparations for the live production of _Scrooge_, the TV executive experiences his own version of the events that haunted Ebenezer Scrooge. Cross is visited by the ghosts of Christmas past, present and future, and shown how miserable he really is, and how unhappy he has made everyone else.

John Glover, Karen Allen, Robert Mitchum and Bobcat Goldthwait add dandy contributions as Murray's helpers, although Carol Kane – sporting angel wings and a good right hook – delivers the comic knockout punch as the Ghost of Christmas Present. Pour an eggnog, too, for whoever had the temerity to cast Buddy Hackett as Scrooge and gymnast Mary Lou Retton as Tiny Tim in the TV special within the movie.

So if you're bored at Christmas, sick of repeats on the TV, you can't go wrong with _Scrooged_. If nothing else, Lee Major's cameo in the opening minutes of the movie are worth the video rental fee.

Memorable dialogue:

Censor: Quite frankly, you can see her nipples.
Frank Cross: I WANT to see her nipples!
Stagehand: You can hardly see the nipples.

Frank Cross: See? And these guys are looking for 'em!

Ghost of Christmas Past: Let's face it, Frank. Garden slugs got more out of life than you.
Frank Cross: Yeah? Name one!

Frank Cross: I never liked a girl well enough to give her 12 sharp knives.

Frank is confronted by the ghost of his old boss
Frank Cross: No, you are a hallucination, brought on by alcohol! Russian Vodka, poisoned by Chernobyl!

James Cross: You know what they say about people who treat other people bad on the way up?
Frank Cross: Yeah, you get to treat 'em bad on the way back down too. It's great, you get two chances to rough 'em up!

[Props man tries to attach antlers to a mouse.]
Props man: I can't get the antlers glued to this little guy. We tried Crazy Glue, but it don't work.
Frank Cross: Did you try staples?

SID AND NANCY

1986 / 111 mins / UK / DVD / Video
Stars: Gary Oldman, Chloe Webb, David Hayman,
Xander Berkley, Drew Schofield, Kathy Burke
Director: Alex Cox
Producer: Eric Fellner
Script: Alex Cox and Abbe Wool

With an intense interest in punk and with his own opinions of how Sid and Nancy became traitors to a revolutionary movement, Alex Cox desperately wanted to tell their story before a Hollywood studio did.

There is no doubt the story of Sid Vicious and Nancy Spungen is one of the most sensational in rock history. On October 12th 1978, as his girlfriend's body lay in a pool of blood on the bathroom floor of Room 101 in New York's Chelsea Hotel, Sid Vicious was in the bedroom, drenched in blood. Four months later, he died of a massive heroin overdose while awaiting trial for Nancy Spungen's murder. He had been released on bail in New York City just 24 hours earlier.

Cox's film achieves great authenticity, charting Sid's introduction to the mayhem world of the Sex Pistols, his obsession with violence, his relationship with Nancy and their decline into heroin-induced paranoia. *Sid and Nancy* has been recognised as the definitive movie on the punk phenomenon, bringing the viewer as close as possible to understanding the ravaged pair. It's not necessary to like punk music to feel sympathy for the tortured, drug-addicted couple or to be carried away by Cox's ability to mine humour out of the most harrowing situations of drink, drugs and sometimes sex.

'I believe most of the stuff about Sid and Nancy is fairly accurate but the early stuff on the punk scene in London is very exaggerated,' admits Cox. 'They didn't have a mosch pit or anything like that, even in London. The dancing would really have been just four or five guys pogoing and listlessly bouncing up and down. Early on in the Britsh punk scene, it wasn't anything like the craziness that developed later on in LA and then in Britain. Also, in the recreation of Malcolm McLaren's publicity stunt with the Pistols on a boat on the River Thames, there's more police and more violence than there was in reality.'

Cox's black, quirky humour, throughout the first half of the film makes us, the viewers, really grow to like this couple. They don't care about anything or anyone – except each other. And, above all else, before we see the horrors of drug addiction really kick in, we see how they have fun, endlessly. There is even a sense of child-like innocence to their ways as they run around like kids having pretend shoot outs on a hotel roof.

On the surface, the lives of Sid and Nancy would seem to bear little relation to our own. But it is the organisation of fantasy that engages us and allows us to identify with characters like Sid and Johnny. The characters are pure rebels and their lifestyles are rebellious acts against banal society and general tedium, which is why we enjoy see Sid shooting all the stuffed shirts in the theatre for the *My Way* video. Loud and adventurous, Sid and Nancy became a walking disaster area, their appearance offering hope that there was more to popular music than air-brushed beauty and glossy videos. Pushing working class opinions into the mainstream, Sid and Nancy, early on, were part of a cultural force to be admired. But, in the end, they spoilt whatever they had with each other and degraded the punk culture by killing themselves with drugs.

In Cox's reconstruction of events, we see how they are each other's downfall. Nancy, an American groupie has arrived in London with little money and a severe drug addiction, and is a bad influence on Sid. He has never done had drugs before meeting Nancy, but within a few days of meeting her, he is as dependent on heroin as she is. Then, within a year of Sid joining the Sex Pistols, his habit starts seriously to affect their performances. During the disastrous American tour, Johnny Rotten breaks up the band.

After recovering from his first overdose, Sid agrees to stay in New York with Nancy who takes on the role of his manager as they try to launch his solo career. They become a fun couple but with no real success. They wind up in the Chelsea Hotel after being rejected by Nancy's family, who are resigned to the fact she can never change

her ways. They try to go straight, but with only each other to turn to, they never manage it. Their lives are reduced to endless amounts of drugs and TV. In the end, they give up. Nancy hounds Sid about ending their lives together, believing it to be the only way out of their living hell. Nine months after the demise of the Sex Pistols, Sid is arrested for stabbing Nancy to death. Whether it was a tragic accident that happened while the pair were too high to get help, no one will ever know, but the film suggests she goaded him to it.

Cox's film ends with an amazing fantasy sequence. As Sid dances with four little black kids on deserted wasteland, in his drugged up brain, Nancy pulls up in a cab. He joins the fantasy by getting into the cab with her. Together, they ride off into the sunset, leaving the black kids boogying to hiphop, the next craze in music history.

Fifteen years on, Cox is still happy with the way the film turned out: 'I'm most impressed by the technical aspects. The art department – Andrew McAlpine in London and Rae Fox and Linda Burbank in the States – is outstanding, particularly Andrew's stage set for *My Way*, and Fox and Burbank's re-creations of the Chelsea Hotel rooms. And the photography of Roger Deakins is extraordinary, particularly the illumination and movement in the final scenes.'

Memorable dialogue:

Record Company Executive:
I wanna job, I wanna job, I wanna
good job,
I wanna job, I wanna job that
pays.
I wanna job, I wanna job, I wanna
real job,
One that satisfies my artistic
needs.

Malcolm: But Sidney's more than a
mere bass player. He's a fabulous
disaster. He's a symbol, a
metaphor, he embodies the dementia
of a nihilistic generation. He's a
fuckin' star.

Opposite: Gary Oldman as Sid in Alex Cox's Sid and Nancy (1986)

SPACEBALLS

1987 / 96 mins / USA / *DVD* / ▭ Video
Stars: Mel Brooks, John Candy, Rick Moranis,
Bill Pulman, Daphne Zuniga
Director: Mel Brooks
Producer: Mel Brooks
Script: Mel Brooks, Thomas Meehan, Ronny Graham

Spaceballs is Mel Brooks' parody of the space adventure genre. Jokes, which come roughly every 30 seconds are all out of the director's borscht-belt post-modern gag book. As well as poking fun at *Star Wars* and *Star Trek* movies, there are plenty of jokes about sequels and movie merchandising: *Spaceballs* dolls, *Spaceballs* breakfast cereal and, of course, the *Spaceballs* flame thrower.

The plot concerns King Roland of the planet Druidia, who is trying to marry his daughter Princess Vespa (Daphne Zuniga) to Prince Valium. But Vespa is kidnapped by the evil race of the Spaceballs. The Spaceballs ask Roland a tremendous ransom: all the air of Druidia (you see, the air of Spaceball had serious pollution problems...). The King decides to offer a generous amount of money to a space rogue, Lone Star, to persuade him to save Vespa.

A cult curiosity because of the in-jokes and references. Brooks' film is mainly a parody of *Star Wars* but there's bits of *Star Trek* and *Planet of the Apes* (1984) thrown in for good measure. The movie also includes some great caricatures including Pizza the Hutt, Brooks as Tony Yogurt, Moranis as Dark Helmet and Candy as Barf the space dog. Brooks' usual spray-gun approach to humour is packed with rib-ticklers and knowing winks to make sure that you catch all the puns.

Memorable dialogue:

Dark Helmet: Raspberry. There's only one man who would dare give me the raspberry: Lone Star!
Dark Helmet: Out of order? FUCK! Even in the future, nothing works!

Lone Star: What the hell was that noise?
Dot Matrix: That was my virgin-alarm. It's programmed to go off before you do!

President Skroob: Why didn't somebody tell me my ass was so big?

Minister: Dearly beloved, we are gathered here today to witness Princess Vespa, daughter of King Roland going right past the altar, heading down the ramp and out the door!

Colonel Sandurz: It's Mega-Maid! She's gone from suck to blow!

Pizza the Hut: Well, if it isn't Lone Star. And his sidekick, Puke.

Yogurt: And may the schwartz be with you!

STRAIGHT TALK

1992 / 87 mins / USA / (Not currently available)
Stars: Dolly Parton, James Woods, Griffin Dunne,
Michael Madsen
Director: Barnet Kellman
Producers: Robert Chartoff, Fred Berner
Script: Craig Bolotin, Patricia Resnick

The honest and straightforward small-town woman Shirlee Kenyon (Parton) has been unlucky in love having married and divorced the same man three times. She's given up on matrimony altogether to live with a boyfriend (Michael Madsen) who is completely indifferent to her, so one day she ups and goes. She gets into her car and heads north to the big city of Chicago. She checks into a fleabag hotel, goes looking for work and talks herself into a position as a receptionist at a radio station.

Through a misunderstanding at the station, she is mistaken for the newly hired advice personality, put on the air and is an instant hit. It's clear she is a natural and she is hired on the spot. With her homespun wit and down-to-earth advice, Shirlee immediately wins the listeners' hearts, but causes hilarious confusion for her ratings-conscious boss.

But the station insists she call herself Doctor and as her popularity grows a local *Chicago Sun-Times* reporter (Woods) starts digging for the truth. Problem is, the more he is around her the more he fancies her. His investigation leads him down South to Dolly's hometown where he learns the truth. But by this time, he's head over heels!

The best scenes in the movie are the ones where the Parton character simply speaks her mind. Her advice is sound, earthy and blunt. She gives it on the air and off. Soon she's such a star that she can move on up into her own high-rise apartment. It's the advice-spilling parts of the movie which have been reclaimed by a faithful gay audience (Parton is a gay icon).

Memorable dialogue:

Dr Shirlee Kenyon: Get down off the cross, honey. Somebody needs the wood.

Dr Shirlee Kenyon: Sometimes you just have to toot your own horn. Otherwise, nobody'll know you're a-coming.

Previous page: Dolly Parton woos the workers on the streets of Chicago in Straight Talk *(1992)*

STRAIGHT TO HELL

1987 / 86 mins / UK / DVD / Video
Stars: Sy Richardson, Joe Strummer,
Dick Rude, Courtney Love, Zander Schloss,
Elvis Costello, Kathy Burke
Director: Alex Cox
Producer: Eric Fellner
Script: Alex Cox, Dick Rude

Straight to Hell has a cast that includes the former lead singer of The Clash, Joe Strummer, rebellious punk outfit, The Pogues, and a then-unknown Courtney Love. The film's inspiration was found by Cox during promotional work for *Sid and Nancy* (1986) at the Cannes Film Festival. Returning to his hotel room, Cox found Strummer with Dick Rude and cameraman Tom Richmond all looking dazed and confused after a protracted drinking session. This image stuck in his mind and formed the starting point for his demented Western. 'I remember all of us saying, 'Fuck it! Let's just go and make a film', recalls producer Eric Fellner. 'Why should we spend years writing it, financing and developing it?' Eventually, Cox wrote the script with Dick Rude, over three days, in an LA hotel. The film was made for Island Pictures, a division of the record company, and was shot over just four weeks in August 1986. But the month in Spain wasn't entirely an easy ride. The funding from Island ($1 million) ran out half way through filming and Eric Fellner ended up financing the rest of the shoot on traveller's cheques and credit cards.

The plot concerns money. After a botched bank robbery, a band of thieves – surly Norwood (Sy Richardson), Willy (Dick Rude) and Simms (Joe Strummer) – head off into the desert. They make their getaway with Velma (Courtney Love), Norwood's girlfriend, who is pregnant with his child. In the middle of the desert, their Honda breaks down and the bumbling foursome take refuge in Blanco Town, which is run by a murderous, incestuous clan of trigger-happy coffee addicts known as the MacMahons, played by The Pogues.

After her small role in *Sid and Nancy*, this was Courtney Love's first leading role. She's very impressive and her character, Velma, is like a tougher version of Nancy Spungen – or, as Love described the part, 'a white-trash pregnant bitch, some weird hillbilly from an incestuous background who's fascinated with charms and magic'.

The cast of *Straight to Hell* is also littered with an array of hip celebrity cameos from such punk luminaries as Elvis Costello (as a coffee-dispensing butler), Grace Jones, Jim Jarmusch and Dennis Hopper, whose character carries a briefcase of automatic weapons and whose name, coincidentally, is the same as the German industrial agent, IG Farben.

Another highlight is the wickedly funny Kathy Burke who plays Sabrina: 'It was great fun', says Burke. 'Cox was nuts on *Straight to Hell*, a complete and utter egomaniac. But the pop stars thought it was great because the set was so anarchic'.

Like Cox's *Repo Man* (1984) and *Sid and Nancy*, *Straight to Hell* has a top soundtrack, with almost everyone in the film having a role in the music. One great performance is that of Fox Harris singing 'Delilah', accompanied by Elvis Costello.

Straight to Hell is wild, enormously grotesque and just plain over-the-top madness. It was way ahead of its time and far too gruesome a comedy for the mid-80s. But after hits like *Reservoir Dogs* (1992), people are starting to watch this weird Western again, thanks to video and DVD re-releases. If you are prepared to unleash these edge-of-sanity frolics on your poor unsuspecting brain, welcome to Cox Country.

Memorable dialogue:

Norwood: If it wasn't for my son in that belly there, I'd drop her like a sack o' potatoes!

Willy: There ain't no rooms!

Preacher: You've been spending too much money on coffee.

Left to right: Joe Strummer, Sy Richardson, Dick Rude in Alex Cox's deranged western Straight to Hell *(1987)*

STRANGE DAYS

1995 / 139 mins / USA / *DVD* / ▭ Video
Stars: Ralph Fiennes, Angela Bassett, Juliette Lewis,
Tom Sizemore, Michael Wincott, Vincent D'Onofrio,
Glenn Plummer
Director: Kathryn Bigelow
Producers: James Cameron, Steven Charles Jaffe
Script: James Cameron, James Cocks

LA., December 30th 1999. The eve of the Millennium. Worldwide tension mounts during the final hours of the century as humanity holds its breath for the odometer to click over to triple zeros. Is it the end of the world or the beginning of a new one?

Lenny (Ralph Fiennes) trades in 'squids': snippets of peoples lives recorded onto Minidisc. His clients can experience all the thrills of being, say, an armed robber without leaving the safety of their own bullet-proof limos. Lenny is the Magic Man, the Santa Claus of the Subconscious. If it can be recorded, it can be experienced: violence, sex, thrills of any kind. 'You can say it, even think it, you can have it', he tells his clients. But as the clock ticks, Lenny finds himself in a maze of paranoia, deception and murder. A prostitute who does 'wire work' for Lenny is killed and he receives a wire of her rape and murder. The clip leads him towards a secret so lethal that it may bring the entire city down in flames, but Lenny's immediate concern is to protect his ex-girlfriend Faith (Juliette Lewis), an up-and-coming singer and the greatest obsession in his life. He enlists the help of the only two friends he has – Mace (Angela Bassett), a security agent-cum-chauffeuse whose steely resolve is the still centre of Lenny's chaotic world, and the dependable and likeable Max (Tom Sizemore), another former cop.

Their extraordinary journey together reaches its climax at the party of the century on the streets of LA as racial tensions and the forces of violence reach flash point. The visuals are cool with some great point-of-view scenes, and it's not too overblown with special effects (for a film that James Cameron controlled).

Strange Days did three things to ensure its cult status. It delivered a hero in the noir tradition. It used a unique vocabulary. Listen out for 'tapehead', 'jacking in' and the movie's spin on 'playback', all reclaimed by fans everywhere. And it had a cool soundtrack. Punk band

Skunk Anansie performs, as does Lewis in a cover of PJ Harvey's 'Rid of Me'. The soundtrack also features Tricky, Deep Forest, Strange Fruit and Peter Gabriel.

Memorable dialogue:

Max: Cheer up. The world's about to end in 10 minutes anyway.

Tick: One man's mundane and boring existence is another man's Technicolor.

Lenny: I am the magic man. I am your link to the subconscious. I have what you want. I can get you what you can't have.

Mace: Memories are meant to fade. They're designed that way for a reason.

Philo: Paranoia is reality seen on a finer scale.

Lenny: His ass is so tight, when he farts only dogs can hear it.

Max: The issue is not whether you are paranoid, look around you Lenny, the issue is whether you are paranoid enough.

Philo: The only time a whore should open her mouth is when she is giving head.

Lenny Nero: Right now his frontal

Ralph Fiennes in a scene from Strange Days *(1995)*

lobes are like two runny eggs.
Max: You put that thing on the 11
o'clock news and by midnight
you'll have the biggest riot in
history. They'll see the smoke
from Canada.

SUMMER OF SAM

1999 / 141 mins / USA / DVD / ▣ Video
Stars: John Leguizamo, Mira Sorvino, Jennifer Esposito,
Adrien Brody, Michael Rispoli, Bebe Neuwirth,
Saverio Guerra, Patti LuPone
Director: Spike Lee
Producers: John Kilik, Spike Lee
Script: Victor Colicchio, Michael Imperioli, Spike Lee

It's 1977, the summer to melt in and New York is in meltdown. The 'Son of Sam' serial killer, David Berkowitz is on the prowl, killing couples in cars. No one knows who he is, so a group of Italian–American friends start getting paranoid about each other.

One of the neighbourhood regulars thinks Son of Sam is in fact Reggie Jackson (the killer uses a .44 handgun; Jackson's number is 44). The local priest is also a suspect; after all, he lives alone and can come and go as he wants.

All of the events of the infamous summer are seen mostly through the eyes of Vinny, a philandering Bronx hairdresser. Until that summer, he sees himself as king of the old neighbourhood – he's a disco god, drives a nice car, has the respect of his old buddies and is married to a beautiful woman who seemingly doesn't know of his affairs. But then his life changes for good.

Vinny believes he had a near-fatal run-in with the Son of Sam while 'parked' with his wife's cousin. Then, his best friend Ritchie returns to the old neighbourhood as, of all things, a punk rocker. As the events of that summer slowly unfold, Vinny ultimately loses his wife, his job and the respect of his old buddies. The movie concludes with Vinny's betrayal of Ritchie, whom the other neighbourhood buddies suspect is the Son of Sam.

Director Spike Lee's serial-killer film isn't about the killer so much as the volatile mood he generates in a close-knit community. Taut viewing indeed, but Lee knows just how to lace it with daring wit, neat character studies and intense situations.

The bulk of this film is devoted to covering the Italian Community in the Bronx. This is where the cult appeal lies. As with most Lee films, a minority group (or subculture, counterculture clan) is detailed and not surprisingly, minority groups are drawn to these films. Lee has recently been quoted as saying 'I've been blessed with the opportunity to express the views of black people who otherwise don't have access to power and the media. I have to take advantage of that while I am still bankable.'

Memorable dialogue:

Ritchie: Evil spelled backwards is live!

The Dog: Kill. Kill. Kill.

Dionna: Can you tell me what he likes? Because I want to make him happy but I don't think he is.
Ruby: You want me to tell you how to fuck your husband?
Dionna: Yeah.

Vinnie: I can't be a whore! I'm a man!

Midnight: Damn, girl, you make me wish I was a lesbian.

JOHN**LEGUIZAMO** ADRIEN**BRODY** MIRA**SORVINO** JENNIFER**ESPOSITO**

NYC '77. Disco in the clubs. Panic in the streets.

SOS
SUMMER OF SAM

The summer of '77 was a killer...

A **40 ACRES** AND A **MULE**
FILMWORKS PRODUCTION
A **SPIKE LEE** JOINT

SWEET SMELL OF SUCCESS

1957 / 95 mins / USA / 📼 Video
Stars: Burt Lancaster, Tony Curtis, Susan Harrison,
Martin Milner, Sam Levene, Barbara Nichols,
Jeff Donnell
Director: Alexander Mackendrick
Producer: James Hill
Script: Clifford Odets, Ernest Lehman

Sidney Falco (Tony Curtis) is a young Broadway hustler whose livelihood depends on placing publicity items for his clients in the New York press. Most important of all gossip journalists is the forbiddingly powerful JJ Hunsecker (Burt Lancaster), a Walter Winchell-styled reporter who has a nationwide readership, and Sidney craving coverage for his clients in Hunsecker's columns.

Hunsecker has a sister (Susan Harrison) who is in love with jazz musician Steve Dallas (Martin Milner) and JJ is eager to break up this romance in order to secure his own perverse relationship with her. Hunsecker manages to pressurise the eager Sidney into destroying this affair: if he fails, he will lose all access to the column. Falco therefore plants lies about Dallas and the ploy works temporarily. But Hunsecker wants Dallas out of Susan's life for good and he promises Sidney total column access if he succeeds. Sidney, without a scruple, attempts JJ's damnable instructions.

Neon lights and shiny street-surfaces convey the seamy side of downtown Manhattan in this staggeringly fine movie about the venality of these denizens of New York. Both satirical and diamond-hard, this masterly and thoroughly entertaining film took its time achieving classic status.

Sweet Smell of Success was photographed by one of Hollywood's greatest cameramen, James Wong Howe; written by Clifford Odets and Ernest Lehman (1955's *The Big Knife*) and directed by Alexander Mackendrick. Born in Boston, Massachusetts, but educated in Scotland, Mackendrick directed some of the finest Ealing Comedies, including *Whisky Galore* (1949) and *The Ladykillers* (1955). Here, he makes great use of the sleazy Manhattan nightspot locations. But precisely because of this bleakness, the film was a box-office flop and is still virtually unknown in the USA. Too cynical for 1957, its racy dialogue gradually appealed over subsequent decades, and, although always critically admired, the movie did not really build up a following until relatively recently.

The themes are still appallingly relevant today in our own world of PR and entertainment journalism, notoriously dominated by crafty agents who make hacks jump through hoops for the latest showbiz angle on the latest shiny star.

Memorable dialogue:

JJ Hunsecker: I'd hate to take a bite out of you. You're a cookie full of arsenic.

[Holding an unlit cigarette]
JJ Hunsecker: Match me, Sidney.

Sidney Falco: Watch me run a 50-yard dash with my legs cut off!

Susan Hunsecker: Someday I'd like to look into your clever little mind and see what you're really thinking.

Steve: It's a dirty job, but I pay clean money for it.

JJ Hunsecker: You're dead, son, you're just not buried!

JJ Hunsecker: President? My big toe would make a better President!

Rita: Here's mud in your column!

Steve: Mr Hunsecker, you've got more twists than a barrel of pretzels!

Sidney Falco: The cat's in the bag and the bag's in the river.

SWINGERS

1996 / 96 mins / USA / DVD / ▭ Video
Stars: Jon Favreau, Vince Vaughn, Ron Livingston,
Patrick Van Horn, Alex Desert, Heather Graham
Director: Doug Liman
Producers: Victor Simpkins
Script: Jon Favreau

This is a story about Mike, a comedian who left his girl in New York when he came to LA to be a star. It's been six months since his girlfriend dumped him and he can't seem to get over it. So, his friends, including Trent (Jon Favreau) and try and get him back on the social scene and forget about his six-year relationship. A few funny digs at life in LA add appeal to this contemporary urban tale, a kind of hip update of *American Graffiti* (1973). The lead actor Jon Favreau wrote the screenplay and director Liman also shot it.

Trent is the main expert on the LA dating scene, littering his advice with phrases such as 'beautiful babies' and 'you're so money'. It's Trent's personal mission to break Mike away from his heartache. At one point, Trent takes him aside and gives him a pep talk: 'I don't want you to be like the guy in the PG-13 movie, you know, the one everybody's REALLY hoping makes it happen. I want you to be like the guy in the rated R movie, the guy you're not too sure about, you're not sure where he's coming from, you don't know what to think.'

By the end, Mike is making good progress and in the final sequence, as he tries to tell Trent his sublime moment of clarity, Trent interrupts him to flirt with a girl at the far end of the bar. Mike simply gazes out of the window, with a very clever smile. Cue end titles.

This is one of those movies that mentions other landmark movies (in this case 1992's *Reservoir Dogs*, 1990's *Goodfellas* and 1995's *Casino*). Let's remember, these guys are trying to make it big in LA. So they're constantly talking about movies. They go on about the kitchen follow-though shot in *Goodfellas* and the slow-motion opener to *Reservoir Dogs*. One comments 'you gotta be nuts to shoot in a casino'. But Doug Liman cleverly has these cinematic moments play out later in his own film. Early on in the movie, Trent and Mike are at a casino in Las Vegas, following a poker game, the whole gang walk to their cars in slow-motion and near the end, Trent, Mike and Sue go out, entering a club through the kitchen.

There were no real stars in this film and it was made for just $200,000. No explosions and no car chases. Nevertheless, it made $4 million at the box office. Peanuts compared with *Titanic* (*Swingers* cost a 100 times less than that movie to make) but great for a low-budget film with no TV or radio spots to help it in the marketplace. *Swingers* was one of the best films to come out of 1996, full of wit and charisma.

Memorable dialogue:

Trent: Look at this, OK? I want you to remember this face. This is the guy behind the guy behind the guy.

Mike: Trent, the beautiful babies don't work the midnight to six shift on a Wednesday. This is like the skank shift.

Mike: That was so fucking money. That was like the Jedi mind-shit.

Trent: Um, a malt Glen Garry for me and my friend here. And if you tell that bartender to go extra easy on the water, this 50 cent piece has your name on it.

Trent: Hey! What're you kicking me for? You want me to ask? All right, I'll ask! Ma'am, where do the high-school girls hang out in this town?

Trent: All I do is stare at their mouths and wrinkle my nose, and I turn out to be a sweetheart.

get a n

ghtlife.

Mid-90s cool: Jon Favreau in the poster for Swingers (1996)

TAPEHEADS

1988 / 93 mins / USA / (Not currently available) / *DVD*
Stars: John Cusack, Tim Robbins, Mary Crosby,
Clu Gulager, Katy Boyer, Jessica Walter
Director: Bill Fishman
Producers: Michael Nesmith, Peter McCarthy
Script: Bill Fishman, Peter McCarthy,
James Herzfeld, Ryan Rowe

Bill Fishman's offbeat alternative comedy *Tapeheads* is considered one of the funniest cult movies of all time. In his book *The 100 Best Films to Rent You've Never Heard Of*, David N Meyer went as far as saying that he worships 'at the alter of Fishman'.

The film stars John Cusack and Tim Robbins as Ivan Alexeev and Josh Tager, two bored security guards who get their kicks by messing around with the closed circuit television. As a result, they find themselves unemployed and instead decide to try and make it in the world of music video. Calling themselves The Video Aces, the pair become producers of rock videos with attitude but have to start with a chicken and waffle commercial, being paid in buckets of fried chicken!

Then they end up working in downtown LA for Mo Fuzz (*Soultrain*'s Don Cornelius), a totally insincere producer willing to give them a chance if they'll work on spec (no money) and whose helpful advice is that 'there's only one thing that adds real production value...tits and ass!'

At first, Ivan and Josh have to get by directing 'living wills', funerals and weddings. Later, one of their proper music promos gets mixed up with one of these 'living wills' but ends up becoming a hit and brings the two wannabes the real fame and recognition they so desperately crave. The dynamic duo are then hired to produce a live televised concert by 'Menudo' which is to be watched by 30 million people around the world. 'Let's get into trouble, baby!'

The film also features some really cool cameo appearances by the likes of Weird Al Yankovic, Ted Nugent, Bobcat Goldthwait, Mike Nesmith, Lyle Alzado and Martha Quinn. The soundtrack features real bands such as Fishbone, the Dead Kennedys and Devo as well as the fictitious Swanky Modes (Junior Walker and Sam Moore) and the Blender Children.

As the mild-mannered Josh, Robbins is just right for the role. Cusack is equally impressive as the smarmy

swindler Ivan, a man he describes as someone with 'very little talent, very little intelligence and lots of ambition. I really get to lower myself into the slime on this one'.

As well as appearing in 80s teen movies such as *Class* (1983) and *One Crazy Summer* (1986), Cusack had already worked with Robbins on *Say Anything* (1989). Both actors found themselves on the edge of the whole Brat Pack phenomenon, appearing in movies where losing one's virginity was a basic requirement. *Tapeheads* was probably the best of all the 80s teen comedies they starred in and, after legal complications resulted in a limited theatrical release, Fishman's film quickly became a much sought after video gem. He followed that film with *Car 54, Where Are You* (1994) which starred Fran Drescher and Rosie O'Donnell and also co-produced the Mario Van Peebles cult western *Posse* (1993).

Back in 1989, the series of press interviews during the publicity for *Tapeheads* can't have helped the film's theatrical life, despite adding another layer of mayhem to Fishman's movie. Robbins and Cusack's oddball behaviour led to a *USA Today* reporter saying he would never interview them again. *Good Morning America* even refused to air an interview, with a spokesman complaining: 'They were obnoxious. The interview was horrible.'

The week of the *Good Morning America* interview there were press reports about Tim Robbins' 'secret' dates with Susan Sarandon and Robbins was adamant he didn't want to talk about his personal life, instructing Joan Lunden not to mention the rumours. 'The rumours were obviously true', says Fishman, 'but Tim didn't want everyone talking about it. So when the show began and Joan's opening question was about his relationship with Susan Sarandon, Tim just really got worked up and made some rather pointed remarks about her and the press. But we all thought it was funny and anarchistic in a Johnny Rotten sort of way. The producers couldn't see the funny side and refused to air it.'

LET *TAPEHEADS* TAKE YOU BACK TO THE AWESOME '80s!

"LET'S GET INTO TROUBLE, BABY!"

JOHN CUSACK   TIM ROBBINS

TAPEHEADS

A funny movie with music.

FIRST TIME EVER ON DVD

199

TAPEHEADS (cont.)

At this point, to any viewers with a cult sensibility the film was beginning to retain great interest. However, the behaviour of Cusack and Robbins helped make sure *Tapeheads* was prevented from a decent run in the cinemas and with very little publicity and a limited release, the film understandably developed its reputation as one of the best comedy films hardly ever seen. In this case, the movie became a cult favourite not simply because of its unique characters and dialogue, but the difficulty in obtaining the title. However, with a video and DVD release in the US through Anchor Bay Entertainment, Fishman's movie is set to become popular with a whole new generation.

Memorable dialogue

Ivan: You've got no ambition! You need what I've got brother.
Josh: Herpes?

Norman Mart: Roses are red. Violets are blue. The Russians have satellite laser weapons. Why can't we too?

THE TERMINATOR

1984 / 108 mins / USA / DVD / ▢ Video
Stars: Arnold Schwarzenegger, Michael Biehn,
Linda Hamilton, Paul Winfield, Lance Henriksen,
Rick Rossovich, Bess Motta
Director: James Cameron
Producer: Gale Anne Hurd
Script: James Cameron, Gale Anne Herd

The story opens in a post-holocaust nightmare, AD 2029, where brainy machines have crushed most of the human populace. From that point, Arnold Schwarzenegger as a cyborg programmed for violence is sent back to the present to kill a young woman named Sarah Connor (Linda Hamilton) whose unborn son is destined to be a great freedom fighter.

With the ability to reconstruct any part of its body maimed or destroyed, the Terminator seems unstoppable. But a human survivor from the bleak future (Michael Biehn) also goes back in time to 1984 in an attempt to save Sarah and the future.

Arnold Schwarzenegger performs in a career-shaping role that led to a string of big-budget sci-fi action films for the rest of the 80s and into the 90s: *Commando* (1985), *Raw Deal* (1986), *Predator* (1987), *The Running Man* (1987), *Red Heat* (1988), *Total Recall* (1990), *Terminator 2: Judgment Day* (1992), *True Lies* (1994) and *Eraser* (1996). Likewise, Cameron's career was launched by the success of this film.

The Terminator was a classic genre film and developed a strong cult interest because (a) it wasn't a big budget movie and (b) despite this, the special effects were great, especially for the early '80s. It had great texture and action. In contrast, the sequel, T2, was made to be a blockbuster. *The Terminator* cost $6 million to make. Its sequel cost around $100 million, more than half of which went towards paying the star and the film's director.

Memorable dialogue:

Terminator: Your clothes, give them to me.

Kyle: I came across time for you Sarah. I love you and I always have.

Kyle: Come with me if you want to live!

Kyle: That Terminator is out there. It can't be bargained with. It can't be reasoned with. It doesn't feel pity, or remorse, or fear. And it absolutely will not stop, ever, until you are dead!

Terminator: I'll be back!

Superintendent: Hey, buddy, you got a dead cat in there or what?
Terminator: Fuck you, asshole.

Sarah Connor: You're terminated, fucker.

Lieutenant Traxler: How do I look?
Detective Vuckovitch: Like shit, boss.

Arnold Schwarzenegger in The Terminator *(1984), which re-launched his career after the* Conan The Barbarian *films*

THE TEXAS CHAINSAW MASSACRE

1974 / 83 mins / USA / DVD / Video
Stars: Marilyn Burns, Allen Danziger, Paul A Partain,
William Vail, Teri McMinn, Gunnar Hansen
Director: Tobe Hooper
Producer: Tobe Hooper
Script: Kim Henkel, Tobe Hooper

Shot in Texas by a then-unknown director Tobe Hooper, *The Texas Chainsaw Massacre* seemed to come out of nowhere. In fact, like a lot of the American horror films of that era – particularly the work of Romero, Carpenter and Craven – they emerged in response to the turbulence of the 60s and 70s, when Americans were out of work and the gas stations out of gas. Released to a shocked public, *Chainsaw* went on to attract rave reviews at Cannes and earn a place in the permanent collection of the Museum of Modern Art in New York.

The script by Hooper and Kim Henkel is a take-off on the same incident that inspired Robert Bloch's novel (and later Alfred Hitchcock's film) *Psycho* (1960). The plot follows a group of travellers who run into trouble in rural Texas. En route to visit their grandfather's grave (which has apparently been ritualistically desecrated), five teenagers drive past a slaughterhouse, pick up (and quickly drop) a sinister hitch-hiker, eat some delicious home-cured meat at a roadside gas station, before ending up at the old family home...where they're plunged into a never-ending nightmare as they meet a family of cannibals who have a high-powered approach to preparing meals. One by one, they wander into the murderous clutches of Leatherface and his trusty chainsaw. Before you know it, they're hung up on hooks to tenderise.

Texas Chainsaw Massacre is the quintessential horror movie of all time. Hooper believes it to be a kind of fairy tale: 'I intended to stylise it like a Grimm's fairy tale', he says. 'You're in some kind of archetype the moment you start seeing it. It's almost like Hansel and Gretel: you pick up the bread crumbs and one person continues to follow the other'.

Along with *Night of the Living Dead* (1968) and *The Exorcist* (1973), Hooper's film helped establish the modern era of horror and many slasher movies of the late 70s and early 80s tried to cash in its success. The first sequel took 12 years to reach the screen.

Memorable dialogue:

Franklin: If I have any more fun today, I don't think I can take it!

Franklin: They just shoot a bullet in their head and then retract it. It's just BOOM-shht-BOOM-shht.
Sally: Franklin, I like meat, please change the subject!

Franklin: I think we just picked up Dracula.

Old Man: There's just some things in life you got to do. Don't mean you have to like it.

Old Man: Those girls... those girls don't wanna go messin' round no old house!

THAT'LL BE THE DAY

1973 / 91 mins / UK / ▭ Video
Stars: David Essex, Rosemary Leach, Ringo Starr,
James Booth, Billy Fury, Keith Moon
Director: Claude Whatham
Producers: David Puttnam, Sanford Lieberson
Script: Ray Connolly

That'll Be the Day is like a British *American Graffiti* (1973) in that it sets out to define England in the late 50s, during the birth of rock 'n' roll, when American chart music began to take hold on the country's youth. David Essex, in his first starring role, plays the laconic hero Jim Maclaine, a bright but restless young boy who drops out of school to work in a seaside amusement park. With the help of his new pal Mike (Ringo Starr), he soon enters a world of cheap sex and petty crime. But when the magic is over and Jim has to return to his former grey, mundane working-class life at home, he must make some difficult choices. The movie ends with Maclaine dumping his young wife and child (as his Second World War-bound father had done at the movie's start) to buy a guitar in a pawn shop. The movie uses the gritty kitchen-sink realism that was popular in British films at the time and captures those uneasy years of youth when school is over but adulthood hasn't really kicked in yet. The movie launched Esssex's recording career – and includes the classic 'Rock On', which was his only US hit

Because *That'll Be The Day* has a Beatle in it, it has enjoyed some cult status, much like John Lennon's turn in *How I Won The War* (1967). The sequel is called *Stardust* (1974), which takes the story into the 60s and crystalises the character's resemblance to John Lennon, detailing Maclaine's rise to fame and subsequent bombing out in the 70s. Keith Moon, as a slightly crazed drummer, appears in both movies.

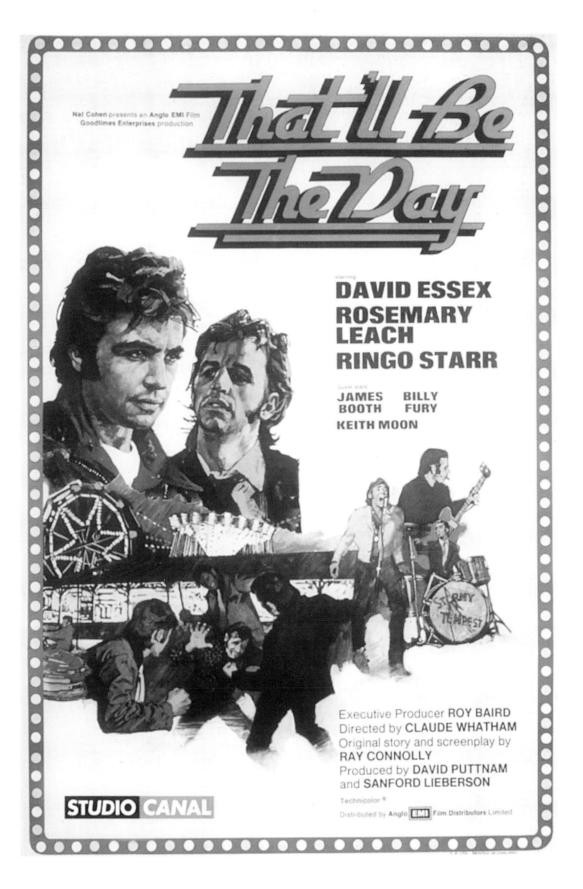

Nat Cohen presents an Anglo EMI Film
Goodtimes Enterprises production

That'll Be The Day

starring

DAVID ESSEX
ROSEMARY LEACH
RINGO STARR

Guest stars
JAMES BOOTH   **BILLY FURY**
KEITH MOON

Executive Producer ROY BAIRD
Directed by CLAUDE WHATHAM
Original story and screenplay by
RAY CONNOLLY
Produced by DAVID PUTTNAM
and SANFORD LIEBERSON

Technicolor ®

Distributed by Anglo EMI Film Distributors Limited

STUDIO CANAL

205

THIS ISLAND EARTH

1955 / 86 mins / USA / 🖵 Video
Stars: Jeff Morrow, Faith Domergue, Rex Reason,
Lance Fuller, Russell Johnson, Douglas Spencer,
Robert Nichols, Karl L Lindt
Director: Joseph Newman
Producer: William Alland
Script: Franklin Cen, Edward G O'Callaghan

This Island Earth tells the tale of test pilot and atomic scientist Dr Cal Meacham (Rex Reason, 1957's *Band of Angels*) who is recruited by a mysterious group of scientists led by the strange, white-haired Exeter (Jeff Morrow, 1956's *The Creature Walks Among Us*). Meacham soon grows suspicious of these 'scientists' and together with fellow atomic researcher Dr Ruth Adams (Faith Domergue, 1974's *House of the Seven Corpses*) soon discovers the shocking truth: Exeter is an alien and he wants Meacham and Adams to help his people survive an interplanetary war!

This movie is considered to be a worthy classic by many and, as with many science-fiction flicks of the 50s, *This Island Earth* takes the exciting possibilities of atomic power and the fears generated by the burgeoning Cold War as the themes that lie beneath the 'aliens from another planet visit Earth' story.

The most memorable image is that of the Mut-Ant, the alien creature that looks like a cross between a lumbering human and, well, an ant. There are also the 'highly advanced' aliens who look just like humans save for their minimalist fashion sense and their huge foreheads. The flying saucers are pretty good too. Shame about the terrible dubbing of Dr Meacham's voice.

Memorable dialogue:

Dr Ruth Adams: It's only Neutron. We call him that because he's so positive.

Dr Cal Meacham: You boys like to call this the pushbutton age. It isn't, not yet. Not until we can team up atomic energy with electronics. Then we'll have the horses as well as the cart.

Joe Wilson: Half an hour late. That's my boss – the only guy in the world who can travel by jet and still be late.

The Monitor: It is indeed typical that you Earth people refuse to believe in the superiority of any world but your own. Children looking into a magnifying glass, imagining the image you see is the image of your true size.
Dr Cal Meacham: Our true size is the size of our God!

Dr Ruth Adams: My mind is my own, and nobody's going to change it! I'm not going into that room!

THIS IS SPINAL TAP

1984 / 82 mins / USA / *DVD* / ▭ Video
Stars: Rob Reiner, Michael McKean, Christopher Guest,
Harry Shearer, RJ Parnell, David Kaff
Director: Rob Reiner
Producer: Karen Murphy
Script: Christopher Guest, Michael McKean,
Harry Shearer, Rob Reiner

This deadpan, spoof rockumentary follows the failing fortunes of the loudest rock band in the world, Spinal Tap. Complete with a never-ending stream of expiring drummers, character clashes and flashbacks to the early days of the band, this is a well-observed, well-written film.

Shot in faux cinema verité with director Rob Reiner as fictional film-maker Marti DiBergi, the film lampoons just about every rock 'n' roll cliché (not to mention every rockumentary cliché) in the book as it follows these fallen rock idols from one disastrous gig to the next. During their tour, the band get lost in the tunnels underneath a stadium concert site, one of them manages to get stuck in a malfunctioning stage prop, and all of them are thoroughly embarrassed when a supposedly full-sized version of the rocks at Stonehenge arrives at barely knee-height.

Scenes of the tour's descent from desperation into total collapse are interspersed with interviews in which the band members delightfully prattle on inanely about the none-too-illustrious history and dubious vision of Spinal Tap. *This is Spinal Tap* is a striking and acutely hysterical directorial debut for Reiner and a deserved cult classic.

The performances are understated and highly accomplished and you are so convinced by the main characters that you hardly notice the endless array of cameos by wonderful comic character actors such as Angelica Huston, Fran Drescher, Billy Crystal, Bruno Kirby and, most notably, Paul Shaffer in a turn as a Chicago promo man.

Memorable dialogue:

Derek Smalls: It's like fire and ice, basically. I feel my role in the band is to be somewhere in the middle of that, kind of like lukewarm water.

Ian Faith: Certainly, in the topsy-turvy world of heavy rock, having a good solid piece of wood in your hand is often useful.

Nigel Tufnel: Well, this piece is called Lick My Love Pump.

[Asked to write his own epitaph]
David St Hubbins: Here lies David St Hubbins and why not?

Mick Shrimpton: As long as there's, you know, sex and drugs, I can do without the rock 'n' roll.

[Reading a review of Spinal Tap's latest album]
Marti DiBergi: This pretentious ponderous collection of religious rock psalms is enough to prompt the question, 'What day did the Lord create Spinal Tap, and couldn't he have rested on that day too?'

David St Hubbins: Dozens of people spontaneously combust each year. It's just not really widely reported.

[Reading a review of the album *Shark Sandwich*]
Marti DiBergi: Two words: shit sandwich.

207

THREE BUSINESSMEN

1998 / 83 mins / USA / *DVD* / 💾 Video
Stars: Miguel Sandoval, Robert Wisdom, Alex Cox,
Isabel Ampudia, Andrew Schofield, Adrian Kai,
John McMartin, Christine Colvin, Adrian Henri
Director: Alex Cox
Producer: Tod Davies
Script: Tod Davies

After the much publicised dispute with Terry Gilliam over writing credits for *Fear and Loathing* (1998), Cox and Davies set up their own production company. *Three Businessmen* was the first film they made through this new venture and came about after they were approached by Wim Kayzer for a contribution to his Dutch TV series on the theme of beauty and consolation. They were given carte blanche, with control over all aspects of the production: the script, the casting, the locations and the crew. Funding came from VPRO television in Holland, Film Funds Rotterdam and Exterminating Angel.

Three Businessmen is the story of Bennie (Cox) and Frank (Miguel Sandoval), two independent businessmen, who meet in the abandoned restaurant of an hotel in Liverpool. Unable to find food there, they decide to set off in search of an evening meal in the famous British city. But their journey (always via public transport) takes them from Liverpool to Rotterdam, Hong Kong, Tokyo and the desert, even though they're unaware they've ever left England.

Cox's film conveys that familiar feeling of waking up in a hotel room and not knowing where you are, as all around you looks the same – the Hilton hotel logo, the McDonald's sign, the advertisement for Diet Coke or Pizza Hut or Pokemon. *Three Businessmen* is about the subtle dangers of globalisation, a vision of a cold, impersonal world created by international corporate capitalism.

Bennie and Frank are holding on by their fingernails, trying to keep their own centre. All they can do is talk gibberish, about safe subjects such as computers and cars. This, according to Cox, is one of the reasons why the characters don't realise where they are: 'They know if they talk about computers, nobody will be offended. Bennie and Frank never really say anything that can provoke a strong reaction in the other character because we don't want to; we just want to get by. The last thing we want to do is have an argument or really address anything. At one point, Bennie wants to talk about sex, but Frank doesn't want to talk about that. We have so much to hide and so much to conceal. We are so withdrawn and protected'.

With the late introduction of a third businessman, Leroy (Robert Wisdom), the film culminates in an odd take on the story of the Three Wise Men, with all three gathering around a crib complete with new-born baby. Finally, they are led out by a little girl – the little hand of God. As the credits roll, we hear Debbie Harry singing a techno version of 'Ghost Riders in the Sky'.

Interestingly, Cox cites Kubrick's *2001* (1968) as a major influence in the film: 'Although we don't have any special effects, we do have the same sort of mundane dialogue. The point of it is that around the mundane activities of these human beings, something exceptional and unusual is about to occur; but will the humans ever be aware of it? In our film, we are aware of it for about two and a half seconds, before we revert back to our former selves and carry on exactly as before'.

Sound familiar? *Three Businessmen* is unpredictable, dislocating and disturbing. It gives you the sense that something is wrong, terribly wrong, with the world. After watching this movie (recent video and DVD releases on both sides of the Atlantic are the only way), you'll have absorbed something strangely revolutionary. You may even be contemplating methods to overthrow the government.

Memorable dialogue:

Bennie: Cheerio mate!

Frank: I think this means we're
not in Liverpool any more.

Barmaid: It's the drug-dealers!

Alex Cox, Miguel Sandoval and Robert Wisdom in Cox's 1998 'serious comedy' Three Businessmen

Frank (Miguel Sandoval) tells Bennie (Alex Cox) another American dog story in Three Businessmen

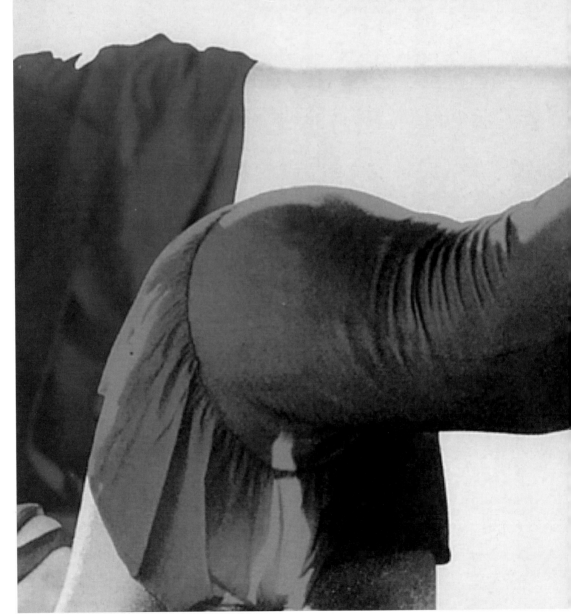

HE VERGE OF A NERVOUS BREAKDOWN!

WN! ⑱

"INVENTIVE DIRECTION, SUPERB LENSING, FINE SCORE
AND TOP TECHNICAL CREDITS MAKE
'TIE ME UP! TIE ME DOWN' A PLEASURE TO WATCH...
...ABRIL AND BANDERAS ARE
COMPELLING TO WATCH".
VARIETY

"ONE OF THE MOST LIVELY
MOVIES SEEN AT
THE BERLIN FESTIVAL...
BOTH ABRIL AND BANDERAS
ARE FINE IN THE
LEADING ROLES".
DEREK MALCOLM
THE GUARDIAN

"CONTROVERSIAL...
BEAUTIFULLY AND
SENSITIVELY HANDLED".
BLITZ

A FILM BY ALMODOVAR

ENTERPRISE PICTURES .... ELDESEO S.A.
ALMODOVAR
TIE ME UP! TIE ME DOWN!
VICTORIA ABRIL ANTONIO BANDERAS
LOLES LEON .... FRANCISCO RABAL
.... JULIETA SERRANO MARIA BARRANCO ROSSY DE PALMA
.... ENNIO MORRICONE .... AGUSTIN ALMODOVAR
.... PEDRO ALMODOVAR
AN ENTERPRISE PICTURES RELEASE

TIE ME UP! TIE ME DOWN!

1990 / 101 mins / Spain / ▭ Video
Stars: Victoria Abril, Antonio Banderas, Loles Leon,
Francisco Rabal, Julieta Serrano, Maria Barranco,
Rossy De Palma
Director: Pedro Almodovar
Producer: Agustin Almodovar
Script: Pedro Almodovar

Tie Me Up! Tie Me Down! is an outrageous comedy about sex and love, and the obsessions that tie it all together, from Academy Award winning writer–director Pedro Almodovar (1999's *All About My Mother*, 1998's *Women on the Verge of a Nervous Breakdown*).

Antonio Banderas (1998's *The Mask of Zorro*) stars as Ricky, recently released from a mental ward and longing to settle down with a loving wife and family. For his bride, he chooses B-movie queen Marina (Victoria Abril), whom he kidnaps and holds prisoner. As their bizarre relationship develops, they discover an uncommon love that is bound by more than just pleasure and pain.

Almodovar is an expert on women. They are central to all of his movies. 'I listen to their conversations in buses and subways', says the director. 'Bergman knows how to show women. It's easier for me to show myself – my immediate, spontaneous emotions – through them. No other male Spanish director talks about the "female universe", and there are really only two women directors in Spain. But for me, men are too inflexible. They are condemned to play their Spanish macho role.'

About *Tie Me Up! Tie Me Down!* he adds, 'It's the triumph of matriarchy, in the best sense of the word. Ricky is looking for love and family, but in the last act, it's Marina who decides yes or no. She, with her sister and her mother, set the conditions.'

'The area I come from, La Mancha, is very macho. The women work and don't talk, and the men are gods. But they sit aloof and never get involved with what goes on. The women know what people are; this ambiguity is the way women lead, even when they are treated like slaves.'

When *Tie Me Up! Tie Me Down!* was finished, Almodovar said, 'You don't know it when you start to write a script – you think you're telling a story. But at the end, the story tells you about you. I think of films as premonitions.'

One of Almodovar's most acclaimed comedies, *Tie Me Up! Tie Me Down!* features a star-making performance by Antonio Banderas, as well as explicit scenes of sexuality that created worldwide controversy. Its description as the most politically incorrect Spanish-made movie helped it gain cult status with great success in post-midnight performances.

Memorable dialogue:

Ricky: I have kidnapped you in order to give you the opportunity to get to know me well, because I am sure that you will fall in love with me as I have fallen in love with you.

Ricky: I am twenty-three years old, have fifty thousand Pesetas and I am alone in the world. I would like to be a good husband for you and a good father for your children.

Previous page: Marina (Victoria Abril) in Almodovar's Tie Me Up! Tie Me Down!

TIMES SQUARE

1980 / 111 mins / USA / (Not currently available)
Stars: Tim Curry, Trini Alvarado, Robin Johnson,
Peter Coffield, Herbert Berghof, David Margulies,
Anna Maria Horsford
Director: Alan Moyle
Producer: Robert Stigwood
Script: Jacob Brackman
(based on a story by Alan Moyle and Leanne Unger)

Allan Moyle's 1980 movie *Times Square* is one of the key rock 'n' roll soundtrack movies (artists include Patti Smith, The Pretenders, The Ramones, Lou Reed, XTC, Gary Numan, Suzi Quatro, Joe Jackson, The Cure, Talking Heads and Roxy Music). But it's also developed into a lesbian cult film with screenings at lesbian and gay film festivals in New York and San Francisco, all mainly down to a story revolving around a teenage girl friendship. The movie's poster tag line read: 'In the heart of Times Square, a poor girl becomes famous, a rich girl becomes courageous and both become friends.'

Rich girl Pammy (Trini Alvarado) is the sheltered upper-class daughter of a leading politician, whereas wild cheeky Nicky (Robin Johnson) is a tough runaway off the streets. Admitted to a hospital for the same psychiatric tests, the girls share a room and get to know each other. They run away from the mental institution and forge a relationship on the streets of New York. They create a home for themselves in a dockside warehouse and soon begin enjoying their punk-rock life, romping around Times Square. But it's not long before the powers that be start looking for them.

The impressive soundtrack often provides a romantic commentary on the developing relationship between the two teenage girls. 'You Can't Hurry Love' accompanies their escape from the hospital and when radio DJ Johnny LaGuardia (*Rocky Horror* star, Tim Curry) learns that the two sweethearts have a favourite song he plays it for them. It just so happens to be Suzi Quatro's lesbian anthem 'Rock Hard'.

Lesbian readings of the girl buddy movie were proved significant when screenwriter Jacob Brackman admitted that many erotically charged scenes between Nicky and Pammy were cut from his original script or the final cut of Alan Moyle's movie. Omitted scenes included the pair playing together in the river and other physical contact. However, the main point of the film which still makes it through to the final cut is that they love each other and they're not interested in boys. As their friendship develops, Pammy's first feelings for Nicky are expressed in a poem she writes in her diary: 'Your ribs are my ladder, Nicky, I'm so amazed, I'm so amazed.' Pammy later recites TS Eliot to Nicky and proclaims to her, 'Everything you do, or you say, is poetry. At least I think so.' The romantic tone is undeniable. In that sense, *Times Square* is a great film for any girl who's ever had a crush on another girl. It's also, understandably, a real treat for lesbian youth – a lesbian equivalent to *Beautiful Thing (1996)*.

Director Alan Moyle went on to make *Pump Up the Volume* (1990) and the roots of that film can easily be seen in *Times Square*.

Memorable dialogue:

Nicky: I'm brave, but you're pretty. I'm a freak of fuckin' nature.

Nicky: I can lick your face, I can bite it too, my teeth got rabies, I'm gonna give 'em to you. I'm a damn dog.

Nicky: I got a lot of dumb ideas. But at least I make 'em up myself.

214

TRAINSPOTTING

1996 / 89 mins / UK / DVD / Video
Stars: Ewan McGregor, Ewen Bremner, Johnny Lee
Miller, Kevin McKidd, Robert Carlyle, Kelly MacDonald
Director: Danny Boyle
Producer: Andrew MacDonald
Script: John Hodge

With a strong British cast, *Trainspotting* explores the dark and shocking subculture of Edinburgh with panache and wit that would put Hollywood multimillion dollar blockbusters to shame. With all the madness, humour and insanity of the cult novel by Irvine Welsh (he makes an appearance as the dealer, Mother Superior), relationships crumble and trusts are betrayed, but all with a dark and delicious black humour only the British could create. Produced, directed and adapted by the same production team that brought us *Shallow Grave* (1994), they've come a long way since their tale of junkies in Edinburgh, and so have the cast. Danny Boyle's directed Leonardo DiCaprio. Robert Carlyle is now an OBE. Ewan McGregor is a Jedi Knight.

Before all that, Andrew MacDonald, Danny Boyle and John Hodge put together a cult classic which went a long way in alerting the international film industry that the British are a force to be reckoned with.

Our hero, Mark Renton, is a hopeless case. A junkie, a liar and a thief. The only thing that sets him apart from the people he calls his 'friends' is that he understands he doesn't have much of a life. But that's okay, because he has chosen not to choose life. He's addicted to his world and try as he might, he just can't seem to kick it.

His 'friends' are Spud (Ewen Bremner), a harmless drug addict, Sick Boy (Johnny Lee Miller), an occasional junkie whose main objective is to irritate Renton as much as possible, Begbie (Robert Carlyle), who never touches heroin but is a psychopathic maniac nonetheless, and Tommy (Kevin McKidd), who also never touches heroin – or at least not yet.

So the question remains, will they ever change their ways and do they even want to? As this motley crew haunt the underbelly of Edinburgh, their lives remain entangled in drugs, deals and dealers. As lives are lost and destroyed, Renton can't help but think that there must be a way out of the madness. However, every attempt he makes to cut free thwarted by his own inadequacies, until he dares to make the ultimate break.

Trainspotting features an exceptional soundtrack, including Lou Reed, Iggy Pop, Damon Albarn, New Order, Pulp and Beethoven.

The crew have borrowed heavily from another cult film: Kubrick's *A Clockwork Orange* (1971). The scene in the Volcano nightclub is a direct copy of the Velocet Milk Bar scene in *Clockwork Orange*. The sequence even features a track by Heaven 17 (who took their moniker from the Kubrick classic).

As well as the cool underground soundtrack and cross references to other movies – factors which add cult appeal anyway – *Trainspotting* seemed, at the time, to capture the darkest imagination of disaffected youth. Boyle dared to comically showcase the blissed-out pleasures achieved from shooting up, with no apologies please. 'Otherwise, we wouldn't do it', intones the needle-worshiping Renton. 'After all, we're not fucking stupid.' *Trainspotting* was the perfect movie for teens and twentysomethings in search of a cultish thrill.

Memorable dialogue:

Mark 'Rent-boy' Renton: Choose life. Choose a job. Choose a career. Choose a family. Choose a fucking big television. Choose washing machines, cars, compact disc players and electrical tin openers. Choose good health, low cholesterol and dental insurance. Choose fixed interest mortgage repayments. Choose a starter home. Choose your friends. Choose leisurewear and matching fabrics. Choose DIY and wondering who the fuck you are on a Sunday morning. Choose sitting on that couch watching mind-numbing, spirit-

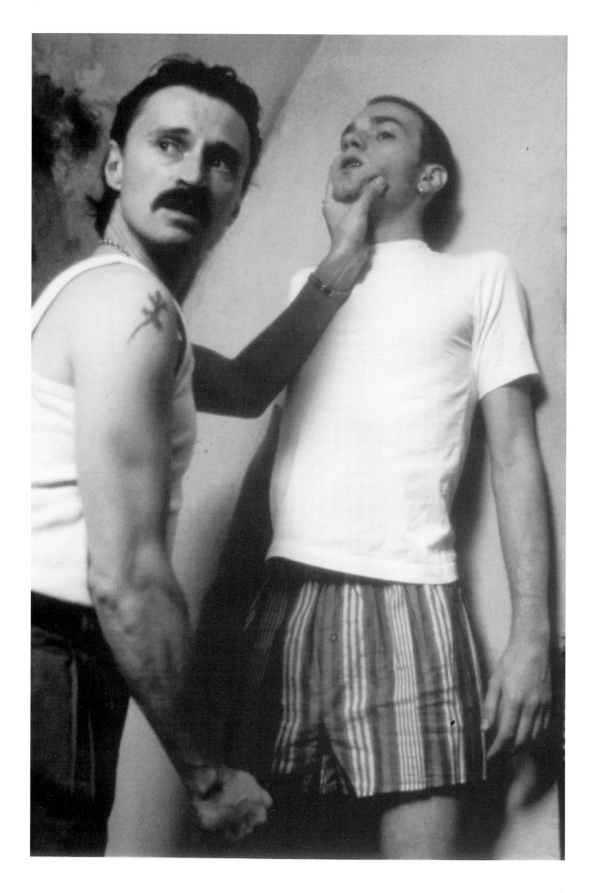

crushing game shows, stuffing junk food into your mouth. Choose rotting away at the end of it all, pushing your last in a miserable home, nothing more than an embarrassment to the selfish, fucked-up brats you spawned to replace yourself. Choose a future. Choose life.… But why would I want to do a thing like that?

Mark 'Rent-boy' Renton: Thank you, your honour. With God's help I'll conquer this terrible affliction.

Mark 'Rent-boy' Renton: I chose not to choose life, I choose something else. And the reasons? There are no reasons, who needs reasons when you've got heroin?

Mark 'Rent-boy' Renton: Phew! I haven't felt that good since Archie Gemmill scored against Holland in 1978!

Mark 'Rent-boy' Renton: We would have injected vitamin C if only they had made it illegal!

Mark 'Rent-boy' Renton: Relinquishing junk. Stage one, preparation. For this you will need one room which you will not leave. Soothing music. Tomato soup, 10 tins of. Mushroom soup, eight tins of, for consumption cold. Ice cream, vanilla, one large tub of. Magnesia, milk of, one bottle. Paracetamol, mouthwash, vitamins. Mineral water, Lucozade, pornography. One mattress. One bucket for urine, one for faeces and one for vomitus. One television and one bottle of Valium. Which I've already procured from my mother. Who is, in her own domestic and socially acceptable way also a drug addict. And now I'm ready. All I need is one final hit to soothe the pain while the Valium takes effect.

Left: Robert Carlyle and Ewan McGregor in Danny Boyle's Trainspotting *(1996)*

THE USUAL SUSPECTS

1995 / 108 mins / USA / DVD / Video
Stars: Stephen Baldwin, Gabriel Byrne,
Benecio Del Toro, Kevin Pollak, Kevin Spacey,
Chaz Palminteri, Pete Postlethwaite, Suzi Amis
Director: Bryan Singer
Producers: Bryan Singer, Michael McDonnell
Script: Christopher McQuarrie

The Usual Suspects was directed and produced by Bryan Singer, who was just 26 at the time of filming. It centres on five criminals brought together for a police line-up.

As in all traditional cult movie fare, each character has a distinct personality, which we glean via a series of flashbacks. There's the veteran who's trying to go clean (Gabriel Byrne); the impulsive, eagle-eyed gunman (Stephen Baldwin); the bilious, self-serving hardware specialist (Kevin Pollak); the mush-mouthed Benecio Del Toro; and the nebbish, weasely cripple (Kevin Spacey). In each case, the movie's casting can't be beat.

The Usual Suspects delivers the usual action scenes, including a complicated New York robbery in which these new colleagues swiftly make off with a few million dollars in gems. But the movie swerves onto a different road when an elegant Pakistani man (Pete Postlethwaite) walks into their secret quarters with a briefcase full of incriminating details about each of them. This is where we learn of a mob legend named Keyser Soze, a seemingly omnipotent criminal mastermind who is so enigmatic nobody even knows what he looks like.

The plot's full of twists and turns and left many annoyed that it was so hard to follow, even star, Gabriel Byrne: 'I know the story. I know exactly what happened from scene to scene and yet I was sitting in the theatre saying, "Oh, my god. Maybe he did it."'

The audience may have to strain to hear some of Del Toro's dialogue, but then, so did the other actors. Recalls Singer, 'Gabriel came to me and said, "We don't want to mess with this process, you know, but we can't understand what he's saying." I said, "If you don't understand him, ask him. In fact in this scene, ask him. Kevin ask him – to let the audience know we're in on it."'

While the average Hollywood film costs $30 million, Singer made this one for under $6 million. He shot it in just 35 days, using existing locations in Los Angeles and New York. Flashbacks, plot twists and even some mumbled dialogue may make *The Usual Suspects* difficult to follow, but it's also made audiences want to see it time and time again.

Memorable dialogue:

Verbal Kint: What the cops never figured out, and what I know now, was that these men would never break, never lie down, never bend over for anybody. Anybody.

Keaton: I'm a businessman now.
Cop: Yeah? What's that, the restaurant business? No. From now on, you're in the gettin'-fucked-by-us business.

Verbal Kint: Oh gee, thanks Dave, bang-up job so far. Extortion, coercion; you'll pardon me if I ask you to kiss my pucker.

Kobayashi: One cannot be betrayed if one has no people.

Fenster: He'll flip ya. He'll flip ya for real.

Verbal Kint: Big fat guy, I mean like orca fat.

Verbal Kint: The greatest trick the devil ever pulled was convincing the world he didn't exist.

Fred Fenster: So who the goddamned piss-hell stole the fuckin' truck?

VAMP

1986 / 94 mins / USA / (Not currently available)
Stars: Chris Makepeace, Sandy Baron, Robert Rusler,
Dedee Pfeiffer, Gedde Watanabe, Grace Jones
Director: Richard Wenk
Producer: Donald P. Borchers
Script: Richard Wenk

Vamp is a tongue-in-cheek, camp and kinky cult exploitation movie which borrows from equally camp and kinky cult movies. It boasts appearances by such cult luminaries as Grace Jones, who plays the nasty ringleader Katrina and the popular bodybuilder Lisa Lyon as a stripper named Cinnamon. The film also features original furniture by Keith Haring and Andy Warhol.

Vamp is the story of three college freshmen (Chris Makepeace as Keith, Robert Rusler as AJ and Gedde Watanabe as Duncan) who go to a sleazy bar looking for strippers to entertain their friends. They have problems with transportation, biker gangs, and worst of all, the staff of the bar, all of whom seem to be vampires, with Grace Jones playing the head vampire. Her role is kind of an extended cameo appearance, often in frightful-looking fangs and contact lenses, dancing the night away at a seedy strip joint called The After Dark Club. Just about everybody who works there is among the undead.

Sandy Baron is one of the best things about the movie. As the cockroach-eating nightclub owner Vic, he gets most of the laughs, although Dedee Pfeiffer (Michelle's younger sister) is also good as a waitress who's chasing Makepeace and may or may not be one of the vampires.

As well as being influenced by the old EC comic of the 50s, Wenk's fast-paced film also owes a considerable debt to *Vampire Circus* (1972), as shown in the scene where Jones performs an erotic dance painted in zebra-stripes.

`Memorable` `dialogue:`
    AJ: Do I look like a mosquito?

VAMPYROS LESBOS

1970 / 86 mins / Spain-Germany / _DVD_ / ▣ Video
Stars: Ewa Stroemberg, Paul Muller, Soledad Miranda,
Dennis Price
Director: Jess Franco
Script: Jaime Chavarri, Jess Franco

A classic 70s sleazefest starring cult German actress Soledad Miranda as Nadine, a vampire with impeccable taste, a taste for beautiful young women that is. With her many charms she entices her victims back to her island for a spot of necro-nookie.

Vampyros Lesbos is a Spanish-German production that was released in Europe as _El Signo Del Vampiro_ in 1970. Jess Franco's (credited as Franco Manera) film is a masterpiece of multiple European exploitation genres. A hit in Europe, its leading lady, Soledad Miranda, was all set to become a major star. But she was killed in a car crash shortly after the film's completion. Franco's film was released in Spain in a sanitised version, but released uncut in Germany.

Vampyros Lesbos is full of glamour, soft-core sex and lounge music. It's all very surreal, coupling weird art-house imagery with psychedelic soft-core and dream sequences to create a genuinely unique movie. The emphasis is on sex and intrigue, so it won't appeal to hardcore horror fans, although if you're a fan of Hammer, you'll dig this!

Vampyros Lesbos has a cool cult soundtrack: sink your teeth into the groovy 70s world of sexadelic German duo Manfred Hubler and Siegfried Schwab (aka Vampyros Sound Incorporation) with their 'The Lions and the Cucumba'. Segments of the soundtrack were used by Quentin Tarantino in _Jackie Brown_ (1997).

Memorable dialogue:
Memmet: She went to the woman on the island – when she came back she was crazy.

Right: Soledad Miranda strikes again in Jess Franco's Vampyros Lesbos _(1970)_

VIRTUOSITY

1995 / 106 mins / USA / *DVD* / ▭ Video
Stars: Russell Crowe, Denzel Washington, Kelly Lynch,
Stephen Spinella, William Forsythe, Louise Fletcher
Director: Brett Leonard
Producer: Gary Lucchesi
Script: Eric Bernt

A mad professor and computer programmer called Lindenmeyer (Stephen Spinella) re-creates his virtual reality personification as an android, SID 6.7 (*Gladiator* star Russell Crowe). Sid was devised as a virtual-reality cop-training tool, but when the project is threatened with shutdown after a rather nasty software bug emerges, Lindenmeyer sets Sid loose on the world with the help of nanotechnology. It turns a virtual Sid into a real one formed from glass.

Denzel Washington plays Parker Barnes, a murderer and ex-cop sprung from jail to track down and terminate SID 6.7. Barnes was previously jailed for slaughtering bystanders in his revenge killing of the evil hostage terrorist whose DNA now forms part of SID, a computer composite of infamous killers' personality traits. As Barnes' criminologist sidekick, Kelly Lynch is surprisingly convincing.

Virtuosity is Brett Leonard's follow-up to *Lawnmower Man* (1992), another movie based in a computer-generated world. *Virtuosity* offers up another media-age satire by making Sid a narcissistic camera-hound; he can't seem to decide whether he'd rather be a psycho killer or a TV star. Leonard also adds a few throwaway references to other movies and in one scene, Sid dons mid-70s attire, and 'Saturday Night Fever' starts to play.

Virtuosity's cult status has been helped enormously by the rapid rise to stardom of lead actor Russell Crowe.

Memorable dialogue:
Sid 6.7: Just because I'm carrying the joy of killing your family inside me doesn't mean we can't be friends.

WATERS, JOHN

Director, writer
Born 29 April 1946, Baltimore

Growing up in Baltimore in the 50s Waters was completely obsessed by violence and gore, both real and on the screen. With his weird counterculture friends acting, he began making silent 8mm and 16mm films in the mid-60s; he screened these in rented Baltimore church halls to underground audiences drawn by word-of-mouth and street leafleting campaigns. He gathered together interested friends and neighbours to form his own stock company, the undisputed star of which was Harris Glenn Milstead, a former high-school chum and 300-pound cross-dresser who billed himself as Divine.

Success came when *Pink Flamingos* (1972), a deliberate exercise in ultra-bad-taste made for just $10,000, took off in 1973, helped no doubt by lead actor Divine's infamous dog-shit-eating scene. He continued to make low-budget shocking movies with his Dreamland repertory company, until Hollywood cross-over success came with *Hairspray*

in 1988. Universal Pictures noted its resounding success and duly obliged by handing over $8 million to Waters to direct a hipper, funnier variation of *Grease*. The result was *Cry-Baby* (1990), starring Johnny Depp alongside his regulars, Mink Stole, Patty Hearst and ex-porno star Traci Lords.

Obviously, having 'gone Hollywood', some changes were made. Not that he actually went to Hollywood, shooting the Depp movie in his beloved Baltimore again. But the ditching of the grotesque elements associated with Waters' films was clearly designed to bring his sensibilities to mainstream audiences. Waters' manic energy was still on show however.

Waters' *Serial Mom* (1994) with Kathleen Turner was even more glossy and the Edward Furlog and Christina Ricci comedy *Pecker* (1998) was also fairly tame, although it was at least still set in Baltimore. See Filmography, p.240.

WAYNE'S WORLD

1992 / 95 mins / USA / 🖵 Video
Stars: Mike Myers, Dana Carvey, Rob Lowe,
Tia Carrere, Brian Doyle-Murray, Lara Flynn Boyle,
Kurt Fuller, Colleen Camp, Donna Dixon
Director: Penelope Spheeris
Producer: Lorne Michaels
Script: Mike Myers, Bonnie Turner, Terry Turner

Wayne's World derives from cult sketches on the American television show *Saturday Night Live* (shown on NBC in the US and various satellite channels in the UK) and survives the transition to movie length by clever manipulation of cinema conventions and a tiny bit of a plot.

Wayne and Garth (Myers and Carvey) two long-haired, suburban, rockin' teenagers, live a life of partying and have their own public-access cable television show. The show is completely improvised. It just wouldn't occur to the pair to prepare. They might profile the Top 10 babes of the year or even discuss the news. They're completely spaced out in the media-barraged white-youth culture, their entire references based on syndicated TV shows of the 70s, heavy-metal bands and TV commercials.

Not unlike the less funny *Bill and Ted* (1989), they have invented their own dudes' slang expressions and trademark facial contortions. The widest known Wayne 'n' Garthism is their use of 'not'. As in: *Wayne's World* is a superb achievement in film-making, an allegorical conundrum that will make you question yourselves and all around you... Not!'

A slimy television executive Benjamin Oliver (Rob Lowe) decides to exploit the show. He wants to buy Wayne's show for a network and sanitise it beyond all value. Wayne and Garth's friendship is severely tested and all threatens to come apart at the seams. The good guys of course save the day in the end. Look out for cameo roles by Meatloaf, Ed O'Neil (Al Bundy), (an intellectual) Alice Cooper and supermodel robobabe Donna Dixon.

Memorable dialogue:

Wayne: Garth, marriage is punishment for shoplifting in some countries!

Wayne: I mean, Led Zeppelin didn't write tunes that everyone liked.

They left that to the Bee Gees.

Wayne: I say hurl. If you blow chunks and she comes back, she's yours. If you spew and she bolts, then it was never meant to be.

Wayne: Hi. My name is Wayne Campbell. I live in Aurora, Illinois, which is a suburb of Chicago. Excellent! I have had plenty of Joe jobs, nothing I would call a career or anything. Let me put it this way: I have an extensive collection of name tags and hairnets. Yes, I still live with my parents, which I admit is both bogus and sad. But I have this awesome cable access show, and I still know how to party. Ahh, the mirth-mobile.

Wayne: Does this guy know how to party or what?

Garth: Ribbed for her pleasure. Ewww!

Garth: Hey Phil, if you're gonna spew, spew into this.

Garth: That is a babe! She makes me feel kinda funny, like when we used to climb the rope in gym-class.

[Talking about Claudia Schiffer]

Wayne: She's a babe.
Garth: She's magically babelicious.
Wayne: She tested very high on the stroke-ability scale.

Wayne: Exsqueeze me? Baking powder?

Russell: It will be Terry's job to give the actors their hand cue.
Wayne: Excuse me, Russell, but I believe I requested the hand job...

Benjamin: So Garth, how do you like being in a studio?
Garth: Ahm, it's like a new pair of underwear, you know... At first it's constrictive, but after a while it becomes a part of you.

WENDERS, WIM (ERNST WILHELM WENDERS)

Director
Born 14 August 1945, Dusseldorf, Germany

'Sex and violence was never really my cup of tea; I was always more into sax and violins,' Wenders once stated. 'Hollywood film-making has become more and more about power and control. It's really not about telling stories. That's just a pretence. But ironically, the fundamental difference between making films in Europe versus America is in how the screenplay is dealt with. From my experiences in Germany and France, the script is something that is constantly scrutinised by the film made from it. Americans are far more practical. For them, the screenplay is a blueprint and it must be adhered to rigidly in fear of the whole house falling down. In a sense, all of the creative energy goes into the screenplay so one could say that the film already exists before the film even begins shooting. You lose spontaneity. But in Germany and France, I think that film-making is regarded as an adventure in itself.' (The Internet Movie Database).

Wim Wenders first came to prominence with films that focused on post-war Germany and the Americanisation of its culture; his work neither condemns nor celebrates the American cultural influence on post-war German youth, but there is always a stark awareness. 'The Yanks have colonised our subconscious,' says one of the characters in *Kings of the Road* (1976).

Wenders' first critically praised feature was a strange tale called *Die Angst des Tromanns beim Elfmeter/The Goalie's Anxiety at the Penalty Kick* (1971) and was followed by an adaptation of *Der Scharlachrote Buchstabe/The Scarlet Letter* (1972). His three road movies of the 70s (Wenders' own production company is called Road Movies), *Alice in den Stadten/Alice in the Cities* (1974), *Falsche Bewegung/Wrong Move* (1975), and the mammoth *Im Lauf der Zeit/Kings of the Road* (1976), all dealt with Wenders' strong interest in cinema and rock and roll.

Der Amerikanische Freund/The American Friend (1977) was the first of Wenders' films to achieve noticeable cult status and featured American actor Dennis Hopper along with appearances by Wenders' directorial heroes Nicholas Ray and Samuel Fuller. It tells the tale of a Stetson-wearing nihilistic art smuggler (Hopper) and a friendship with a German craftsman.

Next, Wenders left Germany for the US, the country that had intrigued him so much. However, things didn't go very smoothly; his film *Hammett,* begun in 1978, was hit by problems from the start. Two thirds of the troubled film was abandoned in rough cut and re-shot. Producer, Francis Ford Coppola, reportedly asked for the changes to be made. It was finally released in 1983. Wenders then used his first experience in the US film industry for his 1982 movie *Der Stand der Dinge/The State of Things*, which offered a bleak look at film-making.

Wenders won international acclaim for 1984's *Paris, Texas*, the story of a drifter (Harry Dean Stanton), lost and speechless for the first 20 minutes, shell-shocked by the separation from his wife (Natassia Kinski) who he seaches for in order to bond with his seven-year-old son. With a haunting soundtrack by Ry Cooder, this richly atmospheric film was beautifully photographed by Robby Muller and earned the Palme D'Or at Cannes.

Returning to Germany, Wenders next directed *Wings of Desire* (1987), a fable of angels hovering over Berlin, one of them so disillusioned by his inability to alleviate suffering that he falls in love with a beautiful trapeze artist and opts for mortality. Peter Falk appears as a film-maker with a secret celestial past. This brilliant film was widely praised and earned Wenders a Best Director award at Cannes.

By this time Wenders had become one of the cult directors of the 80s, while his films were becoming ever more successful with the public. Also in 1987, Wenders published his first book, *Written in the West*, which reflects his fascination with the American West. This collection of photographs was followed by many other books – collections of essays, reflections on film-making, other photo and art books, companion books to his movies and more.

In 1991 he completed a long-time project, *Until the End of the World*, a science-fiction drama shot in more than five countries and featuring an international cast led by William Hurt. In the same year he received the Friedrich Wilhelm Murnau Award in Bielefeld.

Fashion designer Yohji Yamamoto was the subject of his documentary *Notebook on Cities and Clothes* (1989), his fourth cinematographic diary. This was followed by a collaboration with Michelangelo Antonioni, *Beyond the Clouds* (1995). Other projects in this period included the follow-up to *Wings of Desire – Far Away, So Close* (1993), with key original cast members reprising their roles.

From 1991 to 1996 he was the Chairman of the European Film Academy and was subsequently elected as its president. Since 1993 he has been teaching as an honorary professor at the HFF (Academy of Film and Television) in Munich.

Since then, having settled in Los Angeles, he has filmed his movies mainly in the US and in English, most notably *The End of Violence* (1997), the award-winning music documentary *Buena Vista Social Club* (1999) and *The Million Dollar Hotel* (2000).

After 30 years of film-making, flitting between Germany and the US, Wenders still retains the air of an outsider in both countries: 'Originality now is rare in the cinema', he says, 'and it isn't worth striving for because most work that does this is egocentric and pretentious. What is most enjoyable about the cinema is simply working with a language that is classical in the sense that the image is understood by everyone. I'm not at all interested in innovating film language, making it more aesthetic. I love film history, and you're better off learning from those who preceeded you'.

Still one of the most important directors on the international scene, Wenders says he'll always produce his own films and avoid finding himself at the distributor's mercy: 'You must become a producer if you want any control over the fate of your work. Otherwise, it becomes another person's film and he does with it what he pleases. I only had one experience like that and I will never repeat it.' See Filmography, p.240.

WHITE OF THE EYE

1987 / 110 mins / UK / (Not currently available)
Stars: David Keith, Cathy Moriarty, Art Evans,
Rosenberg, Alberta Watson, Michael Greene
Director: Donald Cammell
Producers: Cassion Elwes, Brad Wyman
Script: Donald Cammell, China Cammell

White Of The Eye stars David Keith as Paul White, an Arizona-based ex-drifter turned hi-fi repairman who is implicated when local women are killed in a series of grisly murders. Lots of red herrings are thrown in and Cammell has delivered one of the most genuinely suspenseful films of the 80s.

With rapid cross-cutting in time and space, grainy flashbacks, subliminal imagery and other interesting camerawork, *White of the Eye* is definitely not the standard slasher movie.

Cammell took the source novel, *Mrs White*, and created a whole new psychic arena. 'The novel explored this woman's feelings as she discovers that her husband is insane, and yet she is completely dominated by him,' he explained. 'Well, I rethought all that and decided it was more interesting to have her deeply in love, so that when she discovers he's a serial killer, she has to make that decision to leave him or confront him and continue to love him. Even to the point where he degenerates into bestiality.'

Like 1970's *Performance* (the film Cammell co-directed with Nicolas Roeg), *White Of The Eye* has an eerie visual style and, although the final denouement is hard to make sense of, this thriller was a welcome return to the screen for one of the world's most under-rated directors. Cammell committed suicide in 1996, disillusioned with film studio execs' interference in his work.

True to form, the release of *White of the Eye* was delayed by a bankruptcy suit. Brando even stepped in when the film was threatened with cuts by the American censor, asking, 'If a film-maker of this order and subtlety and taste is not encouraged, what hope have we?' Although it was well received by the critics, and later achieved cult status on video, *White Of The Eye* died at the box office.

Memorable dialogue:

Mike: You can't change a channel, future or past.

THE WICKER MAN

1973 / 102 mins / UK / DVD / ▭ Video
Stars: Edward Woodward, Christopher Lee,
Britt Ekland, Diane Cilento, Ingrid Pitt, Lindsay Kemp
Director: Robin Hardy
Producer: Peter Snell
Script: Anthony Shaffer

The term 'cult classic' is bandied around a lot nowadays, but Robin Hardy's film really does deserve the description. Provocative and bizarre, *The Wicker Man* is not only worshipped by loyal admirers, it's also a film *about* a cult – a creepy pagan community whose inhabitants believe that making love is the best way to fertilise the earth. The harrowing screenplay is by Liverpool-born writer Anthony Shaffer, celebrated author of *Sleuth* and *Frenzy*. His script for this feature is remarkable – a devastatingly original sexual parable full of shock and horror.

Edward Woodward stars as Sergeant Howie, a strait-laced police officer and devout Christian based on the Scottish mainland. He receives an anonymous letter from the remote offshore community of Summerisle, asking him to investigate the disappearance of a young girl called Rowan Morrison (Geraldine Cowper). Howie arrives at the Scottish island to find a secretive, tightly knit neo-pagan society – a world where couples copulate on gravestones, women breast feed in a desecrated church and young children are taught about the importance of the phallus. He is shocked by the islanders' open sexuality and devotion to pre-Christian gods.

Christopher Lee, as the completely amoral Byronesque leader of the island, Lord Summerisle, simply wants to 'turn and live with animals. They are so placid and self-contained. They do not lie awake in the dark and weep for their sins. They do not make me sick discussing their duty to God. Not one of them kneels to another or to his own kind that lived thousands of years ago. Not one of them is respectable or unhappy, all over the earth.'

Britt Ekland (dubbed into Scottish by Leslie Mackie) is the innkeeper's sexually rampant daughter, Willow. 'Some things in their natural state,' she says, 'have the most *vivid* colours.' She flaunts herself in front of Howie to test this virginal victim. Diane Cilento also puts in a fine performance as the strict local schoolmarm. Ingrid Pitt is the deceptively innocent librarian.

The Wicker Man was shot entirely on location. Said director Robin Hardy: 'The semi-tropical agricultural background gave no difficulty, but the village had to be a composite of 15 or 20 different places. In the course of securing ideal locations, we shot in 27 different spots within a radius of 33 miles from the production base of Newton Stewart, Wigtownshire.'

As the mystery of the missing girl unravels, Howie begins to suspect that she is a victim of human sacrifice. But it soon becomes apparent that Rowan Morrison was never missing and Howie has been completely misled by the whole community. In the film's apocalyptic finale, the truth is revealed when he meets the Wicker Man. As the respected film historian Ian Connich has noted: 'It is in the film's dramatic conclusion in which the hunter becomes the hunted, or the saviour the sacrifice, that audience participation and identification reaches a crisis point.'

Disorientated, viewers must adjust to Howie's loss of control. As Lord Summerisle remarks, Howie has been 'a King for a day'. The viewer has therefore also lost control, making what happens all the more terrifying.

What makes the film so unsettling is that, unlike *The Exorcist* (also released in 1973) in which God is awarded victory over demonic possession, there is no restoration of confidence in *The Wicker Man*. As Howie burns, he has only the ultimate test of faith. Of course, there is no escape. In the last shock sequence, we see the Wicker Man crammed with geese, cows and bleating lambs. 'Oh God, no! Jesus Christ!' cries Sergeant Howie.

One critic, David McGillivray, writing at the time of the film's release described what he saw as: 'An encouraging achievement for those who had begun to despair of the British cinema.' Meanwhile, *Cinefantastique* dubbed it the *Citizen Kane* of horror films. Later, the film's cult reputation began to develop as a new generation became fascinated with the themes and roots of Scottish paganism and culture. In Britain there are now fan clubs,

Wicker Man conventions and magazines as well as special screenings of the film for both die-hard fans and regular cinema-goers. There's even been an in-depth BBC documentary which reunited the main players and a re-release of the film's distinctive soundtrack by Paul Giovanni. Also, the love song Ekland sings to entice Woodward has been covered by the Sneaker Pimps. Interestingly, the novel of *The Wicker Man* by both Hardy and Shaffer, wasn't published until five years after the release of the film. In the US, Burning Man festivals have been established in the Nevada desert with New Age cultists burning wicker men.

The Wicker Man is also a film praised highly by the original cast members. The film was made when Christopher Lee was at the height of his career. Lee still maintains that it 'was the best-scripted film I ever took part in'. Edward Woodward, riding high as TV's *Callan* in the 70s went on to further fame and fortune as *The Equaliser*, one of the most popular drama series on US television in the 80s. It was a role he won after the wife of the studio head remembered him as Sergeant Howie.

Originally, *The Wicker Man* was given a very poor theatrical release and British Lion failed to show the picture to the press. It was shown only in truncated versions, usually either the 87-minute or the 95-minute print rather than the intended 102-minute version, cut by 15 minutes on the advice of cult auteur Roger Corman. The excised 15 minutes of footage included a crucial early scene in which Edward Woodward is introduced and the viewer told he's engaged to be married but not yet 'known a woman'. His colleagues gossip that he's 'keeping himself pure' for his wedding night.

While one of the cut versions commences with a title that simply reads: 'Sunday the 29th of April 1973', the original 102-minute film opens with a much longer printed statement: 'The Producer would like to thank The Lord Summerisle and the people of his island off the west coast of Scotland for this privileged insight into their religious practices and for their generous co-operation in the making of this film.' Lord Summerisle is, of course, a fictional character but this statement and extensive use of exterior locations disturbingly suggest that what we are about to see is based on real events. When the opening credits appear over shots of Howie's seaplane en route to the Scottish isle, we see a huge expanse of water and islands, as if to reinforce the remoteness of Summerisle – a place very difficult to escape from.

As a result of the emerging cult fascination with the film, the original film-making team, together with various other parties, began the search for the original 102-minute print. This was a hard task, seeing as though much of the unedited footage from 1973 had been used as landfill for the M4 motorway! Nevertheless, a rare copy of the original version was eventually tracked down at an auction house in America and a recent release on video and DVD by Anchor Bay provides the longest version now in existence, an opportunity for the legions of fans to see the film as the director had originally intended.

Memorable dialogue:

May Morrison: Can I do anything for you, Sergeant?
Sergeant Howie: No, I doubt it, seeing you're all raving mad!

May Morrison: You'll simply never understand the true nature of sacrifice.

Sergeant Howie: But they are are naked!
Lord Summerisle: Naturally! It's much too dangerous to jump through the fire with your clothes on!

WISE BLOOD

1979 / 108 mins / USA / West Germany /
(Not currently available)
Stars: Brad Dourif, Ned Beatty, Harry Dean Stanton,
Amy Wright, John Huston
Director: John Huston
Producers: Michael Fitzgerald, Kathy Fitzgerald
Script: Benedict Fitzgerald

John Huston's *Wise Blood* is an excellent adaptation of Flannery O'Connor's first novel. Army veteran Hazel Motes (Brad Dourif) is released from the armed services and returns to his heavily religious home town in the Deep Evangelical South. There, he begins a private spiritual battle against the religiosity of the community and, in particular, against Asa Hawkes, the 'blind' preacher (Stanton), and his degenerate 15-year-old daughter (Susan Tyrell). In desperation, Hazel founds and promotes his own religion, 'The Church Without Christ', and the extraordinary narrative moves towards its savage and macabre resolution.

Wise Blood was John Huston's first film after *Fat City* (1972) and also set in small-town America. Part comedy, part tragedy, part philosophical farce, Huston manages to imbue this version of O'Connor's remarkable novel with the same zest with which it was written: a haunting meld of O'Connor's Gothic approach to human relationships and Huston's pessimistic view of human endeavours. Disturbing and grim in its portraits, *Wise Blood* is nevertheless masterful storytelling and includes some fine performances. It features some of the best cult movie actors around, including Brad Dourif in his first lead role and Harry Dean Stanton (1984's *Paris, Texas* and 1984's *Repo Man*). And, like all great cult movies, there's a director's cameo; Huston (who bills himself here as Jhon Huston) appears as a preacher.

It is admirable that the ageing Huston chose to make a film as dark and as interesting as this so late in his career. He presents Hazel's quest for salvation seriously, as a sincere search for faith in a crass and commercial world.

Memorable dialogue:

Hazel: A man don't need justification if he's got a good car.

WITHNAIL AND I

1986 / 108 mins / UK / ▭ Video
Stars: Richard E Grant, Paul McGann, Richard
Griffiths, Ralph Brown, Michael Elphick
Director: Bruce Robinson
Producer: Paul M Heller
Script: Bruce Robinson

Bruce Robinson's film *Withnail and I* is a drug- and booze-fuelled tale of two out-of-work young actors, Withnail and I, at the end of the 60s. Full of characterisation, quotable lines and excellently played set pieces it quickly became a cult classic, loved by fans of quirky indie films and students everywhere.

The Withnail character is actually based on Robinson's late housemate Vivian MacKerrell, an outrageous drunk who Robinson described as: 'a wild aristocratic figure, highly educated'.

Withnail (a camped-up Richard E Grant) and I (an on-the-edge Paul McGann), tired out by their lives of idleness, drugs, booze and squalor, decide to take a 'holiday' at Withnail's Uncle Monty's country home. But, in this tale of a friendship in decline, their rustic life becomes even more of a nightmare than the one they left behind.

Withnail has a drink problem so severe he'll down a can of lighter fluid in order to get a fix. On the day of the shoot, the production team reportedly substituted the can's contents for vinegar, a fact unknown to Grant, which probably explains his stunned reaction.

During pre-production, Robinson made his two lead actors go out and get drunk so they would have a 'chemical memory' of what it was like for future reference. Grant, usually tee-total, was prepared to suffer for his art and gave one of the finest performances of his career.

Both McGann and Grant are superb and the supporting actors are equally impressive, with Richard Griffiths as the homosexual Uncle Monty and Michael Elphick as an eel-carrying poacher.

Grant suddenly became one of Hollywood's favourite 'English' actors and went on to work with the likes of Martin Scorsese (1993's *The Age of Innocence*); Robert Altman (1992's *The Player*) and Francis Ford Coppola (1992's *Bram Stoker's Dracula*).

Ralph Brown also scored as drug dealer Danny. Mike Myers cast him in a similar role for *Wayne's World 2* (1993) and George Lucas hired him for *The Phantom Menace* (1999).

Director Bruce Robinson has fared less well in recent years. His Withnail follow-up, *How to Get Ahead in Advertising* (1989), bombed while his Hollywood debut *Jennifer 8* (1992) fared even less well. More recently, the director has made a return to acting, playing an ageing rock star in *Still Crazy* (1998).

Vulgar, nostalgic, acidly funny, with a strong 60s flavour, as with all cult movies, *Withnail and I* is full of quotable one-liners. The film also contains plenty of drug references, bad language and drink (particularly the legendary Camberwell Carrot). Devoted fans have gone from the usual memorable line quoting to actually taking up the *Withnail and I* drinking challenge, which involves drinking all the drinks (including lighter fluid) as they are consumed on screen. Because of these cult factors, its place on late-night TV and posters on student walls is assured for a long time.

Memorable dialogue:

Peter: My thumbs have gone weird!

Withnail: Free to those that can afford it, very expensive to those that can't.

Withnail: I feel like a pig shat in my head.

Withnail: Don't threaten me with a dead fish.

Withnail: We want the finest wines available to humanity, we want them here, and we want them now!
Withnail: I demand to have some booze!
Monty: As a youth I used to weep in butcher's shops.

Monty: Come on lads, let's get home, the sky's beginning to bruise, night must fall and we shall be forced to camp.

Withnail: I think a drink, don't you?

Peter: Even a stopped clock tells the right time twice a day, and for once I'm inclined to believe Withnail is right. We are indeed drifting into the arena of the unwell.

Withnail: I have a heart condition. If you hit me, it's murder.

Monty: Flowers are simply tarts; prostitutes for the bees.

YOUNG EINSTEIN

1988 / 89 mins / Australia / (Not currently available)
Stars: Yahoo Serious, Odile Le Clezio, John Howard,
Pee Wee Wilson, Su Cruikshank
Director: Yahoo Serious
Producers: Yahoo Serious, Warwick Ross, David Roach
Script: David Roach, Yahoo Serious

On a remote Tasmanian apple farm, the young wild-haired genius, Albert Einstein, splits the atom to make the world's first bubbled beer. Did you know that Einstein invented not only the theory of relativity but rock 'n' roll and surfing as well? That he was born in the Outback and had a fondness for cat pies? Not only that but when he wasn't dating Marie Curie he found time to save his nuclear brewery from an evil businessman wanting to use it to blow up the world.

In 1988 Yahoo Serious became the first Australian to write, direct, produce and star in a feature film. *Young Einstein* was a national and international hit both critically and at the box office. Made on a shoestring budget which Yahoo pulled together by selling his car and borrowing cameras, *Young Einstein* went on to gross over $100 million and reach number one in many countries including Australia, UK, France, Germany and Canada during 1989-90. In America *Young Einstein* was one of the most successful Australian movies ever released and became a cult classic. The movie's soundtrack, produced by Yahoo, went double platinum.

In February 1989 Yahoo was featured on the cover of *Time* magazine. In the same year he was the cover of *MAD* magazine, made his own MTV show in New York and in a satire on TV reporting, he interviewed himself on *60 Minutes*.

Yahoo's latest movie *Mr Accident* (2000) is a dangerous romantic comedy about free range eggs, refrigerators and whether Mankind is alone in the Universe.

Memorable dialogue:

Young Einstein: Two objects cannot occupy the same space and the same time.

ZACHARIAH

1971 / 93 mins / USA / *DVD* / ▭ Video
Stars: John Rubinstein, Pat Quinn, Don Johnson,
Country Joe and The Fish, Doug Kershaw,
The James Gang, The New York Rock Ensemble,
Whit Lightnin', William Challee
Director: George Englund
Producer: George Englund
Script: Joe Massot, Phillip Austin

This is the movie to watch if you fancy seeing (an admittedly very sexy-looking) Don Johnson (circa 1971) in black cowboy garb!

The first and only electric Western is built on a base of solid rock with a musical score and cast headed by such music greats as Country Joe and The Fish, Elvin Jones, The James Gang and Cajun singer Doug Kershaw.

The adventure begins when Zachariah (John Rubinstein), who just received a mail order gun, convinces his friend Matthew (Don Johnson) to ride off with him on the trail of the Crackers (Country Joe and The Fish), a roving band of bandits. At a saloon where the Crackers are entertaining, a cowboy picks a fight with Zachariah who outdraws and kills him. Based on the success of the first showdown, Zachariah decides that he is good gunfighter material. He and Matthew set out on a trail of gun-slinging adventures, including encounters with the infamous Job Cain (Elvin Jones) and his gang (The James Gang).

Experience this unique Western and the surreal visions of two gunfighters on their journey through the West. Englund's homoerotic cowboy film features lots of partial sets, and abstract buildings made of plywood. This may be a profound statement on the fragility of modern life, or it may just be the by-product of a small budget. Hmmm...I wonder.

Memorable dialogue:

Matt: Faaaarrrr out!

ZUCKER, DAVID

Director, writer
Born 16 October 1947, Milwaukee

As one of the creators of *Airplane!*, *Top Secret* and the *Naked Gun* movies, David Zucker taught audiences not to be satisfied with fewer than two belly laughs per minute. He's been writing, as well as directing and producing, his exceedingly unique style of comedies ever since *Kentucky Fried Movie* (1977) first impressed audiences. Over the years, as his work has developed, he's coined a description of it, 'Guerrilla comedy', also often referred to around his office, he says, as 'Take No Prisoners comedy'.

'Most comedies are just situational, with jokes added in', Zucker comments. 'And that's fine. But I like comedy that doesn't let up, that just unrelentingly keeps going after you'.

Zucker grew up in Shorewood, Wisconsin, a suburb of Milwaukee, where he and his brother Jerry entertained family and friends with comic Super-8 home movies. David studied film-making at the University of Wisconsin, in Madison, and made several student films with Jerry and friend, Jim Abrahams. After graduation, in 1972, they moved to LA and scraped together the cash – $28,000 – to produce a short reel of some of their best Kentucky Fried material. Soon they found backers to finance their first movie in 1977 with John Landis as director and Robert K Weiss as producer. A collection of short parodies, *Kentucky Fried Movie* became a hit independent release.

Their next project was *Airplane!* (1980), and this time the trio insisted on directing their screenplay themselves. The resulting film – a masterpiece of off-the-wall comedy spoofing airplane disaster flicks – became one of the surprise hits of that year. 'No one at the studio thought *Airplane!* would do anything', Zucker remembers quite fondly. 'It was just this really small movie. But there was a real feeling of excitement on the set. It turned out pretty well'.

Zucker, Abrahams and Zucker next created and produced the TV series, *Police Squad!*, a parody of cop shows, which starred Leslie Nielsen. Although only six episodes were made, the series received two Emmy nominations. When it was cancelled by ABC executives, it was David Zucker who came up with the idea of turning it into a feature film, but for the time being it was put on the back burner.

Top Secret! (1984) was released next, an hilarious parody of every conceivable genre – teenage rock stars, espionage, war and the love story. Val Kilmer played Nick Rivers, a rock 'n' roll star invited to entertain culturally deprived teenagers. Lucy Getteridge co-starred as Hillary Flammond, an activist in the French Resistance whose comrades include Deja Vu and Latrine. In the same year, Zucker, Abrahams and Zucker agreed to direct the comparatively 'straight' *Ruthless People*.

The Naked Gun finally came to the screen in 1988. David and Jerry Zucker and Jim Abrahams, along with Pat Proft, wrote the script, while David Zucker made his solo directing debut. Zucker also directed the sequel *The Naked Gun 2¹/₂: The Smell of Fear* (1991).

Jerry Zucker makes his own movies (*Ghost*) and Jim Abrahams his (*Hot Shots!*). David is the one who continued alone with the *Naked Gun* series. After over 20 years of making raucous comedies, he still refuses to get serious. 'Years ago when we made movies as ZAZ', Zucker recalls, 'I think the idea of group film-making had such an impact that many people today believe we still shower together. We may have then, but the truth is that we each have long since left the nest and separately have made our own movies with our own teams for over 10 years'.

The ZAZ team having gone their separate ways, Zucker next directed *BASEketball* (1998) starring the creators of the cult TV series *South Park*, Trey Parker and Matt Stone, in which two losers from Milwaukee invent a new game, playing basketball, using baseball rules. It's an outrageous satire of professional sports, bridging the comedic generation gap with sight gags and gross-out bodily-function jokes. As well as the film attracting the usual cult crowd, the actual game of Baseketball in the movie took off as well. (in Baseketball, shots can be taken from single, double, triple and home run lines. A successful shot gets a man on base, and a missed shot is an out, unless it's tipped in by the opposing team, in which case it's a double play.) Leagues have been formed, a scoreboard built, uniforms made and an entire season and playoff schedule drawn up. 'We always knew how stupid the whole thing was, yet you're guys, and you compete,' Zucker says. 'It was nerve-wracking. Guys would have knots in their stomachs before a game. Everybody wanted to win.'

Zucker's most recent film, another comedy, was *The Guest* (2001). See Filmography, p.240.

FILMOGRAPHY

ALLEN, WOODY
Hollywood Ending (2002)
Curse of the Jade Scorpion, The
    (2001)
Small Time Crooks (2000)
Sweet and Lowdown (1999)
Celebrity (1998)
Deconstructing Harry (1997)
Everyone Says I Love You (1996)
Mighty Aphrodite (1995)
Don't Drink the Water (1994) (TV)
Bullets Over Broadway (1994)
Manhattan Murder Mystery (1993)
Husbands and Wives (1992)
Shadows and Fog (1992)
Alice (1990)
Crimes and Misdemeanors (1989)
New York Stories (1989)
    (segment 3)
Another Woman (1988)
September (1987)
Radio Days (1987)
Hannah and Her Sisters (1986)
Purple Rose of Cairo, The (1985)
Broadway Danny Rose (1984)
Zelig (1983)
Midsummer Night's Sex Comedy, A
    (1982)
Stardust Memories (1980)
Manhattan (1979)
Interiors (1978)
Annie Hall (1977)
Love and Death (1975)
Sleeper (1973)
Everything You Always Wanted to
    Know About Sex (1972)
...aka Everything You Always
    Wanted to Know About Sex But
    Were Afraid to Ask (1972)
Men of Crisis: The Harvey Wallinger
    Story (1971) (TV)
Bananas (1971)
Take the Money and Run (1969)
What's Up, Tiger Lily? (1966)

ANDERSON, LINDSAY
Is That All There Is? (1993)
Ritorno di Robin Hood, Il (1991)
    aka Robin Hood: Quest for the
    Crown (1991)
Glory! Glory! (1989) (TV)
Whales of August, The (1987)
Wish You Were There (1985)
Britannia Hospital (1982)
Look Back in Anger (1980)
Old Crowd, The (1979) (TV)
aka Six Plays by Alan Bennett: The
    Old Crowd (1979) (TV) (UK:
    series title)
In Celebration (1975)
O Lucky Man! (1973)
Home (1972) (TV)
If... (1968)
Singing Lesson, The (1967)
    aka Raz, dwa, trzy (1967) (Poland)

White Bus, The (1966)
    aka Red, White and Zero (1966)
    (USA)
This Sporting Life (1963)
Every Day Except Christmas (1957)
Children Upstairs, The (1955)
Energy First (1955)
Foot and Mouth (1955)
Green and Pleasant Land (1955)
Henry (1955)
Hundred Thousand Children, A
    (1955)
£20 a Ton (1955)
Thursday's Children (1954)
O Dreamland (1953)
Three Installations (1952)
Trunk Conveyor (1952)
Wakefield Express (1952)
Idlers That Work (1949)
Meet the Pioneers (1948)

BARTEL, PAUL
Shelf Life (1993)
Scenes from the Class Struggle in
    Beverly Hills (1989)
Longshot, The (1986)
Lust in the Dust (1985)
Amazing Stories (1985) TV Series
    (episodes Secret Cinema
    (1986), Gershwin's Trunk
    (1987))
Not for Publication (1984)
Comic Strip Presents, The (1982) TV
    Series
Eating Raoul (1982)
Cannonball (1976)
... aka Carquake (1976) (UK)
Death Race 2000 (1975)
Private Parts (1972)
... aka Blood Relations (1972)
    (USA)
Naughty Nurses (1969)
Secret Cinema, The (1969)

BROOKS, MEL (as director only)
Dracula: Dead and Loving It (1995)
Robin Hood: Men in Tights (1993)
... aka Sacré Robin des bois (1993)
    (France)
Life Stinks (1991)
... aka Life Sucks (1991) (USA)
Spaceballs (1987)
History of the World: Part I (1981)
High Anxiety (1977)
Silent Movie (1976)
Young Frankenstein (1974)
Blazing Saddles (1974)
Twelve Chairs, The (1970/I)
Producers, The (1968)

BURTON, TIM
Planet of the Apes (2001)
Sleepy Hollow (1999)
Mars Attacks! (1996)
Ed Wood (1994)
Batman Returns (1992)
Edward Scissorhands (1990)
Batman (1989)
Beetlejuice (1988)

Alfred Hitchcock Presents (1985)
    TV Series (episode Jar, The)
Amazing Stories (1985) TV Series
    (episode Family Dog)
Pee-Wee's Big Adventure (1985)
Aladdin and His Wonderful Lamp
    (1984) (TV)
Frankenweenie (1984)
Hansel and Gretel (1982) (TV)
Vincent (1982)

CARPENTER, JOHN
Ghosts of Mars (2001)
Vampires (1998)
Escape from L.A (1996)
In the Mouth of Madness (1995)
Village of the Damned (1995)
Body Bags (1993) (TV) (segments
    Gas Station, The and Hair)
Memoirs of an Invisible Man
    (1992)
They Live (1988)
Prince of Darkness (1987)
Big Trouble in Little China (1986)
Starman (1984)
Christine (1983)
Thing, The (1982)
Escape from New York (1981)
Fog, The (1980)
Elvis (1979) (TV)
Someone's Watching Me! (1978)
    (TV)
Halloween (1978)
Assault on Precinct 13 (1976)
Dark Star (1974)
Warrior and the Demon (1969) (as
    Johnny Carpenter)

CHEECH AND CHONG
Best Buds (1998)
Far Out Man (1990)
Born in East LA (1987)
Get Out of My Room (1985)
Cheech & Chong's The Corsican
    Brothers (1984)
Still Smokin' (1983)
Cheech & Chong's Nice Dreams
    (1981)
Cheech & Chong's Next Movie
    (1980)
Up in Smoke (1978)

COEN BROTHERS
To the White Sea (2002)
Man Who Wasn't There, The (2001)
O Brother, Where Art Thou? (2000)
Big Lebowski, The (1998)
Fargo (1996)
Hudsucker Proxy, The (1994)
Barton Fink (1991)
Miller's Crossing (1990)
Raising Arizona (1987)
Blood Simple (1984)

CORMAN, ROGER
Frankenstein Unbound (1990)
Deathsport (1978) (uncredited)
Red Baron, The (1971)
Bloody Mama (1970)

Gas-s-s-s (1970)
De Sade (1969) (uncredited)
Target: Harry (1969)
Time for Killing, A (1967) (uncredit-
    ed)
Trip, The (1967/II)
St. Valentine's Day Massacre, The
    (1967)
Wild Angels, The (1966)
Tomb of Ligeia, The (1965)
Masque of the Red Death, The
    (1964)
Secret Invasion, The (1964)
Haunted Palace, The (1963)
Raven, The (1963)
Terror, The (1963)
X (1963)
Young Racers, The (1963)
Premature Burial, The (1962)
Tower of London (1962)
Tales of Terror (1962)
Creature from the Haunted Sea
    (1961)
Intruder, The (1961)
Pit and the Pendulum (1961)
Atlas (1960)
House of Usher (1960)
Last Woman on Earth (1960)
Little Shop of Horrors, The (1960)
Ski Troop Attack (1960)
Wasp Woman, The (1960)
Bucket of Blood, A (1959)
I, Mobster (1958)
Machine-Gun Kelly (1958)
Saga of the Viking Women and
    Their Voyage to the Waters of
    the Great Sea Serpent, The
    (1958)
Teenage Caveman (1958)
War of the Satellites (1958)
Carnival Rock (1957)
Naked Paradise (1957)
Rock All Night (1957)
She Gods of Shark Reef (1957)
Sorority Girl (1957)
Teenage Doll (1957)
Undead, The (1957)
Attack of the Crab Monsters (1957)
Not of This Earth (1957)
Day the World Ended, The (1956)
Gunslinger (1956)
It Conquered the World (1956)
Oklahoma Woman, The (1956)
Apache Woman (1955)
Beast with a Million Eyes, The
    (1955) (uncredited)
Swamp Women (1955)
Five Guns West (1955)

COX, ALEX
Revengers Tragedy (2001)
Hard Look, A (2000) (TV)
Kurosawa: The Last Emperor (1999)
Three Businessmen (1998)
Death and the Compass (1996)
Winner, The (1996)
Patrullero, El/Highway Patrolman
    (1991)
Straight to Hell (1987)

Walker (1987)
Sid and Nancy (1986)
Repo Man (1984)
Sleep Is for Sissies (1980)

CRONENBERG, DAVID
Spider (2002)
Camera (2000/I)
eXistenZ (1999)
Crash (1996)
M. Butterfly (1993)
Naked Lunch (1991)
Scales of Justice (1990) TV Series
　(episodes *Regina vs Logan*
　(1990), *Regina vs Horvath*
　(1990))
Dead Ringers (1988)
Friday the 13th (1987) TV Series
　(episode *Faith Healer*)
Fly, The (1986)
Dead Zone, The (1983)
Videodrome (1983)
Scanners (1981)
Brood, The (1979)
Fast Company (1979)
Rabid (1977)
Teleplay (1976) TV Series (episode
　Italian Machine, The (1976))
Peep Show (1975) TV Series
　(episodes *Lie Chair, The* (1976),
　Victim, The (1976))
Shivers (1975)
Programme X (1972) TV Series
　(episode *Secret Weapons*
　(1972))
Don Valley (1972) (TV)
Fort York (1972) (TV)
In the Dirt (1972) (TV)
Lakeshore (1972) (TV)
Scarborough Bluffs (1972) (TV)
Winter Garden (1972) (TV)
Jim Ritchie Sculptor (1971) (TV)
Letter from Michelangelo (1971)
　(TV)
Tourettes (1971) (TV)
Crimes of the Future (1970)
Stereo (1969)
From the Drain (1967)
Transfer (1966)

FERRARA, ABEL
R-Xmas (2001)
New Rose Hotel (1998)
*Subway Stories: Tales from the
　Underground* (1997) (TV) (seg-
　ment *Love on the A Train*)
Blackout, The (1997)
California (1996)
Funeral, The (1996)
Addiction, The (1995)
Dangerous Game (1993)
Body Snatchers (1993)
Bad Lieutenant (1992)
King of New York (1990)
Cat Chaser (1988)
China Girl (1987)
Crime Story (1986) TV Series
Crime Story (1986) (TV)
Gladiator, The (1986) (TV)

Miami Vice (1984) TV Series
　(episode *Dutch Oven, The*
　(1985))
Fear City (1984)
Ms. 45 (1981)
Driller Killer (1979)
Nine Lives of a Wet Pussy (1977)
　(as L, Jimmy Boy)
Not Guilty: For Keith Richards
　(1977)

FRIEDKIN, WILLIAM
Hunted, The (2001)
Rules of Engagement (2000)
12 Angry Men (1997) (TV)
Jade (1995)
Blue Chips (1994)
Jailbreakers (1994) (TV)
Guardian, The (1990)
Tales from the Crypt (1989) TV
　Series
Rampage (1988)
CAT Squad: Python Wolf (1988)
　(TV)
CAT Squad (1986) (TV)
To Live and Die in LA (1985)
Twilight Zone, The (1985) TV Series
　(episode *Nightcrawlers* (1985))
Deal of the Century (1983)
Cruising (1980)
Brink's Job, The (1978)
Sorcerer (1977)
*Fritz Lang Interviewed by William
　Friedkin* (1974)
Exorcist, The (1973)
French Connection, The (1971)
Boys in the Band, The (1970)
Birthday Party, The (1968)
Night They Raided Minsky's, The
　(1968)
Good Times (1967)
*Time-Life Specials: The March of
　Time* (1965) (TV Series)
Alfred Hitchcock Presents (1955)
　(TV Series)

GILLIAM, TERRY
Good Omens (2002)
Fear and Loathing in Las Vegas
　(1998)
*Monty Python & the Quest for the
　Holy Grail* (1996) (VG)
12 Monkeys (1995)
Fisher King, The (1991)
*Adventures of Baron Munchausen,
　The* (1988)
Brazil (1985)
Crimson Permanent Assurance, The
　(1983)
*Monty Python's The Meaning of
　Life* (1983) (segment *Crimson
　Permanent Assurance, The*)
Time Bandits (1981)
Jabberwocky (1977)
Monty Python and the Holy Grail
　(1975)
*And Now for Something
　Completely Different* (1971)
Monty Python's Flying Circus

(1969) TV Series (cartoon
　sequences)

HOOPER, TOBE
Night Visions (2000) TV Series
Crocodile (2000)
Others, The (2000) TV Series
　(episode *Souls On Board*)
Apartment Complex, The (1999)
　(TV)
Perversions of Science (1997) TV
　Series
Dark Skies (1996) TV Series
Nowhere Man (1995) TV Series
Mangler, The (1995)
Body Bags (1993) (TV) (segment
　Eye)
Tobe Hooper's Night Terrors (1993)
I'm Dangerous Tonight (1990) (TV)
Tales from the Crypt (1989) TV
　Series
Spontaneous Combustion (1989)
Freddy's Nightmares (1988) TV
　Series
Texas Chainsaw Massacre 2, The
　(1986)
Invaders from Mars (1986)
Amazing Stories (1985) TV Series
　(episode *Miss Stardust* (1987))
Equalizer, The (1985) TV Series
Lifeforce (1985)
Poltergeist (1982)
Funhouse, The (1981)
Dark, The (1979) (uncredited)
　(replaced by John Cardos)
Salem's Lot (1979) (TV)
Eaten Alive (1976)
Texas Chainsaw Massacre, The
　(1974)

HOPPER, DENNIS
Chasers (1994)
Hot Spot, The (1990/I)
Catchfire (1989) (as Alan Smithee)
Colors (1988)
Out of the Blue (1980)
Last Movie, The (1971)
Easy Rider (1969)

JARMUSCH, JIM
*Ghost Dog: The Way of the
　Samurai* (1999)
Year of the Horse (1997)
Dead Man (1995)
Coffee and Cigarettes III (1993)
Night on Earth (1991)
Mystery Train (1989)
Coffee and Cigarettes II (1986)
Coffee and Cigarettes (1986)
Down by Law (1986)
Stranger Than Paradise (1984)
New World, The (1982)
Permanent Vacation (1981)

KUBRICK, STANLEY
Eyes Wide Shut (1999)
Full Metal Jacket (1987)
Shining, The (1980)
Barry Lyndon (1975)

Clockwork Orange, A (1971)
2001: A Space Odyssey (1968)
*Dr Strangelove or: How I Learned
　to Stop Worrying and Love the
　Bomb* (1963)
Lolita (1962)
Spartacus (1960)
Paths of Glory (1957)
Killing, The (1956)
Killer's Kiss (1955)
Fear and Desire (1953)
Seafarers, The (1952)
Flying Padre (1951)
Day of the Fight (1951)

LYNCH, DAVID
Mulholland Drive (2001)
Straight Story, The (1999)
Lost Highway (1997)
Lumière et compagnie (1995)
Hotel Room (1993) TV Series
On the Air (1992) TV Series
Twin Peaks: Fire Walk with Me
　(1992)
*Industrial Symphony No. 1: The
　Dream of the Broken Hearted*
　(1990) (TV)
American Chronicles (1990) TV
　Series
Wild at Heart (1990)
Twin Peaks (1990) TV Series
Twin Peaks (1990) (TV)
Cowboy and the Frenchman, The
　(1989)
Français vus par..., Les (1988) (TV)
Blue Velvet (1986)
Dune (1984)
Elephant Man, The (1980)
Eraserhead (1977)
Amputee, The (1974)
Grandmother, The (1970)
Alphabet, The (1968)
Six Figures Getting Sick (1966)

MALICK, TERRENCE
Thin Red Line, The (1998)
Days of Heaven (1978)
Badlands (1973)
Lanton Mills (1969)

MEYER, RUSS
*Beneath the Valley of the Ultra-
　Vixens* (1979)
Up! (1976)
Supervixens (1975)
Blacksnake! (1973)
Seven Minutes, The (1971)
Beyond the Valley of the Dolls
　(1970)
Cherry, Harry and Raquel! (1969)
Finders Keepers, Lovers Weepers!
　(1968)
Vixen (1968)
Common Law Cabin (1967)
Good Morning... and Goodbye!
　(1967)
Mondo Topless (1966)
Faster, Pussycat! Kill! Kill! (1965)
Motor Psycho (1965)

Mudhoney (1965)
Lorna (1964)
Fanny Hill (1964)
Europe in the Raw (1963)
Heavenly Bodies! (1963)
Wild Gals of the Naked West!
    (1962)
Erotica (1961)
Eve and the Handyman (1961)
Immoral Mr. Teas, The (1959)

RAIMI, SAM

Spider-Man (2002)
Gift, The (2000)
For Love of the Game (1999)
Simple Plan, A (1998)
Quick and the Dead, The (1995)
Army of Darkness (1993)
Darkman (1990)
Evil Dead II (1987)
Crimewave (1985)
Evil Dead, The (1982)
Clockwork (1978)
Within the Woods (1978)
It's Murder! (1977)

ROEG, NICOLAS

Sound of Claudia Schiffer, The
    (2000)
Samson and Delilah (1996) (TV)
Hotel Paradise (1995)
Full Body Massage (1995) (TV)
Two Deaths (1995)
Heart of Darkness (1994) (TV)
Young Indiana Jones Chronicles,
    The (1992) TV Series (episode
    Paris, October 1916)
Cold Heaven (1991)
Witches, The (1990)
Sweet Bird of Youth (1989) (TV)
Track 29 (1988)
Aria (1987) (segment *Un ballo in*
    maschera)
Castaway (1987)
Insignificance (1985)
Eureka (1982)
Bad Timing (1980)
Man Who Fell to Earth, The (1976)
Don't Look Now (1973)
Walkabout (1970)
Performance (1970)

ROMERO, GEORGE A.

Bruiser (2000) (V)
Night of the Living Dead: 30th
    Anniversary Edition (1999)
Dark Half, The (1993)
Due occhi diabolici (1990) (episode
    The Facts in the Case of Mr.
    Valdemar)
Monkey Shines (1988)
Day of the Dead (1985)
Tales from the Darkside (1984) TV
    Series
Creepshow (1982)
Knightriders (1981)
Dawn of the Dead (1979)
Martin (1978)
Crazies, The (1973)

Season of the Witch (1972/)
There's Always Vanilla (1972)
Night of the Living Dead (1968)

RUSSELL, KEN

Fall of the House of Usher, The
    (2001)
Lion's Mouth (2000)
Dogboys (1998) (TV)
Ken Russell 'In Search of the
    English Folk Song' (1997)
Tales of Erotica (1996) (segment
    Insatiable Mrs. Kirsch, The
    (1993))
Alice in Russialand (1995) (TV)
Classic Widows (1995) (TV)
Mindbender (1995)
Insatiable Mrs. Kirsch, The (1993)
Mystery of Doctor Martinu, The
    (1993) (TV)
Lady Chatterley (1992) (TV)
Secret Life of Sir Arnold Bax (1992)
    (TV)
Prisoner of Honor (1991) (TV)
Whore (1991)
Strange Affliction of Anton
    Bruckner, The (1990) (TV)
Women and Men: Stories of
    Seduction (1990) (TV)
British Picture, A (1989) (TV)
Méphistophélès (1989) (TV)
Rainbow, The (1989)
Salome's Last Dance (1988)
Lair of the White Worm, The (1988)
Aria (1987) (segment *Nessun*
    dorma)
Gothic (1986)
Vaughan Williams (1986)
Crimes of Passion (1984)
Planets, The (1983) (TV)
Altered States (1980)
Clouds of Glory: The Rime of the
    Ancient Mariner (1978) (TV)
Clouds of Glory: William and
    Dorothy (1978) (TV)
Valentino (1977)
Lisztomania (1975)
Tommy (1975)
Mahler (1974)
Savage Messiah (1972)
Boy Friend, The (1971)
Devils, The (1971)
Music Lovers, The (1971)
Dance of the Seven Veils (1970)
    (TV)
Women in Love (1969)
Song of Summer (1968) (TV)
Billion Dollar Brain (1967)
Dante's Inferno (1967) (TV)
Isadora Duncan, the Biggest
    Dancer in the World (1966) (TV)
Don't Shoot the Composer (1966)
    (TV)
Always on Sunday (1965) (TV)
Bartok (1964) (TV)
Diary of a Nobody (1964) (TV)
Dotty World of James Lloyd, The
    (1964) (TV)
Lonely Shore (1964) (TV)

Debussy Film, The (1963) (TV)
French Dressing (1963)
Watch the Birdie (1963) (TV)
Elgar (1962) (TV)
Lotte Lenya Sings Kurt Weill (1962)
    (TV)
Mr. Chesher's Traction Engines
    (1962) (TV)
Pop Goes the Easel (1962) (TV)
Preservation Man (1962) (TV)
Antonio Gaudi (1961) (TV)
London Moods (1961) (TV)
Old Battersea House (1961) (TV)
Prokofiev (1961)
Architecture of Entertainment
    (1960) (TV)
Cranks at Work (1960) (TV)
House in Bayswater, A (1960)
Light Fantastic, The (1960) (TV)
Marie Rambert Remembers (1960)
Miner's Picnic, The (1960) (TV)
Shelagh Delaney's Salford (1960)
    (TV)
Gordon Jacob (1959) (TV)
Guitar Craze (1959) (TV)
McBryde and Coquhoun: Two
    Scottish Painters (1959)
Poet's London (1959) (TV)
Portrait of a Goon (1959) (TV)
Variations on a Mechanical Theme
    (1959) (TV)
Lourdes (1958)
Monitor (1958) TV Series
Amelia and the Angel (1957)
Knights On Bikes (1956) (incom-
    pleted)
Peepshow (1956)

WATERS, JOHN

Cecil B. DeMented (2000)
Pecker (1998)
Serial Mom (1994)
Cry-Baby (1990)
Hairspray (1988)
Polyester (1981)
Desperate Living (1977)
Female Trouble (1974)
Pink Flamingos (1972)
Multiple Maniacs (1970)
Diane Linkletter Story, The (1969)
Mondo Trasho (1969)
Eat Your Make Up! (1967)
Roman Candles (1966)
Hag in a Black Leather Jacket
    (1964)

WENDERS, WIM

Blues, The (2002) (mini) TV Series
In America (2001)
Vill passiert (2001)
Million Dollar Hotel, The (2000)
Buena Vista Social Club (1999)
Willie Nelson at the Teatro (1998)
End of Violence, The (1997)
Gebrüder Skladanowsky, Die (1995)
Lumière et compagnie (1995)
Al di là delle nuvole/Beyond the
    Clouds (1995)

Lisbon Story (1994)
In weiter Ferne, so nah! /Far Away,
    So Close (1993)
Arisha, der Bär und der steinerne
    Ring (1992)
Bis ans Ende der Welt/Until the End
    of the World (1991)
Night & Day (1990) (TV)
Aufzeichnungen zu Kleidern und
    Städten/Notebook on Cities
    and Clothes (1989)
Himmel über Berlin, Der/Wings of
    Desire (1987)
Tokyo-Ga (1985)
Docu Drama (1984)
Paris, Texas (1984)
Chambre 666 (1982) (TV)
Hammett (1982)
Reverse Angle (1982) (TV)
Stand der Dinge, Der/The State of
    Things (1982)
Lightning Over Water (1980)
Amerikanische Freund, Der/The
    American Friend (1977)
Im Lauf der Zeit/Kings of the Road
    (1976)
Haus für uns, Ein (1974) (mini) TV
    Series (episodes *Aus der*
    Familie der Panzerechsen, Insel,
    Die)
Falsche Bewegung/False Move
    (1975)
Alice in den Städten (1974)
Scharlachrote Buchstabe, Der
    (1972)
Angst des Tormannes beim
    Elfmeter, Die/Goalkeeper's Fear
    of the Penalty (1971)
Polizeifilm (1970) (TV)
Summer in the City (1970)
Alabama: 2000 Light Years (1969)
Drei Amerikanische LP's (1969) (TV)
Silver City (1969)
Klappenfilm (1968)
Same Player Shoots Again (1968)
Victor I (1968)
Schauplätze (1967)

ZUCKER, DAVID

Guest, The (2001)
BASEketball (1998)
High School High (1996) (uncredit-
    ed)
For Goodness Sake (1993)
Naked Gun 2 ¹/₂: The Smell of Fear,
    The (1991)
Naked Gun: From the Files of Police
    Squad!, The (1988)
Ruthless People (1986)
Top Secret! (1984)
Police Squad! (1982) TV Series
Airplane! (1980)